OUR INTELLECTUAL STRENGT

'ENGLISH-CANADIAN LITERATURE'/'FRENCH-CANADIAN LITERATURE'

Literature of Canada

Poetry and Prose in Reprint

Douglas Lochhead, General Editor

Our Intellectual Strength and Weakness

JOHN GEORGE BOURINOT

'English-Canadian Literature'

THOMAS GUTHRIE MARQUIS

'French-Canadian Literature'

CAMILLE ROY

Introduction by Clara Thomas

UNIVERSITY OF TORONTO PRESS

© University of Toronto Press 1973
Toronto and Buffalo
Printed in Canada
ISBN 0-8020-1950-1 (cloth)
ISBN 0-8020-6175-3 (paper)
ISBN Microfiche 0-8020-0294-3
LC 72-91693

Preface

Yes, there is a Canadian literature. It does exist. Part of the evidence to support these statements is presented in the form of reprints of the poetry and prose of the authors included in this series. Much of this literature has been long out of print. If the country's culture and traditions are to be sampled and measured, both in terms of past and present-day conditions, then the major works of both our well-known and our lesser-known writers should be available for all to buy and read. The Literature of Canada series aims to meet this need. It shares with its companion series, The Social History of Canada, the purpose of making the documents of the country's heritage accessible to an increasingly large national and international public, a public which is anxious to acquaint itself with Canadian literature — the writing itself — and also to become intimate with the times in which it grew.

DL

OUR INTELLECTUAL STRENGTH AND WEAKNESS

'ENGLISH-CANADIAN LITERATURE'/'FRENCH-CANADIAN LITERATURE'

Clara Thomas

Introduction

Nothing in our history is as constant as the sound of the Canadian voice celebrating in triumph or in tears, our past, our present, and our destiny. To read John George Bourinot's *Our Intellectual Strength and Weakness* (1893), Thomas Guthrie Marquis' 'English-Canadian Literature' (1913) and Camille Roy's 'French-Canadian Literature' (1913) is to mark the introduction and establishment of guidelines, critical and cultural rationalizations and contingencies, that structure and inform our ways of looking at ourselves and our literature throughout its succession of important documents – through E.K. Brown's *On Canadian Poetry* (1943) to Northrop Frye's 'Conclusion' to *The Literary History of Canada* (1965). A 'peaceable kingdom' is Bourinot's goal and promise just as the 'garrison mentality,' made manifest in a shoddy, shopkeeping materialism, is his villain, the enemy of all cultural light. Critics of successive generations developed in their insistence on the release of literature from a rigidly formulated and largely ornamental role in the life of a people rather than in their summarizing analyses of the intellectual and cultural states of our nation.

Twenty-five years after Confederation, John George Bourinot delivered his 'Short Review of the Intellectual Development of the New Dominion' as a presidential address to the Royal Society of Canada. He was returning to a topic which was of prime interest to him – his *Intellectual Development of The Canadian People: An Historical Review* had been published in 1881. His address, called *Canada's Intellectual Strength and Weakness*, and printed as the first in a series of Royal Society Monographs, is a

vii

wide-ranging view of our cultural situation by a distinguished man of letters. It is unique in its easy incorporation of our two nations, two languages, and two cultures into one unified, expansive, and optimistic vision.

Mr (later Sir John George) Bourinot was born in Nova Scotia and educated at the University of Toronto; he was the founder and editor of *The Halifax Herald* and Clerk of the House of Commons from 1880 until his death in 1902. He was the first authority of his day on Canadian constitutional history and his impressive list of historical texts and commentaries were all based, as Norah Story testifies, 'on the facts of constitutional history.' Emotionally and actively, Bourinot was an Imperialist, closely associated with the goals of Charles Mair, George Taylor Denison, George Monro Grant, George Parkin, and the many others whose aspirations for Canada have been recently and splendidly documented in Carl Berger's *Sense of Power*.

The literature of imperialism was characterized by a profound emotional attachment to Canada. Far from denigrating Canadian things, Imperialists were positively utopian in their expectations and it was exactly this overestimation of Canadian capacities which enabled them to believe that their country would become 'the future centre and dominating portion of the British empire.' The only difference among them on this matter was the words and metaphors they used to express it.[1]

This was a time when Canada seemed still to be Charles G.D. Roberts' 'Child of Nations, giant-limbed,' still malleable to the guidance of wise leaders and with everything to be hoped for in its potential development. Likewise, this was a time when a man like Bourinot saw himself, quite without self-inflation, as such a leader. To him, the function of a 'Man of Letters' was a well-defined responsibility, eminently honourable and admirable – not quite an attitude of 'all knowledge is my province,' but certainly a feeling that 'my country's achievements and her destiny are one with my own, my opportunity and my responsibility.' Today such a confidence of tone is no more than a dim and enviable memory; but we can still recognize and respectfully acknowledge Bourinot's ideal, the range of his grasp of cultural matters, and the precision of his detail.

The group of men to whom he spoke had first come together as the Royal Society in 1882. They saw themselves, ideally, as 'a union of leading representatives of all those engaged in literature and science in the several provinces.' Membership had at first been limited to eighty Fellows who had written 'memoirs of merit or rendered eminent service to literature and science' and had subsequently been raised to one hundred. Still, for all his obvious pride in the Society, Bourinot found it necessary in his speech to defend its fellowship against a continuing and pervasive stigma of élitism. He insisted that it had been established 'in no spirit of isolation from other literary and scientific men,' that it could not be allowed to dwindle into a 'sort of literary or scientific picnic by allowing every man or woman who had, or believed they had, some elementary scientific or other knowledge to enter its ranks.' He finally closed the argument with a statement which, for him, was unequivocal and not to be challenged: 'If there is an intelligent democracy anywhere it is the Republic of Letters,' and in summary, he assembles impressive evidence for the Royal Society's first decade of achievement as published in its 'Transactions,' from the Abbé Cuoq's work on the Algonquin language to the geological findings of Sir William Dawson and the anthropological studies of Sir Daniel Wilson.

The most constant of Bourinot's own prepossessions is his determined biculturalism. He is a devoted student of the details and the accomplishments of French Canada's past, drawing from his knowledge conclusions of romantic idealism and projecting a future of glorious unity between Canada's two founding races. The French régime constituted for him the 'heroic days' of Canada:

...days of heroic endeavour, since we see in the vista of the past a small colony whose total population at no period exceeded eighty thousand souls, chiefly living on the banks of the St Lawrence between Quebec and Montreal, and contending against great odds for the supremacy on the continent of America.

Furthermore, he casts over the past and the present of Quebec a mantle of gentle nostalgia, seeing it as the pathetic, deserted child-colony, a vision that was already well established in his day through the work of François-Xavier Garneau and that has since been reaffirmed a thousand times over in literature and the rhetoric of politics.

The struggle for life was very bitter up to the last hours of French supremacy in a country constantly exposed to the misfortunes of war and too often neglected by a king who thought more of his mistresses than of his harrassed and patient subjects across the sea.

Bourinot, in fact, sets out to be a revisionist historian. He balances his generation's view of Columbus, the 'great Discoverer,' whose 'purpose was so great and his success so conspicuous that both have obscured his human weakness,' with his own insistence that,

As Canadians, however, now review the character of the great Genoese, and of his compeers and successors in the opening up of this continent, they must, with pride, come to the conclusion that none of these men can compare in nobility of purpose, in sincere devotion to God, King and Country, with Champlain, the sailor of Brouage, who became the founder of Quebec and the father of New France.

But however we assess Bourinot's historical and emotional bias, we must also admit and admire his encyclopaedic knowledge of the French-Canadian cultural achievement. We are just now recognizing the validity of an assertion as confident as, for example, this one: 'the English colonies of America cannot present us with any books which, for faithful narrative and simplicity of style, bear comparison with the admirable work of Champlain, explorer and historian, or with those of the genial and witty advocate Marc Lescarbot.'

The early intellectual supremacy of a very few French over the great mass of people in the English colonies of North America is a matter of great pride to Bourinot and, by inference, to all Canadians. And yet he holds it as an article of faith that the French province could only realize its best future under British rule.

The germs of intellectual life were necessarily dormant among the mass of the people, for they never could produce any rich fruition until they were freed from the spirit of absolutism which distinguished French supremacy, and were able to give full expression to the natural genius of their race under the inspiration of the Liberal Government of England in these later times.

The peroration of Bourinot's address returns to the two races, his confidence in the continuance of the French language and the necessity for 'friendly rivalry on the part of the best minds among French and English Canadians which will best stimulate the genius of their people in art, history, poetry and romance.' Above all, he urges on both English and French a will to unity.

It is for the respective nationalities not to stand aloof from one another, but to unite in every way possible for common intellectual improvement, and give sympathetic encouragement to the study of the two languages and to the mental efforts of each other.

Carl Berger analyzes the elements that were combined in the Imperialists' attempt to harmonize our two races and cultures as 'some sincerity, ingenuity and not a little blindness.'[2] In the long perspective of history he proves, of course, to be right; but Bourinot's is a benign and a generous vision and it is pleasant both to contemplate and to honour a Canadian past when there were such men, not seeking for the Canadian identity, but confident that they had found it and equally confident that it was their mission 'to bring reality into alignment with their vision.'[3]

It is obvious from its beginning and it is only to be expected from the Royal Society's decorum, that Bourinot's address will be in its overall effect a vote of confidence for the future of Canadian culture. What is particularly impressive, however, is his combination of precise information, discursiveness, and range in his areas of comparison. The first third of a sixty-page address consists of a general cultural survey beginning with an

xii

informed comparison of Canada's situation and America's; the next third is almost equally divided between a commentary on poetry and fiction in English and French and a history of the Royal Society and its achievements; the final third assembles wide-ranging information and opinions about the state of the nation's education, literary criticism, libraries, and art galleries. In our specialized professional terminology Bourinot would be more fittingly called a cultural historian than a literary critic, although in his day the wing-spread of a 'critic' was very broad and he is obviously and avowedly of the genus Matthew Arnold. The literature of a country is best defined, he believes, with the breadth of Arnold's definition and in Arnold's own words:

All knowledge that reaches us through books is literature. But as I do not mean, by knowing ancient Rome, knowing merely more or less of Latin *Belles-Lettres*, and taking no account of Rome's military, and political, and legal, and administrative work in the world; and as, by knowing ancient Greece, I understand knowing her as the giver of Greek art, and the guide to a free and right use of reason and to scientific methods, and the founder of our mathematics and physics, and astronomy and biology, I understand knowing her as all this, and not merely knowing certain Greek poems, and histories, and treatises and speeches, so as to the knowledge of modern nations also.

Those rampant enemies of culture whom Arnold called the Philistines are Bourinot's prime adversaries too and he finds their insidious inroads everywhere in a new, raw nation.

...an over-weening confidence in itself and home-made methods, an over-estimate of material success and a corresponding indifference to things of the mind – and the by-product of this, a parochial, depreciating, denigratory spirit inhibiting the efforts of its own and preferring the foreign second-rate to the home-made first-rate.

The hearings of the Royal Commission on Publishing in 1971 reverberated with echoes of his remarks on the state of literary criticism: 'Let me frankly insist that we have far too much hasty and slovenly literary work done in Canada'; and with the direction of his summation of the problem: 'at least if we could have in the present state of our intellectual development, a criticism in the press which would be truthful and just ... the effect would be probably in the direction of encouraging promising writers, and weeding out some literary dabblers.'

Our cultural laments have been remarkably constant and unmistakably the contemporary voice still speaks Bourinot's nineteenth-century message. The obstacles in the way of Canadian literary endeavours are still interminably listed in his very words.

Our population is still small and separated into two distinct nationalities, who for the most part necessarily read books printed in their own tongue ... a book published in Canada then has a relatively limited clientele in the country itself, and cannot meet much encouragement from publishers in England and the United States ... publishers are apt to look askance at a book when it is offered to them from the colonies. ... But the time has long since passed for sneers at colonial self-government or colonial intellect...

Where Bourinot does sharply diverge from present-day critical orthodoxy, at least in the free nations of the world, is in his conception of the writer's role in the life and culture of a nation. A work of literature to him is not to be judged, primarily, as an illumination of the experiences of individual men and women, nor as a criticism of life contemporary to its living. It is to be valued critically and culturally according to the fulfillment of its particular functions and responsibilities – and these are inspirational and commemorative. To him the artist has pre-eminently a public role and a public duty, for literature is the ornament of life and of nationhood. Moreover, in literature a nation's best immortality resides: 'The garners of Sicily are empty now, but the bees of all climes still fetch honey from the tiny garden-plot of Theocritus.'

A nineteenth-century concept of nationhood and culture, an Imperialist's devotion to Canada, and a loyalty to 'la patrie' which, though most often voiced by Laurier in his time, was not restricted to those of Laurier's tongue, are all a part of Bourinot's determining position. He finds a qualified, but certain achievement among our poets – among the colonies we have outdone Australia, for instance – and the patriotic verses of Howe, Frechette, Roberts, and Edgar 'are worth a good many political speeches in parliament so far as their effects upon the hearts and sympathies is concerned.'

However, his standard of greatness in poetry is measured ultimately against the epic or heroic narrative – Longfellow's *Evangeline* has 'captured the world,' and he sees in the Canadian past vast untapped resources for our truly aspiring poets:

Description of our meadows, prairies and forests, with their wealth of herbage and foliage, or artistic sketches of pretty bits of lake scenery have their limitations as respects their influence on a people. Great thoughts or deeds are not bred by scenery.

It is interesting that the heroic and narrative tradition in Canadian poetry has proved to be very strong and that Dorothy Livesay's essay, 'The Documentary Poem: A Canadian Genre,'[4] can be read as a confirmation and a documentation of Bourinot's ambitions for the genre.

The novel he views with great caution, as a necessary but doubtful offshoot of true literature: 'It is inevitable that a busy people, and especially women distracted with house-hold cares, should always find that relief in this branch of literature which no other reading can give them.' In comparison, any history which is written with painstaking attention to sources, 'picturesqueness' of narration, philosophic insight into politics and statesmanship and comprehension of the life and character of a people — 'such a history has assuredly a much deeper and more useful purpose in the culture and education of the world than any work of fiction can possibly have, even when animated by a lofty genius.' The fictional works of James De Mille and Sara Jeanette Duncan do, however, prove the existence of some imagination and humour in the Canadian mind, 'though one sees little of those qualities in the press or in public features.' Thomas Chandler Haliburton is granted comic genius for his Sam Slick, though Bourinot introduces 'The Clockmaker' as a part of his tribute to the versatility of Joseph Howe, its publisher, and not as we see it — a landmark achievement in itself and in the development of a Canadian literature.

The idiosyncracies of Bourinot's views and opinions are woven into the fabric of his address and they are entirely a part of its haunting 'age of gold' charm. He wrote with confidence on Canadian life and letters from an over-arching view of history which fused men and the concept of nationhood into a benign, progressing whole. To read him is to admire the confidence of his informing vision, to regret its passing and also to regret the twentieth century's erosion of all such buoyant dreams.

Two decades later, Thomas Guthrie Marquis wrote the chapter 'English-Canadian Literature' for the compendium history of Canada, *Canada and its Provinces* (1913), edited by Adam Shortt and A.B. Doughty. Each of the twenty volumes in this large undertaking had its own editor and each chapter was a separate entity written by a specialist in its particular field. The whole enterprise was a complicated piece of committee-work and its finished volumes are a solid memorial of success for such committee-enterprises, the first of its kind in the country. A mere twenty years in time can be a lost world apart in scholarly decorum. The entire project, Marquis' specialized assignment, and his handling of it, separate us completely from the over-vision of the man of letters and move us to the specializing, compartmentalizing – and separating – nature of scholarship in our own time. We gain in clarity, in organization, and perhaps in sheer bulk of informative detail, but we lose both the charm and the reassurance that light the wide sweep of Bourinot's circle.

Section six, Volumes 11 and 12, of the history is called *The Dominion: Missions Arts and Letters.* Seven of its chapters are on the various religions, denominations, and their works across Canada: the other six cover our culture – painting and sculpture, music and theatre, architecture, 'The Higher National Life, a study of the civilizing and refining influences at work in "a

Commercial Democracy feverishly busy in the development of half a continent" ' and on our two literatures – firmly divided. 'French-Canadian Literature' was written by Mgr Camille Roy, the very eminent Professor of Literature at Laval. It seems likely that a firm editorial hand finally presided over all these chapters, tailoring each one of them into a clear and impersonal expository style. While it is entirely credible that Marquis should have written as his chapter reads, it is incredible that he and Mgr Roy should have written the same kind of English, with the same tone and rhythm, in the same matter-of-fact, entirely admirable, but non-commital style. The weight of Camille Roy's emotional allegiance and conviction remains, however, in the many French quotations which no editor could alter, and pre-eminently in his quotation from Laurier, defining the loyalty of the French Canadian:

> J'aime la France qui nous a donné la vie, j'aime l'Angleterre qui nous a donné la liberté; mais la première place dans mon cœur est pour le Canada, ma patrie, ma terre natale. ... Vous en conviendrez avec moi, le sentiment national d'un pays n'a de valeur que par l'orgueil qu'il sait inspirer à ses enfants. En bien! nous l'avons, nous, Canadiens, cet orgueil de notre pays...

His final paragraph too rises above the matter-of-fact, linking him once again to Bourinot in a credo of conviction about the place and function of literature in the life of a nation.

> French Canadian literature is eminently moral. It bears the stamp of the Christian spirit in which its works were conceived. In it Catholic thought is expressed without timidity – with that apostolic boldness which is its characteristic ... taken

as a whole, the literature is indeed Canadian ... in it the life of the people is reflected and perpetuated. Many of its works, the best in prose and in verse, breathe the perfume of the soil and are the expression — original, sincere, and profound — of the Canadian spirit.

In contrast, the shaping principle of Marquis' work is a notion of the world of literature as an arena of competition, a literary Olympic Games always in progress, the standards set by the accepted canon of great English authors, and Canadians to be measured against these standards — measured, cajoled, rejected, applauded, but finally, regretfully, found wanting. Nothing could differ more markedly from Camille Roy's idealistic peroration than the chilling materialism of Marquis' final paragraph, though frequent warnings against Canada's over-weening materialism have tolled constantly throughout his work.

But there are still rich literary fields to be cultivated; and with the increase of wealth and the consequent increase of leisure, with better educational establishments, Canadian authors will have a home market for their productions, and will doubtless be able to do as good work as is done in other parts of the English-speaking world.

There was of course a very great difference in audience or reader-expectation between Bourinot in 1893 and Marquis and Roy in 1913, the one speaking to a small and élite group of Canada's cultivated and outstanding men and women, the others charged with clearly informing a larger and far more conglomerate group of readers. Marquis' words seldom tease us into interpretations of his frame of mind or his entire cultural environment. Rather, the organization of his material into History, Biography,

Travels and Exploration, General Literature, Fiction, and Poetry is admirably self-defining. Within each category he provides a great deal of information that has a convincing ring of well-researched authenticity. It is surprising, in fact, that over the past twenty-five years, when scholarship in both history and literature has steadily advanced in this country, Marquis' comments and the authors he chose to list have not been more thoroughly heeded; that, for instance, we have just now got a reprint of G.M. Grant's *Ocean to Ocean*, of which he speaks so highly.

By 1913 the reading of fiction had become a leading popular entertainment and its publishing an important business. As Gordon Roper has pointed out in *The Literary History of Canada*, 'until 1880 about 150 Canadians published over 250 volumes of fiction ... during the years 1880 to 1920, more than 400 Canadians published over 1,400 volumes of fiction.'[5] Marquis is beyond condescending to it as a housewives' panacea and yet a taint still hangs about the novel and he must rationalize its existence before he can discuss it.

> The average reader desires knowledge with a sugar coating, and, as a result, men and women of imaginative bent of mind and literary skill find the story the best means of giving pleasure and instruction. History, politics, manners and customs, psychology, pathology, science and even theology have all been served up with the sauce of fiction.

However, once embarked, he charts the hopeful course of Canadian fiction, marking the year 1890 'as the dividing line between the early writers, more or less provincial in their art, and the modern school, influenced by world standards.' He faithfully lists and comments on works of fiction from its beginnings in English-

Canadian literature, *The History of Emily Montague* to *Anne of Green Gables* which in 1908 'took the reading public by storm.'

Some of his insights have been explored by later critics – his justifying of a place for Susanna Moodie among fiction-writers, for instance – but numbers of his comments are still to be investigated, and all together they constitute a continuing and valuable body of source material for scholars. His opinions have been sharply modified by later critics. We would not, for instance, be likely to accord Sara Jeanette Duncan 'a place well towards the front rank of modern humorists,' but his high regard for Miss Duncan's work certainly suggests that she would bear closer investigation than we have yet given her.

Marquis' chapter concludes with a consideration of 'the chief glory of Canadian literature' – its poetry. Here he gives the impression of both confidence and pride, and the enthusiasm and sensitivity of his commentary elevates the tone and effect of his entire article. It is here also that his position as a critic is most clearly visible: he assigns no prescriptive role, theme, or series of themes to the poet, who is artistically free as Bourinot would not leave him free; yet he also binds the poet, both to an accepted canon of good taste and to standards of excellence which seem to have been once and forever set.

Roberts' 'Ave,' written to commemorate the death of Shelley, he considers great, not only as a Canadian poem, 'but it is also important as an English elegy and is worthy of study alongside of such a poem as Matthew Arnold's "Thyrsis".' Camille Roy deplored the French-Canadian writer's tendency to 'imitate the artistic forms of French thought' and to 'reproduce that which is most characteristic and least capable of assimilation, in the literature of the ancient motherland,' but Marquis obviously considered literary relations of this order a mark of poetic competence. Bliss Carman, he says, is a sort of twentieth-century blend of Omar Khayyàm, Shelley, and Robert Browning, 'with Tennyson's art thrown in to give a delicate flavour to the whole. Not that he is as supremely great as any of these.' In the use of 'nature poet' as a term of highest praise for Lampman, Marquis is equally far from today, when the words have hackneyed sound and limiting connotation (something like the term 'woman novelist'), and from Bourinot's brusque, dismissing 'great deeds are not bred by scenery.'

Lampman, however, he treats with an enthusiastic sensitivity that is, at times, productive of fresh insights for our own time. He quotes 'Heat' entire and comments: 'With a rapid pencil the poet has here limned a common Canadian country scene with the vigour and truth of a Millet.' That sentence alone makes several beckoning gestures: the long-abandoned notion of the poem as a 'word-picture' is there; so is a lost landscape of the imagination, common to both Marquis and Lampman, where Millet was an obvious standard of excellence for paintings of 'vigour and truth'; and ironically, at the point of highest praise there is also the lingering implied inferiority – 'a common Canadian country scene.'

There are many such comments throughout Marquis' entire work and they still invite many-sided critical and cultural investigations. But in review of his effectiveness, it is his very naming for which we must be most grateful. The level quality of his prose and the quantity and precision of his detail inspire confidence in the justice of his choices. Though subsequent scholar-critics have adjusted the balance of his judgments in some cases and considerably expanded his research in others, there can be no discrediting of the documentary value of his material. Without his gathering, much might have been lost to us. These works of Bourinot, Marquis, and Roy are all 'classics' in our literary and cultural history. Their marked differences in purpose, in tone, and in effect give priceless evidence for a lively variety, and against a monotone dullness, in the cultural history of Canada. In any period of dynamic nationalism there will still be those who insist on the writer's patriotic function and duty; in the rampant tides of a materialistic society, there will always be the temptation to judge literary work excellent by its success as a marketable commodity; and we will always in some measure seek to bring reality into alignment with our visions. Amidst it all, we can be blessedly sure that our writers will continue, as they always have done, to record the experience of life in this country, to illuminate it for us and sometimes to transcend the local, or the regional, or the national, into the timeless and universal experience of men and women everywhere. To be able to follow them, to understand and, sometimes, to interpret them to others will continue to be the critic's only real function and his constant challenge.

NOTES

1 Carl Berger, *The Sense of Power: Studies in the Ideas of Canadian Imperialism 1867 to 1914* (Toronto 1970), 261
2 Ibid., 145
3 Ibid., 265
4 Dorothy Livesay, 'The Documentary Poem: A Canadian Genre,' in *Contexts of Canadian Criticism*, ed. Eli Mandel (Toronto 1971), 267-81
5 Gordon Roper, 'New Forces: New Fiction, 1880-1920,' *Literary History of Canada: Canadian Literature in English*, gen. ed. Carl F. Klinck (Toronto 1965)

Our Intellectual Strength and Weakness

JOHN GEORGE BOURINOT

Royal Society of Canada Series.

OUR INTELLECTUAL

STRENGTH AND WEAKNESS

A SHORT HISTORICAL AND CRITICAL REVIEW OF LITERATURE,
ART AND EDUCATION IN CANADA,

BY

J. G. BOURINOT, C.M.G., LL.D., D.C.L., D.L. (LAVAL).

AUTHOR OF "CAPE BRETON AND ITS MEMORIALS OF THE FRENCH REGIME," AND OF
SEVERAL WORKS ON FEDERAL AND PARLIAMENTARY GOVERNMENT
IN THE DOMINION OF CANADA.

MONTREAL:
FOSTER BROWN & CO.

LONDON:
BERNARD QUARITCH.

1893

PREFATORY NOTE.

This monograph on the intellectual development of the Dominion was delivered in substance as the presidential address to the Royal Society of Canada at its May meeting of 1893, in Ottawa. Since then the author has given the whole subject a careful revision, and added a number of bibliographical and other literary notes which could not conveniently appear in the text of the address, but are likely to interest those who wish to follow more closely the progress of culture in a country still struggling with the difficulties of the material development of half a continent. This little volume, as the title page shows, is intended as the commencement of a series of historical and other essays which will be periodically reproduced, in this more convenient form for the general reader, from the large quarto volumes of the Royal Society of Canada, where they first appear.

OTTAWA, 1st October, 1893.

GAZETTE PRINTING COMPANY, MONTREAL.

To my Friends

SIR J. W. DAWSON, (C.M.G., F.R.S.C., LL.D.)

AND

MONSIGNOR HAMEL, (M.A., F.R.S.C.),

WHO REPRESENT THE CULTURE AND LEARNING OF THE ENGLISH AND FRENCH
ELEMENTS OF THE CANADIAN PEOPLE,

I dedicate

THIS SHORT REVIEW OF THE INTELLECTUAL DEVELOPMENT
OF THE NEW DOMINION.

ANALYSIS OF CONTENTS.

I.—P. 1.

Introductory remarks on the overestimate of material success in America; citation from an oration on the subject by James Russell Lowell; application of his remarks to Canadians.

II.—P. 4.

Three well defined eras of development in Canada; the French regime and its heroic aspect; the works of Champlain, Lescarbot, Potherie, Le Clercq, Charlevoix and others; evidences of some culture in Quebec and Montreal; the foundation of the Jesuit College and the Seminaries; Peter Kalm on the study of science; the mental apathy of the colony generally in the days of French supremacy.

III.—P. 9.

The period of political development from 1760-1840, under English government; low state of popular education; growth of the press; influence of the clergy; intellectual contests in legislative halls; publication of "Sam Slick"; development of a historical literature.

IV.—P. 14.

An era of intellectual as well as material activity commences in 1840, after the con cession of responsible government; political life still claims best intellects; names of prominent politicians and statesmen from 1840-1867; performance in literature and science; gross partisanship of the press; poems of Crémazie, Howe, Sangster and others; histories of Christie, Bibaud, Garneau and Ferland.

V.—P. 19.

Historical writers from 1867-1893—Dent, Turcotte, Casgrain, Sulte, Kingsford, etc.; Canadian poets—LeMay, Reade, Mair, Roberts, Carman and others; critical remarks on the character of French and English Canadian poetry; comparison between Canadian and Australian writers; patriotic spirit of Canadian poems.

VI.—P. 27.

Essay writing in Canada; weakness of attempts at fiction; Richardson's "Wacousta"; De Gaspé's "Anciens Canadiens"; Kirby's "Golden Dog"; Marmette's "F. de Bienville," among best works of this class; Professor De Mille and his works; successful efforts of Canadians abroad—Gilbert Parker, Sara Jeannette Duncan and L. Dougall; general remarks on literary progress during half a century; the literature of science in Canada eminently successful.

2

BIBLIOGRAPHICAL, ART AND GENERAL NOTES.

(1) P. 61.—Lowell's remarks on the study of the Liberal Arts.
(2) P. 61.—Jamestown, Va.
(3) P. 61.—Champlain's Works ; his character compared with that of Captain John Smith.
(4) P. 62.—Lescarbot's " Histoire de la Nouvelle France."
(5) P. 62.—Charlevoix's " Histoire et Description Générale de la Nouvelle France."
(6) P. 63.—Hutchinson's " History of Massachusetts."
(7) P. 63.—Sagard's " Le Grand Voyage," etc.
(8) P. 63.—P. Boucher's " Mœurs et Productions de la Nouvelle France."
(9) P. 63.—Jesuit Relations.
(10) P. 63.—Père du Creux, " Historia Canadensis."
(11) P. 63.—La Potherie's " Histoire de l'Amérique Septentrionale."
(11a) P. 63.—The Jesuit Lafitau and his work on Indian customs.
(12) P. 64.—C. le Clercq, " Etablissement de la Foy."
(13) P. 64.—Cotton Mather's " Magnalia."
(13a) P. 64.—Dr. Michel Sarrazin.
(13b) P. 64.—Peter Kalm and the English colonies.
(14) P. 65.—Education in Canada, 1792-1893.
(15) P. 65.—Upper Canada, 1792-1840.
(16) P. 66.—Canadian Journalism.
(17) P. 66.—Howe's Speeches.
(18) P. 66.—" Sam Slick."
(19) P. 66.—Judge Haliburton's History of Nova Scotia.
(20) P. 66.—W. Smith's History of Canada.
(21) P. 67.—Joseph Bouchette's Topographical Works on Canada.
(22) P. 67.—M. Bibaud's Histories of Canada.
(23) P. 67.—Thompson's Book on the War of 1812-14.
(24) P. 67.—Belknap's History of New Hampshire.
(25) P. 67.—The poet Crémazie.
(26) P. 68.—Chauveau as a poet.
(27) P. 69.—Howe's Poems.
(28) P. 69.—The poets Sangster and McLachlan.
(29) P. 69.—Charles Heavysege's Works.
(30) P. 69.—Todd's Parliamentary Government.
(31) P. 69.—Christie's History of Lower Canada.
(32) P. 70.—Garneau's History of Canada.
(33) P. 70.—Ferland and Faillon as Canadian Historians.
(34) P. 70.—Dent's Histories of Canada.

xii BIBLIOGRAPHICAL, ART AND GENERAL NOTES.

OUR INTELLECTUAL
STRENGTH AND WEAKNESS.

A SHORT REVIEW OF

LITERATURE, EDUCATION AND ART IN CANADA

I.

I cannot more appropriately commence this address than by
a reference to an oration delivered seven years ago in the great
hall of a famous university which stands beneath the stately
elms of Cambridge, in the old " Bay State " of Massachusetts : a
noble seat of learning in which Canadians take a deep interest,
not only because some of their sons have completed their education within its walls, but because it represents that culture and
scholarship which know no national lines of separation, but
belong to the world's great Federation of Learning. The orator
was a man who, by his deep philosophy, his poetic genius, his
broad patriotism, his love for England, her great literature and
history, had won for himself a reputation not equalled in some
respects by any other citizen of the United States of these later
times. In the course of a brilliant oration in honour[1]* of the two
hundred and fiftieth anniversary of the foundation of Harvard,
James Russell Lowell took occasion to warn his audience against
the tendency of a prosperous democracy " towards an overweening
confidence in itself and its home-made methods, an overestimate

---

[1]* In all cases the references are to the Notes in the Appendix.

of material success and a corresponding indifference to the things of the mind." He did not deny that wealth is a great fertilizer of civilization and of the arts that beautify it ; that wealth is an excellent thing since it means power, leisure and liberty ; "but these," he went on to say, "divorced from culture, that is, from intelligent purpose, become the very mockery of their own essence, not goods, but evils fatal to their possessor, and bring with them, like the Nibelungen Hoard, a doom instead of a blessing." "I am saddened," he continued, "when I see our success as a nation measured by the number of acres under tillage, or of bushels of wheat exported ; for the real value of a country must be weighed in scales more delicate than the balance of trade. The garners of Sicily are empty now, but the bees from all climes still fetch honey from the tiny garden-plot of Theocritus. On a map of the world you may cover Judea with your thumb, Athens with a finger-tip, and neither of them figures in the Prices Current ; but they still lord it in the thought and action of every civilized man. Did not Dante cover with his hood all that was Italy six hundred years ago ? And if we go back a century, where was Germany outside of Weimar ? Material success is good, but only as the necessary preliminary of better things. The measure of a nation's true success is the amount it has contributed to the thought, the moral energy, the intellectual happiness, the spiritual hope and consolation of mankind."

These eloquently suggestive words, it must be remembered, were addressed by a great American author to an audience, made up of eminent scholars and writers, in the principal academic seat of that New England which has given birth to Emerson, Longfellow, Bancroft, Prescott, Motley, Hawthorne, Holmes, Parkman, and many others, representing the brightest thought and intellect of this continent. These writers were the product of the intellectual development of the many years that had passed since the pilgrims landed on the historic rock of Plymouth. Yet, while Lowell could point to such a brilliant array of historians, essayists, poets and novelists, as I have just named, as the latest results of New England culture, he felt compelled to utter a word of remonstrance against that spirit of materialism that was then as now abroad in the land, tending to stifle those generous intellectual aspirations which are best calculated to make a people truly happy and great.

Let us now apply these remarks of the eminent American poet and thinker to Canada—to ourselves, whose history is even older than that of New England; contemporaneous rather with that of Virginia, since Champlain landed on the heights of Quebec and laid the foundations of the ancient capital only a year after the English adventurers of the days of King James set their feet on the banks of the river named after that sovereign and commenced the old town which has long since disappeared before the tides of the ocean that stretches away beyond the shores of the Old Dominion. [2] If we in Canada are open to the same charge of attaching too much importance to material things, are we able at the same time to point to as notable achievements in literature as results of the three centuries that have nearly passed since the foundation of New France? I do not suppose that the most patriotic Canadian, however ready to eulogize his own country, will make an effort to claim an equality with New England in this respect; but, if indeed we feel it necessary to offer any comparison that would do us justice, it would be with that Virginia whose history is contemporaneous with that of French Canada. Statesmanship rather than Letters has been the pride and ambition of the Old Dominion, its brightest and highest achievement. Virginia has been the mother of great orators and great presidents, and her men of letters sink into insignificance alongside of those of New England. It may be said, too, of Canada, that her history in the days of the French regime, during the struggle for responsible government, as well as at the birth of confederation, gives us the names of men of statesmanlike designs and of patriotic purpose. From the days of Champlain to the establishment of the confederation, Canada has had the services of men as eminent in their respective spheres, and as successful in the attainment of popular rights, in moulding the educational and political institutions of the country, and in laying broad and deep the foundations of a new nationality across half a continent, as those great Virginians to whom the world is ever ready to pay its meed of respect. These Virginian statesmen won their fame in the large theatre of national achievement—in laying the basis of the most remarkable federal republic the world has ever seen ; whilst Canadian public men have laboured with equal earnestness and ability in that far less conspicuous and brilliant arena of colonial development, the eulogy of which has to be written in the histories of the future.

II.

Let me now ask you to follow me for a short time whilst I review some of the most salient features of our intellectual progress since the days Canada entered on its career of competition in the civilization of this continent. So far there have been three well defined eras of development in the country now known as the Dominion of Canada. First, there was the era of French Canadian occupation which in many respects had its heroic and picturesque features. Then, after the cession of Canada to England, came that era of political and constitutional struggle for a larger measure of public liberty which ended in the establishment of responsible government about half a century ago. Then we come to that era which dates from the confederation of the provinces—an era of which the first quarter of a century only has passed, of which the signs are still full of promise, despite the prediction of gloomy thinkers, if Canadians remain true to themselves and face the future with the same courage and confidence that have distinguished the past.

As I have just said, the days of the French regime were in a sense days of heroic endeavour, since we see in the vista of the past a small colony whose total population at no period exceeded eighty thousand souls, chiefly living on the banks of the St. Lawrence, between Quebec and Montreal, and contending against great odds for the supremacy on the continent of America. The pen of Francis Parkman has given a vivid picture of those days when bold adventurers unlocked the secrets of this Canadian Dominion, pushed into the western wilderness, followed unknown rivers, and at last found a way to the waters of that southern gulf where Spain had long before, in the days of Grijalva, Cortez and Pineda, planted her flag and won treasures of gold and silver from an unhappy people who soon learned to curse the day when the white men came to the fair islands of the south and the rich country of Mexico. In these days the world, with universal acclaim has paid its tribute of admiration to the memory of a great Discoverer who had the courage of his convictions and led the way to the unknown lands beyond the Azores and the Canaries. This present generation has forgiven him much in view of his heroism in facing the dangers of unknown seas and piercing their mysteries. His purpose was so great, and his success so conspicuous, that both have obscured his human weakness. In some respects he was wiser than the age in which he lived ; in others he was the product of the greed and the superstition of that age ; but we who owe him so much forget the frailty of the man in the sagacity of the Discoverer. As Canadians, however, now review the character of the great Genoese, and of his compeers and successors in the opening up of this continent, they must, with pride, come to the conclusion that none of these men can compare in nobility of purpose, in sincere devotion to God, King and Country, with Champlain, the sailor of Brouage, who became the founder of Quebec and the father of New France.

In the daring ventures of Marquette, Jolliet, La Salle and Tonty, in the stern purpose of Frontenac, in the far-reaching plans of La Galissonière, in the military genius of Montcalm, the historian of the present time has at his command the most attractive materials for his pen. But we cannot expect to find the signs of intellectual development among a people where there was not a single printing press, where freedom of thought and action was repressed by a paternal absolutism, where the struggle for life was very bitter up to the last hours of French supremacy in a country constantly exposed to the misfortunes of war, and too often neglected by a king who thought more of his mistresses than of his harassed and patient subjects across the sea. Yet that memorable period—days of struggle in many ways —was the origin of a large amount of literature which we, in these times, find of the deepest interest and value from a historic point of view. The English colonies of America cannot present us with any books which, for faithful narrative and simplicity of style, bear comparison with the admirable works of Champlain, explorer and historian,[3] or with those of the genial and witty advocate, Marc Lescarbot,[4] names that can never be forgotten on the picturesque heights of Quebec, or on the banks of the beautiful basin of Annapolis. Is there a Canadian or American writer who is not under a deep debt of obligation to the clear-headed and industrious Jesuit traveller, Charlevoix,[5] the Nestor of French Canadian history? The only historical writer that can at all surpass him in New England was the loyalist Governor Hutchinson, and he published his books at a later time when the French dominion had disappeared with the fall of Quebec.[6] To the works just mentioned we may add the books of Gabriel Sagard,[7] and of Boucher, the governor of Three Rivers and founder of a still eminent French Canadian family;[8] that remarkable collection of authentic historic narrative, known as the Jesuit Relations;[9] even that tedious Latin compilation by Père du Creux,[10] the useful narrative by La Potherie,[11] the admirable account of Indian life and customs by the Jesuit Lafitau,[11] and that now very rare historical account of the French colony, the "Etablissement de la Foy dans la Nouvelle France," written by the Recollet le Clercq,[12] probably aided by Frontenac. In these and other works, despite their diffuseness in some cases, we have a library of historical literature, which, when supplemented by the great stores of official documents still preserved in the French archives, is of priceless value as a true and minute record of the times in which the authors lived, or which they described from the materials to which they alone had access. It may be said with truth that none of these writers were Canadians in the sense that they were born or educated in Canada, but still they were the product of the life, the hardships and the realities of New France—it was from this country they drew the inspiration that gave vigour and colour to their writings. New England, as I have already said, never originated a class of writers who produced work of equal value, or indeed of equal literary merit. Religious and polemic controversy had the chief attraction for the gloomy, disputatious puritan native of Massachusetts and the adjoining colonies. Cotton Mather was essentially a New England creation, and if quantity were the criterion of literary merit then he was the most distinguished author of his century ; for it is said that indefatigable antiquarians have counted up the titles of nearly four hundred books and pamphlets by this industrious writer. His principal work, however, was the "Magnalia Christi Americana, or Ecclesiastical History of New England from 1620 to 1698," [13] a large folio, remarkable as a curious collection of strange conceits, forced witticisms, and prolixity of narrative, in which the venturesome reader soon finds himself so irretrievably mystified and lost that he rises from the perusal with wonderment that so much learning, as was evidently possessed by the author, could be so used to bewilder the world of letters. The historical knowledge is literally choked up with verbiage and mannerisms. Even prosy du Creux becomes tolerable at times compared with the garrulous Puritan author.

Though books were rarely seen, and secular education was extremely defective as a rule throughout the French colony, yet at a very early period in its history remarkable opportunities were afforded for the education of a priesthood and the cult of the principles of the Roman Catholic religion among those classes who were able to avail themselves of the facilities offered by the Jesuit College, which was founded at Quebec before even Harvard at Cambridge, or by the famous Great and Lesser Seminaries in the same place, in connection with which, in later times, rose the University with which is directly associated the name of the most famous Bishop of the French regime. The influence of such institutions was not simply in making Canada a most devoted daughter of that great Church, which has ever exercised a paternal and even absolute care of its people, but also in discouraging a purely materialistic spirit and probably keeping alive a taste for letters among a very small class, especially the priests, who, in politics as in society, have been always a controlling element in the French province. Evidences of some culture and intellectual aspirations in the social circles of the ancient capital attracted the surprise of travellers who visited the country before the close of the French dominion. " Science and the fine arts," wrote Charlevoix, " have their turn, and conversation does not fail. The Canadians breathe from their birth an air of liberty, which makes them very pleasant in the intercourse of life, and our language is nowhere more purely spoken." La Galissonière, who was an associate member of the French Academy of Science, and the most highly cultured governor ever sent out by France, spared no effort to encourage a systematic study of scientific pursuits in Canada. Dr. Michel Sarrazin,[13a] who was a practising physician in Quebec for nearly half a century, devoted himself most assiduously to the natural history of the colony, and made some valuable contributions to the French Academy, of which he was a correspondent. The Swedish botanist, Peter Kalm, who visited America in the middle of the last century, was impressed with the liking for scientific study which he observed in the French colony. " I have found," he wrote, " that eminent persons, generally speaking, in this country, have much more taste for natural history and literature than in the English colonies, where the majority of people are entirely engrossed in making their fortune, whilst science is as a rule held in very light esteem." Strange to say, he ignores in this passage the scientific labours of Franklin, Bartram and others he had met in Pennsylvania.[13b] As a fact such evidences of intellectual enlightenment as Kalm and Charlevoix mentioned were entirely exceptional in the colony, and never showed themselves beyond the walls of Quebec or Montreal. The province, as a whole, was in a state of mental sluggishness. The germs of intellectual life were necessarily dormant among the mass of the people, for they never could produce any rich fruition until they were freed from the spirit of absolutism which distinguished French supremacy, and were able to give full expression to the natural genius of their race under the inspiration of the liberal government of England in these later times.

III.

Passing from the heroic days of Canada, which, if it could hardly in the nature of things originate a native literature, at least inspired a brilliant succession of historians, essayists and poets in much later times, we come now to that period of constitutional and political development which commenced with the rule of England. It does not fall within the scope of this address to dwell on the political struggles which showed their intensity in the rebellion of 1837-8, and reached their fruition in the concession of parliamentary government, in the large sense of the term, some years later. These struggles were carried on during times when there was only a sparse population chiefly centred in the few towns of Nova Scotia, New Brunswick, Upper and Lower Canada, on the shores of the Atlantic, on the banks of the St. Lawrence and Lake Ontario, and not extending beyond the peninsula of the present province of Ontario. The cities, or towns rather, of Halifax, St. John, Quebec, Montreal, Kingston and York, were then necessarily the only centres of intellectual life. Education was chiefly under the control of religious bodies or in the hands of private teachers. In the rural districts it was at the lowest point possible,[14] and the great system of free schools which has of late years extended through the Dominion—and is the chief honour of Ontario—was never dreamed of in those times of sluggish growth and local apathy, when communication between the distant parts of the country was slow and wretched, when the conditions of life were generally very hard and rude, when the forest still covered the greater portion of the most fertile districts of Ontario,[15] though here and there the pioneer's axe could be heard from morn to eve hewing out little patches of sunlight, so many glimpses of civilization and better times amid the wildness of a new land even then full of promise.

The newspapers of those days were very few and came only at uncertain times to the home of the farmer by the side of some stream or amid the dense forest, or to the little hamlets that were springing up in favoured spots, and represented so many radiating influences of intelligence on the borders of the great lakes and their tributary streams, on the Atlantic seaboard, or on the numerous rivers that form so many natural highways to the people of the maritime provinces. These newspapers were for years mostly small quarto or folio sheets, in which the scissors played necessarily the all-important part ; but there was, nevertheless, before 1840 in the more pretentious journals of the large towns, some good writing done by thoughtful men who studied their questions, and helped to atone for the very bitter vindictive partisan attacks on opponents that too frequently sullied the press in those times of fierce conflict.[16] Books were only found in the homes of the clergy or of the official classes, and these were generally old editions and rarely the latest publications of the time. Montreal and Quebec, for many years, were the only places where bookstores and libraries of more than a thousand volumes could be seen. It was not until 1813 that a successful effort was made to establish a "social library" at Kingston, Bath, and some other places in the Midland district. Toronto had no library worth mentioning until 1836. What culture existed in those rude days was to be hunted up among the clergy, especially of the Church of England, the Roman Catholic priests of Lower Canada, and the official classes of the large towns. Some sermons that have come down to us, in pamphlets of very common paper—and very few were printed in those days when postage was dear and bookselling was not profitable—have no pretensions to originality of thought or literary style : sermons in remarkable contrast with the brilliant and suggestive utterances of such modern pulpit orators as Professor Clarke, of Trinity. The exhaustive and, generally, closely reasoned sermons of the Presbyterian divine had a special flavour of the Westminster confession and little of the versatility of preachers like Principal Grant in these later times when men are attempting to make even dogma more genial, and to understand the meaning of the sermon in the Mount. Then, as always in Canada, there were found among the clergy of all denominations hardworking, self-denying priests and missionaries who brought from time to time to some remote settlement of the provinces spiritual consolation and to many a household, long deprived of the intellectual nourishment of other days, an opportunity of conversing on subjects which in the stern daily routine of their lives in a new country were seldom or ever talked of. It was in the legislative halls of the provinces that the brightest intellect naturally found scope for its display, and at no subsequent period of the political history of Canada were there more fervid, earnest orators than appeared in the days when the battle for responsible government was at its height. The names of Nelson, Papineau, Howe, Baldwin, Wilmot, Johnstone, Young, Robinson, Rolph and Mackenzie recall the era when questions of political controversy and political freedom stimulated mental development among that class which sought and found the best popular opportunities for the display of their intellectual gifts in the legislative halls in the absence of a great printing press and a native literature. Joseph Howe's speeches [17] displayed a wide culture, an original eloquence, and a patriotic aspiration beyond those of any other man of his time and generation, and would have done credit to the Senate of the United States, then in the zenith of its reputation as a body of orators and statesmen. It is an interesting fact that Howe, then printer and publisher, should have printed the first work of the only great humorist that Canada has yet produced. I mean of course "The Clockmaker," [18] in which Judge Haliburton created "Sam Slick," a type of a Down-east Yankee pedlar who sold his wares by a judicious use of that quality which is sure to be appreciated the world over, "Soft sawder and human natur'." In this work, which has run through ever so many editions, and is still found on the shelves of every well-equipped library and bookstore, Sam Slick told some home truths to his somewhat self-satisfied countrymen who could not help laughing even if the humour touched them very keenly at times. Nova Scotia has changed much for the better since those dull times when the house of assembly was expected to be a sort of political providence, to make all the roads and bridges, and give good times and harvests; but even now there are some people cruel enough, after a visit to Halifax, to hint that there still is a grain of truth in the following reflection on the enterprise of that beautiful port: "How the folks to Halifax take it all out in talkin'—they talk of steam-boats, whalers and railroads—but they all end where they begin—in talk. I don't think I'd be out in my latitude if I was to say they beat the womankind at that. One feller says, I talk of goin' to England—another says, I talk of goin' to the country—while another says, I talk of goin' to sleep. If we Yankees happen to speak of such things we say, 'I'm right off down East;' or 'I'm away off South,' and away we go jist like a streak of lightnin'." This clever humourist also wrote the best history [19]—one of his own province—that had been written in British North America up to that time—indeed it is still most readable, and worthy of a place in every library. In later days the Judge wrote many other books and became a member of the English House of Commons: but "Sam Slick" still remains the most signal illustration of his original genius.

During this period, however, apart from the two works to which I have referred, we look in vain for any original literature worthy of special mention. A history of Canada written by William Smith,[20] a son of an eminent chief justice of New York, and subsequently of Canada, was published in excellent style for those days as early as 1815 at Quebec, but it has no special value except to the collector of old and rare books. Bouchette's topographical and geographical account of Canada[21] illustrated the ability and zeal of an eminent French Canadian, who deserved the thanks of his country, but these well printed books were, after all, mere compilations and came from the English press. Pamphlets were numerous enough, and some of them had literary skill, but they had, in the majority of cases, no permanent value except to the historian or antiquarian of the present day who must sift out all sorts of material and study every phase and incident of the times he has chosen for his theme. Michel Bibaud wrote a history of French Canada,[22] which no one reads in these days, and the most of the other works that emanated from the Canadian press, like Thompson's "War of 1812," [23] are chiefly valued by the historical collector. It was not to be expected that in a relatively poor country, still in the infancy of its development, severely tried by political controversies, with a small population scattered over a long stretch of territory, from Sydney to Niagara, there could be any intellectual stimulus or literary effort except what was represented in newspapers like the *Gazette* of Montreal—which has always maintained a certain dignity of style in its long journalistic career—the *Gazette* and the *Canadien* of Quebec, the *Nova Scotian* of Halifax, or displayed itself in keen contests in the legislatures or court-houses of a people delighting always in such displays as there were made of mental power and natural eloquence. From a literary point of view our American neighbours had, during this period, left us away behind, in fact no comparison can be made between the two countries, laying aside the original creation of Sam Slick. Towards the close of the eighteenth century Belknap published his admirable history of New Hampshire,[24] while the third volume of Hutchinson's history of Massachusetts appeared in 1828, to close a work of rare merit alike for careful research, philosophic acuteness and literary charm. That admirable collection of political and constitutional essays known as the "Federalist" had attained a wide circulation and largely influenced the destinies of the union under the constitution of 1783. Chief Justice Marshall illumined the bench by his great judicial decisions which have won a remarkable place in legal literature, on account of their close, acute reasoning, breadth of knowledge, insight into great constitutional principles, and their immediate influence on the political development of the federal republic. Washington Irving published, as far back as 1819, his "Sketch Book," in which appeared the original creation of Rip Van Winkle, and followed it up with other works which recall Addison's delightful style, and gave him a fame abroad that no later American writer has ever surpassed Cooper's romances began to appear in 1821, and Bancroft published in 1834 the first volume of what is a great history despite its somewhat rhetorical and ambitious style. Hawthorne's "Twice Told Tales" appeared in 1835, but his fame was to be won in later years when he wrote the "Scarlet Letter" and the "House of Seven Gables," the most original and quaint productions that New England genius has yet produced. If I linger for a moment among these men it is because they were not merely American by the influence of their writings; but wherever the English tongue is spoken and English literature is read these writers of a past generation, as it may be said of others of later times, claim the gratitude of the untold thousands whom they have instructed and helped in many a weary and sad, as well as idle hour. They were not Canadians, but they illustrated the genius of this continent of ours.

IV.

It was in the years that followed the concession of responsible government that a new era dawned on Canada—an era of intellectual as well as material activity. Then common schools followed the establishment of municipal institutions in Ontario. Even the province of Quebec awoke from its sullen lethargy and assumed greater confidence in the future, as its statesmen gradually recognized the fact that the union of 1841 could be turned to the advantage of French Canada despite it having been largely based on the hope of limiting the development of French Canadian institutions. and gradually leading the way to the assimilation of the two races. Political life still claimed the best talent and energy, as it has always done in this country ; and, while Papineau soon disappeared from the arena where he had been, under a different condition of things, a powerful disturbing influence among his compatriots, men of greater discretion and wider statesmanship like Lafontaine, Morin and Cartier, took his place to the decided benefit of French Canada. Robert Baldwin, a tried and conservative reformer, yielded to the antagonistic influences that eventually arrayed themselves in his own party against him and retired to a privacy from which he never ventured until his death. William Lyon Mackenzie came back from exile and took a place once more in legislative halls only to find there was no longer scope for mere querulous agitators and restless politicians. Joseph Howe still devoted himself with untiring zeal to his countrymen in his native province, while Judge Wilmot, afterwards governor like the former in confederation days, delighted the people of New Brunswick with his rapid, fervid, scholarly eloquence. James W. Johnstone, long the leader of the Conservative party in Nova Scotia, remarkable for his great flow of language and argument; William Young, an astute politician; James Boyle Uniacke, with all the genius of an Irish orator; Laurence O'Connor Doyle, wit and Irishman; Samuel J. W. Archibald with his silver tongue, afterwards master of the rolls; Adams G. Archibald, polished gentleman; Leonard Tilley with his suavity of demeanour and skill as a politician; Charles Tupper with his great command of language, earnestness of expression and courage of conviction, were the leading exponents of the political opinions and of the culture and oratory of Nova Scotia and New Brunswick. In the upper provinces we had in addition to the names of the distinguished French Canadians I have already mentioned, those of John A. Macdonald, at all times a ready and incisive debater, a great party tactician, and a statesman of generous aspirations, who was destined to die very many years later with the knowledge that he had realized his conception of a federation uniting all the territory of British North America, from Sydney to Victoria, under one government. The names of Allan McNab, Francis Hincks, George Brown, George Etienne Cartier, Alexander Galt, D'Arcy McGee, Louis Sicotte. John Hillyard Cameron, Alexander Mackenzie, Seth Huntington, William McDougall, Antoine Dorion, Alexander Campbell, and of other men, eminent for their knowledge of finance, their powers as debaters, their graceful oratory, their legal acumen, their political skill and their intellectual achievements in their respective spheres, will be recalled by many of those who hear me, since the most eminent among them have but recently disappeared from the stage of active life.

As long as party government lasts in this country men will be divided into political divisions, and objection will be of course time and again taken to the methods by which these and other political leaders have achieved their party ends, and none of us will be always satisfied with the conclusions to which their at times overweening ambition has led them; but, taking them all in all, I believe for one who has lived all my life among politicians and statesmen that, despite their failings and weaknesses, the public men of our country in those days laboured on the whole conscientiously from their own points of view to make Canada happier and greater. Indeed, when I look around me and see what has been done in the face of great obstacles during a half century and less, I am bound to pay this tribute to those who laboured earnestly in the difficult and trying intellectual field of public life.

But this period which brought so many bright intellects into the activities of political life was distinguished also, not merely for the material advance in industry, but notably for some performance in the less hazardous walk of literature. The newspaper press with the progress of population, the increase of wealth, the diffusion of education, the construction of railways and telegraph lines, and the development of political liberty, found itself stimulated to new energy and enterprise. A daily press now commenced to meet the necessities of the larger and wealthier cities and towns. It must be admitted, however, that from a strictly intellectual point of view there was not in some respects a marked advance in the tone and style of the leading public journals. Political partisanship ran extremely high in those days—higher than it has ever since—and grosser personalities than have ever characterized newspapers in this country sullied the editorial columns of leading exponents of public opinion. No doubt there was much brilliant and forcible writing, despite the acrimony and abuse that were too often considered more necessary than incisive argument and logical reasoning when a political opponent had to be met. It was rarely that one could get at the whole truth of a question by reading only one newspaper; it was necessary to take two or three or more on different sides of politics in order to obtain even an accurate idea of the debates in the legislative halls. A Liberal or Conservative journal would consider it beneath its legitimate functions even as a newspaper to report with any fulness the speeches of its political adversaries. Of course this is not newspaper editing in the proper sense of the phrase. It is not the English method assuredly, since the London *Times*, the best example of a well-equipped and well-conducted newspaper, has always considered it necessary to give equal prominence to the speeches of Peel, Russell, Palmerston, Derby, Disraeli, Gladstone—of all the leaders irrespective of party. Even in these days of heated controversy on the Irish question one can always find in the columns of the London press fair and accurate reports of the speeches of Gladstone, Balfour, McCarthy, Chamberlain, Morley and Blake. This is the sound basis on which true and honest journalism must always rest if it is to find its legitimate reward, not in the fickle smiles of the mere party follower, but in the support of that great public which can best repay the enterprise and honesty of a true newspaper. Still, despite this violent partisanship to which bright intellects lowered themselves, and the absence of that responsibility to public opinion expected from its active teachers, the press of Canada, during the days of which I am speaking, kept pace in some essential respects with the material progress of the country, and represented too well the tone and spirit of the mass in the country where the rudiments of culture were still rough and raw. Public intelligence, however, was being gradually diffused, and according as the population increased, and the material conditions of the country improved, a literature of some merit commenced to show itself. The poems of Crémazie,[25] of Chauveau,[26] of Howe,[27] of Sangster[28] and others, were imbued with a truly Canadian spirit—with a love for Canada, its scenery, its history and its traditions, which entitled them to a larger audience than they probably ever had in this or other countries. None of those were great poets, but all of them were more or less gifted with a measure of true poetic genius, the more noteworthy because it showed itself in the rawness and newness of a colonial life. Amid the activities of a very busy period the poetic instinct of Canadians constantly found some expression. One almost now forgotten poet who was engaged in journalism in Montreal wrote an ambitious drama, "Saul," which was described at the time by a British critic as "a drama treated with great poetic power and depth of psychological knowledge which are often quite startling;" and the author followed it up with other poems, displaying also much imagination and feeling, but at no time reaching the ears of a large and appreciative audience. We can-

B

not, however, claim Charles Heavysege [29] as a product of Canadian soil and education, for he was a man of mature age when he made his home in this country, and his works were in no wise inspired by Canadian sentiment, scenery or aspiration. In history Canadians have always shown some strength, and perhaps this was to be expected in view of the fact that political and historical literature—such works as Hamilton's "Federalist" or Todd's "Parliamentary Government" [30]—naturally engages the attention of active intellects in a new country at a time when its institutions have to be moulded, and it is necessary to collect precedents and principles from the storehouse of the past for the assistance of the present. A most useful narrative of the political occurrences in Lower Canada, from the establishment of legislative institutions until the rebellion of 1837-38 and the union of 1841, was written by Mr. Robert Christie, long a publicist of note and a member of the assembly of the province. While it has no claim to literary style it has the great merit of stating the events of the day with fairness and of citing at length numerous original documents bearing on the text. [31] In French Canada the names of Garneau [32] and Ferland [33] have undoubtedly received their full meed of praise for their clearness of style, industry of research, and scholarly management of their subject. Now that the political passion that so long convulsed the public mind in this country has disappeared with the causes that gave it birth, one is hardly prepared to make as much a hero of Papineau as Garneau attempted in his assuredly great book, while the foundation of a new Dominion and the dawn of an era of larger political life, has probably given a somewhat sectional character to such historical work. Still, despite its intense French Canadian spirit, Garneau's volumes notably illustrate the literary instinct and intellectual strength which have always been distinguishing features of the best productions of the able and even brilliant men who have devoted themselves to literature with marked success among their French Canadian countrymen, who are wont to pay a far deeper homage to such literary efforts than the colder, less impulsive English Canadian character has ever shown itself disposed to give to those who have been equally worthy of recognition in the English-speaking provinces.

V.

As I glance over my library shelves I find indeed that historical literature has continued since the days of Garneau and
Ferland, to enlist the earnest and industrious study of Canadians
with more or less success. In English Canada, John Charles
Dent produced a work on the political development of Canada
from the union of 1841 until the confederation of 1867, which
was written with fairness and ability, but he was an Englishman by birth and education, though resident for many years in
the city of Toronto.³⁴ And here let me observe that though such
men as Dent, Heavysege, Faillon, Daniel Wilson, Hunt, D'Arcy
McGee and Goldwin Smith were not born or educated in Canada
like Haliburton, Logan, J. W. Dawson, Joseph Howe, Wilmot,
Cartier, Garneau, or Fréchette, but only came to this country in
the maturity of their mental powers, yet to men of their class
the Dominion owes a heavy debt of gratitude for the ability and
earnestness with which they have elevated the intellectual standard of the community where they have laboured. Although all
of us may not be prepared to accept the conclusions of the historian, or approve the judgment of the political critic ; although
we may regret that a man of such deep scholarship and wide
culture as Goldwin Smith has never yet been able to appreciate
the Canadian or growing national sentiment of this dependency,
yet who can doubt, laying aside all political or personal prejudice, that he, like the others I have named, has stimulated intellectual development in his adopted home, and so far has given
us compensation for some utterances which, so many Canadians
honestly believe, mar an otherwise useful and brilliant career.
Such literary men have undoubtedly their uses, since they seem
specially intended by a wise dispensation of affairs to cure us
of too much self-complacency, and to prevent us from falling
into a condition of mental stagnation by giving us from time to
time abundant material for reflection. So much, by way of
parenthesis, is due to the able men who have adopted Canada
as their home and have been labouring in various vocations to
stimulate the intellectual growth of this Dominion. A most

accurate historical record of the same period of our history as
that reviewed by Dent was made in French about the same
time by Louis Turcotte of Quebec.[35]   Mr. Benjamin Sulte, a member of this society, has also given us the results of many years of
conscientious research in his " Histoire des Canadiens," which
is not so well known as it ought to be, probably on account of
its cumbrous size and mode of publication.[36]   The Abbé Casgrain,
also a member of the society and a most industrious author, has
recently devoted himself with true French Canadian fervour to
the days of Montcalm and Lévis, and by the aid of a large mass
of original documents has thrown much light on a very interesting and important epoch of the history of America.[37]   Dr. Kingsford with patience and industry has continued his history of
Canada, which is distinguished by accuracy and research.[38]   It
is not my intention to enumerate all those names which merit
remark in this connection, for this is not a collection of bibliographical notes,[39] but simply a review of the more salient features
of our intellectual development in the well-marked periods of our
history.   Indeed it is gratifying to us to know that the Royal
Society comprises within its ranks nearly all the historical writers
in Canada, and it would seem too much like pure egotism were I
to dilate on their respective performances.   Of poets since the
days of Crémazie we have had our full proportion, and it is
encouraging to know that the poems of Fréchette,—whose best
work has been crowned by the French Academy,— LeMay, Reade,
Mair, Roberts, Bliss Carman, Wilfred Campbell and Lampman
have gained recognition from time to time in the world of letters
outside of Canada.[40] *   We have yet to produce in English Canada
a book of poems which can touch the sympathies and live on the
lips of the world like those of Whittier and Longfellow, but we
need not despair since even in the country which gave these
birth they have not their compeers.   Some even declare that the
only bard of promise who appears in these days to touch that
chord of nature which makes the whole world kin is James
Whitcomb Riley, the Hoosier poet, despite his tendency to ex-

[40] * A list of Canadian poems which have been printed in books (from 1867-
1893) appears in the Bibliographical Notes (40).

aggerate provincial dialect and make his true poetic genius too subordinate to what becomes at last an affectation and a mere mannerism which wearies by its very repetition. Even in England there is hesitation in choosing a poet laureate ; there are Swinburne, Morris and other poets, but not another Tennyson, and it has been even suggested that the honour might pass to a master of poetic prose, John Ruskin, whose brilliant genius has been ever devoted to a lofty idealism which would make the world much happier and better. At the present time Canadian poets obtain a place with regularity in the best class of American magazines, and not infrequently their verse reaches a higher level than the majority of poetic aspirants who appear in the same field of poetry ; but for one I am not an ardent admirer of American magazine poems which appear too often mere machine work and not the results of that true poetic inspiration which alone can achieve permanent fame.

The poems of the well known American authors, Aldrich, Gilder and Stedman, have certainly an easy rhythmical flow and an artistic finish which the majority of Canadian poetic aspirants should study with far more closeness. At the same time it may be said that even these artists do not often surpass in poetic thought the best productions of the Canadians to whom I have referred as probably illustrating most perfectly the highest development so far among us of this department of *belles-lettres.* It is not often that one comes across more exquisitely conceived poems than some of those written by Mr. John Reade, whom the laborious occupation of journalism and probably the past indifference of a Canadian public to Canadian poetry have for a long while diverted from a literary field where it would seem he should have won a wider fame. Among the verses which one can read time and again are those of which the first lines are

" In my heart are many chambers through which I wander free,
Some are furnished, some are empty, some are sombre, some are light ;
Some are open to all comers, and of some I keep the key,
And I enter in the stillness of the night." [41] *

---

[41] * Given in full in Appendix.

It would be interesting as well as instructive if some competent critic, with the analytical faculty and the poetic instinct of Matthew Arnold or Sainte-Beuve, were to study the English and French Canadian poets and show whether they are mere imitators of the best models of French and English literature, or whether their work contains within itself those germs which give promise of original fruition in the future. It will be remembered that the French critic, though a poet of merit himself, has spoken of what he calls "the radical inadequacy of French poetry." In his opinion, whatever talent the French poets have for strophe and line, their work, as a rule is "too slight, too soon read, too poor in ideas, to influence a serious mind for any length of time." No doubt many others think that, in comparison with the best conceptions of Wordsworth, Shelley, Keats, Emerson, Browning and Tennyson, French poetry is, generally speaking, inadequate for the expression of the most sublime thoughts, of the strongest passion, or of the most powerful imagination, and though it must always please us by its easy rhythm and lucidity of style, it fails to make that vivid impression on the mind and senses which is the best test of that true poetic genius which influences generations and ever lives in the hearts of the people. It represents in some respects the lightness and vivacity of the French intellectual temperament under ordinary conditions, and not the strength of the national character, whose depths are only revealed at some crisis which evokes a deep sentiment of patriotism. "Partant pour la Syrie," so often heard in the days of the last Bonaparte regime, probably illustrated this lighter tendency of the French mind just as the "Marseillaise," the noblest and most impressive of popular poetic outbursts, illustrated national passion evoked by abnormal conditions. French Canadian poetry has been often purely imitative of French models, like Musset and Gauthier, both in style and sentiment, and consequently lacked strength and originality. It might be thought that in this new country poets would be inspired by original conceptions —that the intellectual fruition would be fresh and vigorous like some natural products that grow so luxuriantly on the virginal soil of the new Dominion, and not like those which grow on land which is renewed and enriched by artificial means after centu-

ries of growth.   Perhaps the literature of a colonial dependency,
or a relatively new country, must necessarily in its first stages
be imitative, and it is only now and then an original mind bursts
the fetters of intellectual subordination.   In the United States
Emerson and Hawthorne probably best represent the original
thought and imagination of that comparatively new country,
just as Aldrich and Howells represent in the first case English
culture in poetry, and in the other the sublimated essence of
reportorial realism.   The two former are original thinkers, the
two others pure imitators.   Walt Whitman's poems certainly
show at times much power and originality of conception, but
after all they are simply the creations of an eccentric genius
and illustrate a phase of that Realism towards which fiction
even in America has been tending of late, and which has been
already degraded in France to a Naturalism which is positively
offensive.   He has not influenced to any perceptible extent the
intellect of his generation or elevated the thoughts of his countrymen like the two great minds I have just named.   Yet even
Whitman's success, relatively small as it was in his own country, arose chiefly from the fact that he attempted to be an *American* poet, representing the pristine vigour and natural freedom
of a new land.   It is when French Canadian poets become thoroughly Canadian by the very force of the inspiration of some
Canadian subject they have chosen, that we can see them at their
best.   Fréchette has all the finish of the French poets, and while
it cannot be said that he has yet originated great thoughts which
are likely to live among even the people whom he has so often
instructed and delighted, yet he has given us poems like that on
the discovery of the Mississippi,* which proves that he is capable of even better things if he would always seek inspiration
from the sources of the deeply interesting history of his own country, or enter into the inner mysteries and social relations of his
own people, rather than dwell on the lighter shades and incidents of their lives.   Perhaps in some respects Crémazie had
greater capabilities for the poems of deep passion or vivid imagination than any of his successors in literature ; the few national

* See Appendix to this work, note 40, for an extract from this fine poem.

poems he left behind are a promise of what he could have produced had the circumstances of his later life been happier.* After all, the poetry that lives is the poetry of human life and human sympathy, of joy and sorrow, rather than verses on mountains, rivers and lakes, or sweetly worded sonnets to Madame B, or Mademoiselle C. When we compare the English with the French Canadian poets we can see what an influence the more picturesque and interesting history of French Canada exercises on the imagination of its writers. The poets that claim Ontario for their home give us rhythmical and pleasing descriptions of the lake and river scenery of which the varied aspects and moods might well captivate the eye of the poet as well as of the painter. It is very much painting in both cases ; the poet should be an artist by temperament equally with the painter who puts his thoughts on canvas and not in words. Descriptions of our meadows, prairies and forests, with their wealth of herbage and foliage, or artistic sketches of pretty bits of lake scenery have their limitations as respects their influence on a people. Great thoughts or deeds are not bred by scenery. The American poem that has captured the world is not any one of Bryant's delightful sketches of the varied landscape of his native land, but Longfellow's Evangeline, which is a story of the " affection that hopes, and endures and is patient." Dollard, and the Lady of Fort La Tour are themes which we do not find in prosaic Ontario, whose history is only a century old—a history of stern materialism as a rule, rarely picturesque or romantic, and hardly ever heroic except in some episodes of the war of 1812–15, in which Canadians, women as well as men, did their duty faithfully to king and country, though their deeds have never yet been adequately told in poem or prose. The story of Laura Secord's toilsome journey on a June day eighty years ago [41a] seems as susceptible of strong poetic treatment as Paul Revere's Ride, told in matchless verse by Longfellow.

I think if we compare the best Canadian poems with the same class of literature in Australia the former do not at all lose

* See Appendix to this work, note 40, for an extract from one of his national poems.

by the comparison. Thanks to the thoughtfulness of a friend in South Australia I have had many opportunities of late of studying the best work of Australian writers, chiefly poets and novelists,[42] and have come to the conclusion that at least the poets of both hemispheres—for to fiction we cannot make even a pretense —reflect credit on each country. In one respect indeed Canadians can claim a superiority over their fellow-citizens of the British Empire in that far off Australian land, and that is, in the fact that we have poets, and historians, and essayists, who write the languages of France and England with purity and even elegance ; that the grace and precision of the French tongue have their place in this country alongside the vigorous and copious expression of the English language. More than that, the Canadians have behind them a history which is well calculated to stimulate writers to give utterance to national sentiment. I mean national in the sense of being thoroughly imbued with a love for the country, its scenery, its history and its aspirations. The people of that great island continent possess great natural beauties and riches—flowers and fruits of every kind flourish there in rare profusion, and gold and gems are among the treasures of the soil, but its scenery is far less varied and picturesque than ours and its history is but of yesterday compared with that of Canada. Australians cannot point to such historic ground as is found from Louisbourg to Quebec, or from Montreal to Champlain, the battle ground of nations whose descendants now live under one flag, animated by feelings of a common interest and a common aspiration for the future !

Perhaps if I were at any time inclined to be depressed as to the future of Canada, I should find some relief in those poems by Canadian authors which take frequently an elevated and patriotic range of thought and vision, and give expression to aspirations worthy of men born and living in this country. When some men doubt the future and would see us march into the ranks of other states, with heads bowed down in confession of our failure to hold our own on this continent and build up a new nation always in the closest connection with England, I ask them to turn to the poems of Joseph Howe and read that inspiring

poetic tribute to the mother country, "All hail to the day when
the Britons came over "—

> " Every flash of her genius our pathway enlightens,
> Every field she explores we are beckoned to tread,
> Each laurel she gathers, our future day brightens—
> We joy with her living and mourn with her dead." [43]

Or read that tribute which the French Canadian laureate,
Fréchette, has been fain to pay to the English flag under whose
folds his country has enjoyed so much freedom and protection for
its institutions :

> " Regarde me disait mon père
> Ce drapeau vaillamment porté ;
> Il a fait ton pays prospère
> Et respecte ta liberté.

> " C'est le drapeau de l'Angleterre ;
> Sans tache, sur le firmament,
> Presque à tous les points de la terre
> Il flotte glorieusement."

Or take up a volume by Roberts and read that frequently
quoted poem of which these are the closing lines :

> " Shall not our love this rough sweet land make sure?
> Her bounds preserve inviolate, though we die.
> O strong hearts of the North,
> Let flame your loyalty forth,
> And put the craven and base to an open shame,
> Till earth shall know the Child of Nations by her name."

Even Mr. Edgar has forgotten the astute lawyer and the
politician in his national song, "This Canada of Ours," and has
given expression to the deep sentiment that lies as I have said
in the heart of every true Canadian and forces him at times to
words like these :

> " Strong arms shall guard our cherished homes
> When darkest danger lowers,
> And with our life-blood we'll defend
> This Canada of ours,
> Fair Canada,
> Dear Canada,
> This Canada of ours."

Such poems are worth a good many political speeches even in parliament so far as their effect upon the hearts and sympathies is concerned. We all remember a famous man once said, " Let me make all the ballads, and I care not who makes the laws of a people."

VI.

But if Canada can point to some creditable achievement of recent years in history, poetry and essay-writing —for I think if one looks from time to time at the leading magazines and reviews of the two continents he will find that Canada is fairly well represented in their pages [44]—there is one respect in which Canadians have never won any marked success, and that is in the novel or romance. " Wacousta, or the Prophecy : a Tale of the Canadas," was written sixty years ago by Major John Richardson,[44a] a native Canadian, but it was at the best a spirited imitation of Cooper, and has not retained the interest it attracted at a time when the American novelist had created a taste for exaggerated pictures of Indian life and forest scenery. Of course attempts have been made time and again by other English Canadians to describe episodes of our history, and portray some of our national and social characteristics, but with the single exception of " The Golden Dog,"[45] written a few years ago by Mr. William Kirby, of Niagara, I cannot point to one which shows much imaginative or literary skill. If we except the historical romance by Mr. Marmette, " François de Bienville,"[46] which has had several editions, French Canada is even weak in this particular, and this is the more surprising because there is abundance of material for the novelist or writer of romance in her peculiar society and institutions, and in her historic annals and traditions. But as yet neither a Cooper, nor an Irving, nor a Hawthorne has appeared to delight Canadians in the fruitful field of fiction that their country offers to the pen of imaginative genius. It is true we have a work by De Gaspé, " Les Anciens Canadiens,"[47] which has been translated by Roberts and one or two others, but it has rather the value of historical annals than the spirit and form of true romance. It is the very poverty of our production in what ought to be a rich source of literary inspiration, French Canadian life and history, that has given currency to a work whose signal merit is its simplicity of style and adherence to historical fact. As Parkman many years ago first commenced to illumine the too often dull pages of Canadian history, so other American writers have also ventured in the still fresh field of literary effort that romance offers to the industrious, inventive brain. In the "Romance of Dollard," "Tonty," and the "Lady of Fort St. John," Mrs. Mary Hartwell Catherwood has recalled most interesting episodes of our past annals with admirable literary taste and a deep enthusiasm for Canadian history in its romantic and picturesque aspects.[48] When we read Conan Doyle's "Refugees"—the best historical novel that has appeared from the English Press for years—we may well regret that it is not Canadian genius which has created so fascinating a romance out of the materials that exist in the history of the *ancien régime*. Dr. Doyle's knowledge of Canadian life and history is obviously very superficial; but slight as it is he has used it with a masterly skill to give Canada a part in his story—to show how closely associated were the fortunes of the colony with the French Court,—with the plans and intrigues of the king and his mistresses, and of the wily ecclesiastics who made all subservient to their deep purpose. It would seem from our failure to cultivate successfully the same popular branch of letters that Canadians are wanting in the inventive and imaginative faculty, and that the spirit of materialism and practical habits, which has so long necessarily cramped literary effort in this country, still prevents happy ventures in this direction. It is a pity that no success has been won in this country,—as in Australia by Mrs. Campbell Praed, "Tasma," and many others,—in the way of depicting those characteristics of Canadian life, in the past and present, which, when touched by the imaginative and cultured intellect, will reach the sympathies and earn the plaudits of all classes of readers at home and abroad. Perhaps, Mr. Gilbert Parker,[49] now a resident of London, but a Canadian by birth, education and sympathies, will yet succeed in his laudable ambition of giving form and vitality to the abundant materials

that exist in the Dominion, among the habitants on the old seig-
neuries of the French province, in that historic past of which the
ruins still remain in Montreal and Quebec, in the Northwest with
its quarrels of adventurers in the fur trade, and in the many other
sources of inspiration that exist in this country for the true story-
teller who can invent a plot and give his creations a touch of
reality, and not that doll-like, saw-dust appearance that the vapid
characters of some Canadian stories assume from the very poverty
of the imagination that has originated them.

That imagination and humour have some existence in the
Canadian mind—though one sees little of those qualities in the
press or in public speeches, or in parliamentary debates—we can
well believe when we read "The Dodge Club Abroad," by Professor De Mille,[50] who was cut off in the prime of his intellectual
strength, or "A Social Departure," by Sara Jeannette Duncan,[51]
who, as a sequence of a trip around the world, has given us not
a dry book of travels but a story with touches of genial humour
and bright descriptions of life and nature, and who is now following up that excellent literary effort by promising sketches of East
Indian life. A story which attracted some attention not long
since for originality of conception and ran through several editions, "Beggars All," is written by a Miss L. Dougall, who is said
to be a member of a Montreal family, and though this book does
not deal with incidents of Canadian life it illustrates that fertility
of invention which is latent among our people and only requires
a favourable opportunity to develop itself. The best literature
of this kind is like that of France, which has the most intimate
correspondence with the social life and development of the people
of the country. "The excellence of a romance," writes Chevalier
Bunsen in his critical preface to Gustav Freytag's "Debit and
Credit," "like that of an epic or a drama, lies in the apprehension
and truthful exhibition of the course of human things...............
The most vehement longing of our times is manifestly after a
faithful mirror of the present." With us, all efforts in this
direction have been most common place — hardly above the
average of "Social Notes" in the columns of Ottawa newspapers.

I do not for one depreciate the influence of good fiction on the minds of a reading community like ours ; it is inevitable that a busy people, and especially women distracted with household cares, should always find that relief in this branch of literature which no other reading can give them ; and if the novel has then become a necessity of the times in which we live, at all events I hope Canadians, who may soon venture into the field, will study the better models, endeavour to infuse some originality into their creations and plots, and not bring the Canadian fiction of the future to that low level to which the school of realism in France, and in a minor degree in England and the United States, would degrade the novel and story of every-day life. To my mind it goes without saying that a history written with that fidelity to original authorities, that picturesqueness of narration, that philosophic insight into the motives and plans of statesmen, that study and comprehension of the character and life of a people, which should constitute the features of a great work of this class,—that such a history has assuredly a much deeper and more useful purpose in the culture and education of the world than any work of fiction can possibly have even when animated by a lofty genius. Still as the novel and romance will be written as long as a large proportion of the world amid the cares and activities of life seeks amusement rather than knowledge, it is for the Canadian Scott, or Hawthorne, or " George Eliot," or Dickens of the future, to have a higher and purer aim than the majority of novel writers of the present day, who, with a few notable exceptions like Black, Besant, Barrie, Stephenson or Oli-phant, weary us by their dulness and lack of the imaginative and inventive faculty, and represent rather the demands of the publishers to meet the requirements of a public which must have its new novel as regularly as the Scotchman must have his porridge, the Englishman his egg and toast, and the American his ice-water.

If it were possible within the compass of this address to give a list of the many histories, poems, essays and pamphlets that have appeared from the Canadian press during the first quarter of a century since the Dominion of Canada has been in existence,

the number would astonish many persons who have not followed
our literary activity.   Of course the greater part of this work is
ephemeral in its character and has no special value ; much of the
historical work is a dreary collection of facts and dates which
shows the enterprise of school publishers and school teachers and
is generally wanting in that picturesqueness and breadth of view
which give interest to history and leave a vivid impression on
the mind of the student. Most of these pamphlets have been
written on religious, political or legal questions of the day.
Many of the poems illustrate rather the aspirations of the school
boy or maiden whose effusions generally appeared in the poet's
corner of the village newspaper.   Still there are even among these
mere literary " transients " evidences of power of incisive argument and of some literary style. In fact, all the scientific, historical and poetical contributions of the period in question, make
up quite a library of Canadian literature.   And here let me observe in passing, some persons still suppose that *belles-lettres*, works
of fiction, poetry and criticism, alone constitute literature.   The
word can take in its complete sense a very wide range, for it embraces the pamphlet or monograph on the most abstruse scientific,
or mathematical or geographical or physical subject, as well as
the political essay, the brilliant history, or the purely imaginative
poem or novel.   It is not so much the subject as the form and
style which make them worthy of a place in literature.   One of
the most remarkable books ever written, the " Esprit des Lois "
by Montesquieu, has won the highest place in literature by its
admirable style, and in the science of politics by the importance
of its matter.   The works of Lyell, Huxley, Hunt, Dawson, Tyndall, and Darwin owe their great value not entirely to the scientific ideas and principles and problems there discussed, but also
to the lucidity of style in which the whole subject is presented
to the reader, whether versed or not in science. " Literature is
a large word," says Matthew Arnold,[52] discussing with Tyndall
this very subject ; " it may mean everything written with letters
or printed in a book.   Euclid's Elements and Newton's Principia
are thus literature.   All knowledge that reaches us through
books is literature.   But as I do not mean, by knowing ancient

Rome, knowing merely more or less of Latin *belles-lettres*, and taking no account of Rome's military, and political, and legal, and administrative work in the world; and as, by knowing ancient Greece, I understand knowing her as the giver of Greek art, and the guide to a free and right use of reason and to scientific methods, and the founder of our mathematics, and physics, and astronomy, and biology, I understand knowing her as all this, and not merely knowing certain Greek poems, and histories, and treatises and speeches, so as to the knowledge of modern nations also. By knowing modern nations, I mean not merely knowing their *belles-lettres*, but knowing also what has been done by such men as Copernicus, Galileo, Newton, Darwin." I submit this definition of literature by a great English critic and poet who certainly knew what he was writing about, to the studious consideration of Principal Grant who, in an address to the Royal Society two years ago,[53] appeared to have some doubt that much of its work could be called literature ; a doubt that he forgot for the moment actually consigned to a questionable level also his many devious utterances and addresses on political, religious and other questions of the day, and left him entirely out of the ranks of *littérateurs* and in a sort of limbo which is a world of neither divinity, nor politics, nor letters. Taking this definition of the bright apostle of English culture, I think Canadians can fairly claim to have some position as a literary people even if it be a relatively humble one, on account of the work done in history, *belles-lettres*, political science and the sciences generally Science alone has had in Canada for nearly half a century many votaries who have won for themselves high distinction, as the eminent names on the list of membership of the Royal Society since its foundation can conclusively show. The literature of science, as studied and written by Canadians, is remarkably comprehensive, and finds a place in every well furnished library of the world.

The *doyen* of science in Canada, Sir William Dawson,[54] we are all glad to know, is still at work after a long and severe illness, which was, no doubt, largely due to the arduous devotion of years to education and science. It is not my intention to

refer here to other well-known names in scientific literature, but
I may pause for an instant to mention the fact that one of the
earliest scientific writers of eminence, who was a Canadian by
birth and education, was Mr. Elkanah Billings,[55] palæontologist
and geologist, who contributed his first papers to the *Citizen* of
Ottawa, then Bytown, afterwards to have greatness thrown upon
it and made the political capital of Canada.

VII.

Here I come naturally to answer the questions that may be
put by some that have not followed the history and the work of
the Royal Society of Canada,—What measure of success has it
won? has it been of value to the Canadian people in whose interests it was established, and with whose money it is mainly
supported? Twelve years have nearly passed away since a few
gentlemen, engaged in literary, scientific and educational pursuits, assembled at McGill College on the invitation of the Marquess of Lorne, then governor-general of Canada, to consider the
practicability of establishing a society which would bring together both the French and English Canadian elements of our population for purposes of common study and the discussion of such
subjects as might be profitable to the Dominion, and at the same
time develop the literature of learning and science as far as prac-
ticable.[56] This society was to have a Dominion character—to
form a union of leading representatives of all those engaged in
literature and science in the several provinces, with the principle
of federation observed in so far as it asked every society of note
in every section to send delegates to make reports on the work of
the year within its particular sphere. Of the gentlemen who
assembled at this interesting meeting beneath the roof of the
learned principal of Montreal's well-known university, the majority still continue active friends of the society they aided Lord
Lorne to found ; but I must also add with deep regret that, within
a little more than a year, two of the most distinguished promoters of the society, Dr. Thomas Sterry Hunt and Sir Daniel
Wilson, have been ca lled from their active and successful labours

c

in education, science and letters. As I know perhaps better than any one else, on account of an official connection with the society from the very hour it was suggested by Lord Lorne, no two members ever comprehended more thoroughly the useful purpose which it could serve amid the all-surrounding materialism of this country, or laboured more conscientiously until the very hour of their death by their writings and their influence to make the society a Canadian institution, broad in its scope, liberal in its culture, and elevated in its aspirations. Without dwelling on the qualifications of two men [57] whose names are imperishably connected with the work of their lifetime—archæology, education and chemistry—I may go on to say that the result of the Montreal meeting was the establishment of a society which met for the first time at Ottawa in the May of 1882, with a membership of eighty Fellows under the presidency of Dr. (afterwards Sir) William Dawson, and the vice-presidency of the Honourable P. J. O. Chauveau, a distinguished French Canadian who had won a high name, not only in literature, but also in the political world where he was for years a conspicuous figure ; noted for his eloquence, his culture and his courtesy of manner. The society was established in no spirit of isolation from other literary and scientific men because its membership was confined at the outset to eighty Fellows who had written " memoirs of merit or rendered eminent services to literature or science "—a number subsequently increased to a hundred under certain limitations. On the contrary it asks for, and has constantly published, contributions from all workers in the same fields of effort with the simple proviso that such contributions are presented with the endorsation of an actual member, though they may be read before any one of the four sections by the author himself. Every association, whether purely literature or historical, or scientific, as I have already intimated, has been asked to assist in the work of the society,[58] and its delegates given every advantage at the meetings possessed by the Fellows themselves, except voting and discussing the purely internal affairs of the Royal Society. Some misapprehension appears to have existed at first in the public mind that, because the society was named " The Royal Society of Canada,"

an exclusive and even aristocratic institution was in contempla-
tion. It seems a little perplexing to understand why an objection could be taken to such a designation when the Queen is
at the head of our system of government, and her name appears
in the very first clauses of the act of union, and in every act requiring the exercise of the royal prerogative in this loyal dependency of the crown. As a fact, in using the title, the desire was
to follow the example of similar societies in Australia, and recall
that famous Royal Society in England, whose fellowship is a title
of nobility in the world of science. Certain features were copied
from the Institute of France, inasmuch as there is a division into
sections with the idea of bringing together into each for the purposes of common study and discussion those men who have devoted themselves to special branches of the literature of learning
and science. In this country and, indeed, in America generally,
a notable tendency is what may be called the levelling principle
—to deprecate the idea that any man should be in any way
better than another ; and in order to prevent that result it is
necessary to assail him as soon as he shows any political or intellectual merit, and to stop him, if possible, from attaining that
mental superiority above his fellows that his industry and his
ability may enable him to reach. The Royal Society suffered a
little at first from this spirit of depreciation which is often carried
to an extent that one at times could almost believe that this is a
country without political virtues or intellectual development of
any kind. The claims of some of its members were disputed by
literary aspirants who did not happen for a moment to be en-
rolled in its ranks, and the society was charged with exclusive-
ness when, as a fact, it simply limited its membership, and
demanded certain qualifications, with the desire to make that
membership a test of some intellectual effort, and consequently
more prized by those who were allowed sooner or later to enter.
It would have been quite possible for the society to make itself
a sort of literary or scientific picnic by allowing every man or
woman who had, or believed they had, some elementary scientific or other knowledge to enter its ranks, and have the consequent advantages of cheap railway fares and other subsidiary

advantages on certain occasions, but its promoters did not think that would best subserve the special objects they had in view. At all events, none of them could have been prompted by any desire to create a sort of literary aristocracy. Indeed, one would like to know how any one in his senses could believe for a moment that any institution of learning could be founded with exclusive tendencies in these times, in this or any other country! If there is an intelligent democracy anywhere it is the Republic of Letters. It may be aristocratic in the sense that there are certain men and women who have won fame and stand on a pedestal above their fellows, but it is the world, not of a class, but of all ranks and conditions, that has agreed to place them on that pedestal as a tribute to their genius which has made people happier, wiser and better, has delighted and instructed the artisan as well as the noble.

For twelve years then the Royal Society has continued to persevere in its work ; and thanks to the encouragement given it by the government of Canada it has been able, year by year, to publish a large and handsome volume of the proceedings and transactions of its meetings. No other country in the world can exhibit volumes more creditable on the whole in point of workmanship than those of this society. The papers and monographs that have appeared embrace a wide field of literature—the whole range of archæological, ethnological, historical, geographical, biological, mathematical and physical studies. The volumes now are largely distributed throughout Canada—among the educated and thinking classes—and are sent to every library, society, university and learned institution of note in the world, with the hope of making the Dominion better known. The countries where they are placed for purposes of reference are these :

The United States : every	Costa Rica,	India,
State of the Union and	Uruguay,	Japan,
District of Columbia,	Guatemala,	Australia,
Newfoundland,	Venezuela,	New Zealand,
Mexico,	Chile,	Great Britain and
Brazil,	Peru,	Ireland,

Ecuador,	South Africa,	France,
Italy,	Germany,	Russia,
Greece,	Roumania,	Austria-Hungary,
Norway and Sweden,	Argentine Re-	Mauritius,
Spain,	public,	Denmark.

So well known are these 'Transactions' now in every country that, when it happens some library or institution has not received it from the beginning or has been forgotten in the distribution, the officers of the society have very soon received an intimation of the fact. This is gratifying, since it shows that the world of higher literature and of special research—the world of scholars and scientists engaged in important observation and investigation—is interested in the work that is being done in the same branches in this relatively new country. It would be impossible for me within the limits of this address to give you anything like an accurate and comprehensive idea of the numerous papers the subject and treatment of which, even from a largely practical and utilitarian point of view, have been of decided value to Canada, and I can only say here that the members of the society have endeavoured to bring to the consideration of the subjects they have discussed a spirit of conscientious study and research, and that, too, without any fee or reward except that stimulating pleasure which work of an intellectual character always brings to the mind.

In these days of critical comparative science, when the study of the aboriginal or native languages of this continent has absorbed the attention of close students, the Royal Society has endeavoured to give encouragement and currency to those studies by publishing grammars, vocabularies and other monographs relating to Indian tongues and antiquities. The Abbé Cuoq, one of the most erudite scholars of this continent in this special branch of knowledge, has nearly completed in the 'Transactions' what will be a monumental work of learning on the Algonquin language. A Haida grammar and dictionary are also now awaiting the completion of the Abbé Cuoq's work to be published in the same way. A great deal of light has been thrown on Cartier's and Champlain's voyages in the gulf, and consequently on its cartography, by the labours of the Abbé Verreau, Prof. Ganong and others. The excellent work of the Geological Survey has been supplemented by important contributions from its staff, and consequently there is to be found in the 'Transactions' a large amount of information, both abstract and practical, on the economic and other minerals of the Dominion. Chiefly owing to the efforts of the society, the government of Canada some time ago commenced to take tidal observations on the Atlantic coasts of Canada—an enterprise of great value to the shipping and commercial interests of the country—and has also co-operated in the determination of the true longitude of Montreal which is now being prosecuted under the able superintendence of Professor McLeod. It is in the same practical spirit of investigation and action that the society has published a treatise by that veteran scholar, Dr. Moses Harvey, of St. John's, Newfoundland, on "The Artificial Propagation of Marine Food-fishes and Edible Crustaceans"; and it is satisfactory to understand from a statement made in the House of Commons last session that a question of such deep interest to our great fishing industry in the maritime provinces is likely to result in some practical measure in the direction suggested. The contributions of Sir Daniel Wilson on the "Artistic Faculty in the Aboriginal Races," "The Pre-Aryan American Man," "The Trade and Commerce of the Stone Age," and "The Huron-Iroquois Race in Canada," that typical race of American Indians, were all intended to supplement in a measure that scholarly work, "Prehistoric Man," which had brought him fame many years before. Dr. Patterson of Nova Scotia, a most careful student of the past, has made valuable contributions to the history of Portuguese exploration in North American waters, and of that remarkable lost tribe known as Beothiks or Red Indians of Newfoundland. Sir William Dawson has contributed to almost every volume of the 'Transactions' from his stores of geological learning, while his distinguished son has followed closely in his footsteps, and has made valuable additions to our knowledge, not only of the geology of the Northwest, but also of the antiquities, languages and customs of the Indian tribes of

British Columbia and the adjacent islands. The opinions and theories of Dr. Thomas Sterry Hunt on the "Taconic Question in Geology," and the "Relations of the Taconic Series to the later Crystalline and the Cambrian Rocks," were given at length in the earlier volumes. Mr. G. F. Matthew, of St. John, New Brunswick, who is a very industrious student, has elaborated a work on the "Fauna of the St. John Group." Not only have our geological conditions been more fully explained, but our flora, ferns, and botany generally have been clearly set forth by Professors Lawson, Macoun and Penhallow. All these and many other papers of value have been illustrated by expensive plates, generally executed by Canadian artists. The majority of the names I have just given happen to be English Canadian, but the French language has been represented in science by such eminent men as Hamel, Laflamme and Deville—the two first illustrating the learning and culture of Laval, so long associated with the best scholarship of the province of Quebec. Without pursuing the subject further, let me say, as one who has always endeavoured to keep the interests of the society in view, that such monographs as I have mentioned represent the practical value of its work, and show what an important sphere of usefulness is invariably open to it. The object is not to publish ephemeral newspaper or magazine articles —that is to say, articles intended for merely popular information or purely literary practice—but always those essays and works of moderate compass which illustrate original research, experiment and investigation in all branches of historical, archæological, ethnological and scientific studies, and which will form a permanent and instructive reference library for scholars and students in the same branches of thought and study all over the world. In fact, the essays must necessarily be such as cannot be well published except through the assistance granted by a government, as in our case, or by the liberality of private individuals. The society, in fact, is in its way attempting just such work as is done by the Smithsonian Institute, on a large scale, at Washington, so far as the publication of important transactions is concerned. I admit that sometimes essays have appeared, but many more are offered from time to time, better suited to the periodicals of the day than to the pages of a work of which the object is to perpetuate the labours of students and scholars, and not the efforts of the mere literary amateur or trifler in *belles-lettres*. But while there must be necessarily such limitations to the scope of the ' Transactions,' which are largely scientific in their treatment, room will be always made for papers on any economic, social or ethical subject which, by their acute reasoning, sound philosophy and originality of thought, demand the attention of students everywhere. Such literary criticism as finds place now and then in the dignified old ' Quarterly Review ' or in the ' Contemporary ' will be printed whenever it is written by any Canadian author with the same power of keen analysis and judicious appreciation of the thoughts and motives of an author that we find notably in that charming study of Tennyson's " Princess," by S. E. Dawson,[59] who is a Canadian by birth, education and feeling. No doubt there is room in the Dominion for a magazine combining the features of ' Blackwood,' the ' Contemporary ' and the ' Quarterly Review '; that is to say, poetry, fiction, criticism, reviews of topics of the day, and, in fact, original literary effort of the higher order, which, though mostly ephemeral in its character, must have much influence for the time being on the culture and the education of the public mind. Since the days of the old ' Canadian Monthly,'[60] which, with all its imperfections, contained much excellent work, all efforts in the same direction have been deserving of little encouragement ; and, in fact, if such a venture is to succeed hereafter it must have behind it sufficient capital to engage the assistance of the best Canadian writers, who now send their work to American and English periodicals. Such a magazine must be carefully edited, and not made the dumping-ground for the crude efforts of literary dabblers or for romantic gush and twaddle, but must be such a judicious selection of the best Canadian talent as will evoke comparison with the higher class of periodicals I have mentioned. We have only one literary paper of merit in this country, and that is ' The Week,' which, despite all the indifference that is too apt to meet a journal not influenced by party motives, has kept its literary aim always before it, and endeavoured to do such a work as ' The New York

Nation' has been doing for years under far greater advantages in the neighbouring country with marked success and ability. In the meantime, until a magazine of the character I advocate is established, the 'Transactions of the Royal Society' cannot be expected to occupy the same ground unless it is prepared to give up that important field which it and the societies with which it is associated alone can fill in this country. In one respect, indeed, the Royal Society, in my opinion—and I have endeavoured to impress it on my fellow-members—can reach a much larger class of readers than it is now possible by means of its somewhat formidable though handsomely printed and well illustrated volumes, which necessarily are confined, for the most part, to libraries and institutions, where they can be best consulted by students who find it necessary to inform themselves on such Canadian subjects as the society necessarily treats. It is quite possible that by selecting a more convenient form, say royal octavo, and publishing the purely scientific sections in one volume and the purely literary department in another, a larger inducement will be given to the public to purchase its 'Transactions' at a moderate cost and in a more convenient shape for reading, whenever they contain monographs or large works in which Canadians generally are interested or on which they wish special information. Of course, in making this change care must be taken to maintain the typographical appearance and the character of the scientific illustrations and the usefulness of the cartography. Not only may the Royal Society in this way reach a larger reading public, but it may stimulate the efforts of historic and other writers by giving them greater facilities for obtaining special editions of their works for general sale. As it is now, each author obtains a hundred copies of his paper in pamphlets, sometimes more; and if the form is now made smaller and more handy, to use a common word, he will be induced to order a larger edition at his own cost. Even as it is now, some four or five thousand copies of essays and monographs—in special cases many more—are annually distributed by authors in addition to those circulated in the bound volumes of the 'Transactions'; and in this way any value these works may have is considerably enhanced. If it should be decided to continue the large form, at all events it will be in the interest of the society, and of the author of any monograph or history of more than ordinary value, to print it not only in the 'Transactions' but also in a smaller volume for general circulation. Practically this would meet the object in view—the larger distribution of the best work of the section devoted to historical and general literature. But whether this change is adopted or not,[61] I think the Royal Society, by showing even still greater zeal and earnestness in the work for which it was founded, by co-operating with scholars and students throughout the Dominion, by showing every possible sympathy with all those engaged in the work of art, culture and education, can look forward hopefully to the future ; and all it asks from the Canadian public at large is confidence in its work and objects, which are in no sense selfish or exclusive, but are influenced by a sincere desire to do what it can to promote historic truth and scientific research, and give a stimulus in this way to the intellectual development of this young Dominion, yet in the infancy of its literary life.[58] *

VIII.

This necessarily brief review of the work of the Royal Society could not well be left out of an address like this ; and I can now pass on to some reflections that occur to me on the general subject.

In the literature of biography, so susceptible of a treatment full of human interests and sympathies — as chatty Boswell's " Life of Johnson," and Lockhart's " Life of Scott," notably illustrate—we have little to show, except it be the enterprise of publishers and the zeal of too enthusiastic friends. Nor is it necessary to dwell on the literature of the law, which is becoming in a mea-

---

[58] * In the course of a speech by the Earl of Derby, in answer to a farewell address from the Royal Society, he took occasion to make some remarks with reference to its work and usefulness, which have been given in full in the Appendix (Note 58a) as the impartial opinion of a governor-general who always took a deep interest in all matters affecting the intellectual as well as material development of the Dominion.

sure more of a technical and less of a learned profession in the larger sense, unless, indeed, our university schools of political science eventually elevate it to a wider range of thought. Several excellent books of a purely technical character have been compiled from year to year, but no Kent, or Story, or Cooley has yet appeared to instruct us by a luminous exposition of principle, or breadth of knowledge. Those who know anything of Dr. Ed· ward Blake's great intellectual power, of his wealth of legal learning, of his insight into the operations of political constitutions, cannot deny that he at least could produce a work which might equal in many respects those of the great Americans here named ; but it looks very much at present as if he, and others I could mention, will give up their best years to the absorbing and uncertain struggles of politics, rather than to the literature of that profession to which they might, under different conditions, raise imperishable memorials. From the pulpit many of us hear from time to time eloquent and well reasoned efforts which tell us how much even the class, necessarily most conservative in its traditions, and confined in its teachings, has been forced by modern tendencies to enlarge its human sympathies and widen its intellectual horizon ; but the published sermons are relatively few in number ; and while, now and then, at intervals, after a public celebration, an important anniversary or ceremonial, or as a sequence of a controversy on the merits or demerits of creed or dogma, we see a pile of pamphlets on the counter of a bookstore, we do not hear of any printed book of sermons that appears to have entered of recent years into the domain of human thought and discussion in the great world beyond our territorial limits.

I shall not attempt to dwell at any length on the intellectual standard of our legislative bodies, but shall confine myself to a few general observations that naturally suggest themselves to an observer of our political conditions. Now, as in all times of our history, political life claims many strong, keen and cultured intellects, although it is doubtful whether the tendency of our democratic institutions is to encourage the most highly educated organizations to venture, or remain, should once they venture, in the agitated and unsafe sea of political passion and controversy.

The first parliament of the Dominion, and the first legislatures of the provinces, which met after the federal union of 1867, when the system of dual representation was permissible—a system whose advantages are more obvious now—brought into public life the most brilliant and astute intellects of Canada, and it will probably be a long time before we shall again see assemblages so distinguished for oratory, humour and intellectual power. A federal system was, doubtless, the only one feasible under the racial and natural conditions that met the Quebec Conference of 1864; but, while admitting its political necessity, we cannot conceal from ourselves the fact that the great drain its numerous legislative bodies and governments make upon the mental resources of a limited population—a drain increased by the abolition of dual representation—is calculated to weaken our intellectual strength in our legislative halls, when a legislative union would in the nature of things concentrate that strength in one powerful current of activity and thought. A population of five millions of people has to provide not only between six and seven hundred representatives, who must devote a large amount of time to the public service for inadequate compensation, but also lieutenant-governors, judges and high officials, holding positions requiring intellectual qualifications as well as business capacity if they are properly filled. Apart from these considerations, it must be remembered that the opportunities of acquiring wealth and success in business or professional vocations have naturally increased with the material development of the Dominion, and that men of brains have consequently even less inducement than formerly to enter on the uncertain and too often ungrateful pursuit of politics. We have also the danger before us that it will be with us, as it is in the United States and even in England under the new conditions that are rapidly developing there; the professional politician, who is too often the creation of factions and cliques, and the lower influences of political intrigue and party management, will be found, as time passes, more common in our legislative halls, to the detriment of those higher ideals that should be the animating principles of public life in this young country, whose future happiness and greatness depend so much on the present methods of party government. Be all this as it may be, one may still fairly claim for our legislative bodies that their intellectual standard can compare favourably with that of the Congress at Washington or the state legislatures of Massachusetts and New England generally. After all, it is not for brilliant intellectual pyrotechnics we should now so much look to the legislative bodies of Canada, but rather for honesty of purpose, keen comprehension of the public interests, and a business capacity which can grasp the actual material wants and necessities of a country which has to face the competition, and even opposition, of a great people full of industrial as well as intellectual energy.

Nowhere in this review have I claimed for this country any very striking results in the course of the half century since which we have shown so much political and material activity. I cannot boast that we have produced a great poem or a great history which has attracted the attention of the world beyond us, and assuredly we find no noteworthy attempt in the direction of a novel of our modern life ; but what I do claim is, looking at the results generally, the work we have done has been sometimes above the average in those fields of literature—and here I include, necessarily, science—in which Canadians have worked. They have shown in many productions a conscientious spirit of research, patient industry, and not a little literary skill in the management of their material. I think, on the whole, there have been enough good poems, histories and essays written and published in Canada for the last four or five decades to prove that there has been a steady intellectual growth on the part of our people, and that it has kept pace at all events with the mental growth in the pulpit, or in the legislative halls, where, of late years, a keen practical debating style has taken the place of the more rhetorical and studied oratory of old times. I believe the intellectual faculties of Canadians only require larger opportunities for their exercise to bring forth a rich fruition. I believe the progress in the years to come will be far greater than that we have yet shown, and that necessarily so, with the wider distribution of wealth, the dissemination of a higher culture, and a

greater confidence in our own mental strength, and in the resources that this country offers to pen and pencil. The time will
come when that great river, associated with memories of Cartier,
Champlain, La Salle, Frontenac, Wolfe and Montcalm,—that river
already immortalized in history by the pen of Parkman—will be
as noted in song and story as the Rhine, and will have its Irving
to make it as famous as the lovely Hudson.

Of course there are many obstacles in the way of successful
literary pursuits in Canada. Our population is still small, and
separated into two distinct nationalities, who for the most part
necessarily read books printed in their own tongue. A book
published in Canada then has a relatively limited *clientèle* in the
country itself, and cannot meet much encouragement from publishers in England or in the United States who have advantages
for placing their own publications which no Canadian can have
under existing conditions. Consequently an author of ambition
and merit should perforce look for publishers outside his own
country if he is to expect anything like just appreciation, or to
have a fair chance of reaching that literary world which alone
gives fame in the true sense. It must be admitted too that so
much inferior work has at times found its way from Canada to
other countries that publishers are apt to look askance at a book
when it is offered to them from the colonies. Still, while this
may at times operate against making what is a fairly good bar-
gain with the publisher—and many authors, of course, believe
with reason that a publisher, as a rule, never makes a good bar-
gain with an author, and certainly not with a new one—a good
book will sooner or later assert itself whenever Canadians write
such a book. Let Canadians then persevere conscientiously and
confidently in their efforts to break through the indifference which
at present tends to cramp their efforts and dampen their energy.
It is a fashion with some colonial writers to believe that there
is a settled determination on the part of English critics to ignore
their best work, when, perhaps, in the majority of cases it is the
lack of good work that is at fault. Such a conclusion sometimes
finds an argument in the fact that, when so able a Canadian as
Edward Blake enters the legislative halls of England, some ill-

natured critic, who represents a spirit of insular English snob-
bery, has only a sneer for " this Canadian lawyer " who had
better " stay at home," and not presume to think that he, a mere
colonist, could have anything to say in matters affecting the good
government of the British Empire. But the time has long since
passed for sneers at colonial self-government or colonial intellect,
and we are more likely hereafter to have a Canadian House of
Commons held up as a model of decorum for so-called English
gentlemen. Such able and impartial critical journals as *The
Athenæum* are more ready to welcome than ignore a good book in
these days of second-rate literature in England itself. If we produce such a good book as Mrs. Campbell Praed's " Australian
Life," or Tasma's " Uncle Piper of Piper's Hill," we may be sure
the English papers will do us justice. Let me frankly insist that
we have far too much hasty and slovenly literary work done in
Canada. The literary canon which every ambitious writer should
have ever in his mind has been stated by no less an authority
than Sainte-Beuve : " Devoted to my profession as a critic, I have
tried to be more and more a good and if possible an able workman." A good style means artistic workmanship. It is too soon
for us in this country to look for a Matthew Arnold or a Sainte-
Beuve—such great critics are generally the results, and not the
forerunners, of a great literature ; but at least if we could have
in the present state of our intellectual development, a criticism in
the press which would be truthful and just, the essential characteristics of the two authors I have named, the effect would be
probably in the direction of encouraging promising writers, and
weeding out some literary dabblers. " What I have wished,"
said the French critic, " is to say not a word more than I thought,
to stop even a little short of what I believed in certain cases, in
order that my words might acquire more weight as historical testimony." Truth tempered by consideration for literary genius is
the essence of sound criticism.

We all know that the literary temperament is naturally sensitive to anything like indifference and is too apt, perhaps, to
exaggerate the importance of its calling in the prosaic world in
which it is exercised. The pecuniary rewards are so few, rela-

tively, in this country, that the man of imaginative mind—the purely literary worker—naturally thinks that he can, at least, ask for generous appreciation. No doubt he thinks, to quote a passage from a clever Australian novel—"The Australian Girl"—"Genius has never been truly acclimatized by the world. The Philistines always long to put out the eyes of poets and make them grind corn in Gaza." But it is well always to remember that a great deal of rough work has to be done in a country like Canada before its Augustan age can come. No doubt literary stimulus must be more or less wanting in a colony where there is latent at times in some quarters a want of self-confidence in ourselves and in our institutions, arising from that sense of dependency and habit of imitation and borrowing from others that is a necessity of a colonial condition. The tendency of the absence of sufficient self-assertion is to cramp intellectual exertion, and make us believe that success in literature can only be achieved in the old countries of Europe. That spirit of all-surrounding materialism to which Lowell has referred must also always exercise a certain sinister influence in this way—an influence largely exerted in Ontario—but despite all this we see that even among our neighbours it has not prevented the growth of a literary class famous for its intellectual successes in varied fields of literature. It is for Canadian writers to have always before them a high ideal, and remember that literature does best its duty—to quote the eloquent words of Ruskin—" in raising our fancy to the height of what may be noble, honest and felicitous in actual life ; in giving us, though we may be ourselves poor and unknown, the companionship of the wisest spirits of every age and country, and in aiding the communication of clear thoughts and faithful purposes among distant nations, which will at last breathe calm upon the sea of lawless passion and change into such halcyon days the winter of the world, that the birds of the air may have their nests in peace and the Son of Man where to lay his head."

IX.

Largely, if not entirely, owing to the expansion of our common school system—admirable in Ontario and Nova Scotia, but defective in Quebec—and the influence of our universities and colleges, the average intelligence of the people of this country is much higher than it was a very few years ago ; but no doubt it is with us as with our neighbours—to quote the words of an eminent public speaker whose brilliancy sometimes leads one to forget his higher criticism—I refer to Dr. Chauncey Depew—" Speed is the virtue and vice of our generation. We demand that morning-glories and century plants shall submit to the same conditions and flower with equal frequency." Even some of our universities from which we naturally expect so much seem disposed from time to time to lower their standard and yield too readily to the demand for purely practical education when, after all, the great reason of all education is to draw forth the best qualities of the young man, elevate his intelligence, and stimulate his highest intellectual forces. The animating principle with the majority of people is to make a young man a doctor, a lawyer, an engineer, or teach him some other vocation as soon as possible, and the tendency is to consider any education that does not immediately effect that result as superfluous. Whilst every institution of learning must necessarily yield something to this pervading spirit of immediate utility, it would be a mistake to sacrifice all the methods and traditions of the past when sound scholars at least were made, and the world had so many men famous in learning, in poetry, in romance, and in history. For one I range myself among those who, like James Russell Lowell and Matthew Arnold, still consider the conscientious and intelligent study of the ancient classics—the humanities as they are called—as best adapted to create cultured men and women, and as the noblest basis on which to build up even a practical education with which to earn bread and capture the world. Goldwin Smith very truly says, " A romantic age stands in need of science, a scientific and utilitarian age stands in need of the humanities." [62] The study of Greek, above all others of the humanities, is calculated to stimu-

D

late the higher qualities of our nature. As Matthew Arnold adds
in the same discourse from which I have quoted, " The instinct
for beauty is set in human nature, as surely as the instinct for
knowledge is set there, or the instinct for conduct. If the instinct
for beauty is served by Greek literature and art as it is served by
no other literature or art, we may trust to the instinct of self-
preservation in humanity for keeping Greek as part of our culture." With the same great critic and thinker, I hope that in
Canada " Greek will be increasingly studied as men feel the need
in them for beauty, and how powerfully Greek art and Greek
literature can serve this need." We are as respects the higher
education of this country in that very period which Arnold saw
ahead for America—" a period of unsettlement and confusion and
false tendency "—a tendency to crowd into education too many
matters; and it is for this reason I venture to hope that letters
will not be allowed to yield entirely to the necessity for practical
science, the importance of which I fully admit, while deprecating
it being made the dominant principle in our universities. If we
are to come down to the lower grades of our educational system
I might also doubt whether despite all its decided advantages
for the masses—its admirable machinery and apparatus, its com-
fortable school-houses, its varied systematic studies from form to
form and year to year, its well managed normal and model schools,
its excellent teachers—there are not also signs of superficiality.
The tendency of the age is to become rich fast, to get as much
knowledge as possible within a short time, and the consequence
of this is to spread far too much knowledge over a limited ground
—to give a child too many subjects, and to teach him a little of
everything. These are days of many cyclopædias, historical sum-
maries, scientific digests, reviews of reviews, French in a few lessons, and interest tables. All is digested and made easy to the
student. Consequently not a little of the production of our schools
and of some of our colleges may be compared to a veneer of knowledge, which easily wears off in the activities of life, and leaves
the roughness of the original and cheaper material very perceptible. One may well believe that the largely mechanical system
and materialistic tendency of our education has some effect in

checking the development of a really original and imaginative literature among us. Much of our daily literature—indeed the chief literary aliment of large classes of our busy population is the newspaper press, which illustrates in many ways the haste and pressure of this life of ours in a country of practical needs like Canada. When we consider the despatch with which a large newspaper has to be made up, how reports are caught on the wing and published without sufficient verification, how editorials have to be written *currente calamo*, and often after midnight when important despatches come in, we may well wonder that the daily issue of a newspaper is so well done. With the development of confederation the leading Canadian papers have taken, through the influence of the new condition of things, a larger range of thought and expression, and the gross personalities which so frequently discredited the press before 1867 have now become the exception. If I might refer to an old and enterprising paper as an example of the new order of things, I should point to the Toronto *Globe* under its present editorial management and compare it with two or three decades ago. It will be seen there is a deeper deference to an intelligent public opinion by an acknowledgment of the right of a community to hear argument and reason even on matters of party politics, and to have fair reports of speeches on both sides of a question. In point of appearance, make-up, and varied literary matter—especially in its literary department, its criticisms of new books in all branches of literature—the Australasian press is decidedly superior to that of Canada as a rule. The Melbourne *Argus* and the Sydney *Herald* compare with the best London journals, and the reason is mainly because there is no country press in Australia to limit the enterprise and energy of a newspaper publisher. Perhaps it is as well for the general instruction of a community like ours that there should be a large and active country press, and the people not too much under the guidance of a few great journals in important centres of political thought and action. For one I have more faith in the good sense and reason of the community as a whole than in the motives and disinterestedness of a few leaders in one or more cities or towns. But I must also add that when we consider the influence a widely disseminated press like that of Canada must exercise on the opinions and sentiments of the large body of persons of whom it is the principal or only literature, one must wish that there was more independence of thought and honesty of criticism as well as a greater willingness, or capacity rather, to study a high ideal on the part of the press generally. However improved the tone of the Canadian press may have become of late years, however useful it may be as a daily record of passing events—of course, outside of party politics—however ably it may discuss in its editorial columns the topics of the day, it is not yet an influence always calculated to strengthen the mind and bring out the best intellectual faculties of a reader like a book which is the result of calm reflection, sound philosophic thought, originality of idea, or the elevated sentiment of the great poet or the historian. As a matter of fact a newspaper is too often in Canada a reflex of the average rather than of the higher intelligence of the country, and on no other ground can we explain the space devoted to a football match, or a prize fight, or a murder trial, or degrading incidents in the criminal life of men and women. For one, I am an admirer of athletic and other sports calculated to develop health and muscle, as long as they are not pursued to extremes, do not become the end and aim of youth, or allowed to degenerate into brutality. All of us do not forget the great influence of the Olympian, the Pythian and other public games on the Greek character when the land was " living Greece " indeed ; but we must also remember that art and song had a part in those contests of athletes, that they even inspired the lyric odes of Pindar, that the poet there recited his drama or epic, the painter exhibited his picture, and the intellectual was made a part of the physical struggle in those palmy days of Greek culture. I have not yet heard that any Canadian poet or painter or historian has ever been so honoured, or asked to take part in those athletic games and sports to which our public journals devote a number of pages which have not yet been set apart for Canadian or any literature. The newspaper reporter is nowadays the only representative of literature in our Pythia or Olympia, and he assuredly cannot be said to be a Pindaric singer when he

exalts the triumphs of lacrosse or the achievements of the base-
ball champion.

X.

In drawing to a conclusion I come now to refer to a subject
which is naturally embraced in an address intended to review
the progress of culture in this country, and that is what should
have, perhaps, been spoken of before, the condition of Art in the
Dominion. As our public libraries [63] are small compared with
those in the neighbouring union, and confined to three or four
cities—Montreal being in some respects behind Toronto—so our
public and private art galleries are very few in number and insignificant as respects the value and the greatness of the paintings.
Even in the House of Commons, not long since, regret was
expressed at the smallness of the Dominion contribution, one
thousand dollars only, for the support of a so-called National Art
Gallery at Ottawa, and the greater part of this paltry sum, it
appeared, went to pay, not the addition of good paintings, but
actually the current expenses of keeping it up.   Hopes were
thrown out by more than one member of the government, in the
course of the discussion on the subject, that ere long a much
larger amount would be annually voted to make the gallery
more representative of the best Canadian art, and it was very
properly suggested that it should be the rule to purchase a number of Canadian pictures regularly every year, and in this way
stimulate the talent of our artists.   Montreal at present has one
fairly good museum of art, thanks to the liberality of two or three
of her rich men, but so public spirited a city as Toronto, which
numbers among its citizens a number of artists of undoubted
merit, is conspicuous for its dearth of good pictures even in private collections, and for the entire absence of any public gallery.
In Montreal there are also some very valuable and representative
paintings of foreign artists in the residences of her wealthy men
of business; but whilst it is necessary that we should have
brought to this country from time to time such examples of artistic genius to educate our own people for better things, it is still
desirable that Canadian millionaires and men of means and taste

should encourage the best efforts of our own artists. It is said sometimes—and there is some truth in the remark—that Canadian art hitherto has been imitative rather than creative; but while we have pictures like those of L. R. O'Brien, W. Brymner, F. A. Verner, O. R. Jacobi, George Reid, F. M. Bell-Smith, Homer Watson, W. Raphael, Robert Harris, C. M. Manly, J. W. L. Forster, A. D. Patterson, Miss Bell, Miss Muntz, J. Pinhey, J. C. Forbes, Paul Peel—a young man of great promise too soon cut off—and of other excellent painters,[64]* native born or adopted Canadians, illustrating in many cases, as do those of Mr. O'Brien notably, the charm and picturesqueness of Canadian scenery, it would seem that only sufficient encouragement is needed to develop a higher order of artistic performance among us. The Marquess of Lorne and the Princess Louise, during their too short residence in the Dominion, did something to stimulate a larger and better taste for art by the establishment of a Canadian Academy and the holding of several exhibitions; but such things can be of little practical utility if Canadians do not encourage the artists who are to contribute. It is to be hoped that the same spirit of generosity which is yearly building commodious science halls, and otherwise giving our universities additional opportunities for usefulness, will also ere long establish at least one fine art gallery in each of the older provinces, to illustrate not simply English and Foreign art, but the most original and highly executed work of Canadians themselves. Such galleries are so many object lessons — like that wondrous " White City " which has arisen by a western lake as suddenly as the palaces of eastern story — to educate the eye, form the taste and develop the higher faculties of our nature amid the material surroundings of our daily life No doubt the creative and imaginative faculties of our people have not yet been developed to any noteworthy extent; the poems and paintings of native Canadians too frequently lack, and the little fiction so far written is entirely destitute of the essential elements of successful and permanent work in art and literature. But the deficiency in this respect has arisen not from the poverty of Cana-

[64] * Some extended notes on the artists of Canada and their work appear in the Appendix, note 64.

dian intellect, but rather from the absence of that general distribution of wealth on which art can alone thrive, the consequent
want of galleries to cultivate a taste among the people for the
best artistic productions, and above all from the existence of that
spirit of intellectual self-depreciation which is essentially colonial,
and leads not a few to believe that no good work of this kind can
be done in mere dependencies.

The exhibition of American art at the world's fair is remarkable on the whole for individual expression, excellent colour and
effective composition. It proves to a demonstration that the
tendency is progressive, and that it is not too much to expect
that a few decades hence this continent will produce a Corot, a
Daubigny, a Bonnat, a Bouguereau or a Millais. Not the least
gratifying feature of the exhibition has been the revelation to the
foreign world—and probably to many Canadians as well—that
there is already some artistic performance of a much higher order
than was believed to exist in Canada, and that it has been
adjudged worthy of special mention among the masterpieces that
surround the paintings of our artists. This success, very moderate as it is, must stimulate Canadian painters to still greater
efforts in the future, and should help to create a wider interest
in their work among our own people, heretofore too indifferent
to the labours of men and women, whose rewards have been
small in comparison with the conscientiousness and earnestness
they have given to the prosecution of their art.

The opportunities which Canadian artists have had of com-
paring their own work with that of the most artistic examples at
the exhibition should be beneficial if they have made of them
the best possible use. American and French art was particularly
well represented at the exhibition, and was probably most interesting from a Canadian point of view, since our artists would
naturally make comparisons with their fellow-workers on this
continent, and at the same time closely study the illustrations of
those French schools which now attract the greater number of
students from this country, and have largely influenced—perhaps
too much so at times—the later efforts of some well-known painters among us. A writer in the New York *Nation* has made some

comparisons between the best works of the artists of France and the United States, which are supported by the testimony of critics who are able to speak with authority on the subject. The French notably excel " in seriousness of purpose and general excellence of work from a technical point of view, especially in the thorough knowledge of construction in both the figure and landscape pictures." On the other hand, the artists of the United States " show more diversity of aim and individuality of expression, as well as colour feeling." Some two or three Canadian artists give examples of those very qualities—especially in their landscapes —which, according to the New York critic, distinguish the illustrations of the art of the United States. As a rule, however, there is a want of individuality of expression, and of perfection of finish, in the work of Canadian artists, as even their relatively imperfect representation at Chicago has shown. The tendency to be imitative rather than creative is too obvious. Canadian painters show even a readiness to leave their own beautiful and varied scenery that they may portray that of other countries, and in doing so they have ceased in many cases to be original. But despite these defects, there is much hope in the general performance of Canadians even without that encouragement and sympathy which the artists of the United States have in a larger measure been able to receive in a country of greater wealth, population and intellectual culture.

Not only does the exhibition of paintings in the world's fair make one very hopeful of the future artistic development of this continent, but the beauty of the architectural design of the noble buildings which contain the treasures of art and industry, and of the decorative figures and groups of statuary that embellish these buildings and the surrounding grounds, is a remarkable illustration of the artistic genius that has produced so exquisite an effect in general, whatever defects there may be in minor details. A critic in the July number of the ' Quarterly Review,' while writing " in the presence of these lovely temples, domes, and colonnades under the burning American sky which adds a light and a transparency to all it rests upon," cannot help echoing the regret that this vision of beauty is but for a season, and expressing the hope that some one of the American money kings "may perpetuate his name on marble, by restoring, on the edge of this immense capital, amid parks and waters, that great central square which, were it only built of enduring materials, would stand without a rival in modern architecture." Perhaps the fine arts in the Dominion — where sculpture would be hardly heard of were it not for the French Canadian Hébert — may themselves even gain some stimulus from the examples of a higher conception of artistic achievement that is shown by this exhibition to exist in a country where a spirit of materialism has obtained the mastery so long. Canadian architecture hitherto has not been distinguished for originality of design—much more than art it has been imitative. In Montreal and Quebec the old buildings which represent the past have no architectural beauty, however interesting they may be to the antiquarian or the historian, and however well many of them harmonize with the heights of picturesque Quebec. Montreal is assuredly the most interesting city from an architectural point of view in Canada, simply for the reason that its architects have, as a rule, studied that effect of solidity and simplicity of design most in keeping with the grand mountain and the natural scenery that give such picturesqueness to an exceptionally noble site. While we see all over Canada— from Victoria on the Pacific to Halifax on the Atlantic [64a] *—the evidences of greater comfort, taste and wealth in our private and public buildings, while we see many elaborate specimens of ecclesiastical art, stately piles of legislative halls, excellent specimens of Gothic and Tudor art in our colleges, expensive commercial and financial structures, and even civic palaces, yet they are often illustrative of certain well defined and prevalent types of architecture in the eastern and western cities of the United States. It cannot be said that Canada has produced an architect of original genius like Henry Hobson Richardson, who was cut off in the commencement of his career, but not before he had given the continent some admirable specimens of architectural art, in which his study of the Romanesque was specially conspicuous, and probably led the way to a higher ideal which has reached some

* See in Appendix 64a references to our notable public edifices.

realization in the city which must too soon disappear like the fabric of a vision, though one can well believe that, unlike a dream, it will leave a permanent impress on the intellectual development of the people who have conceived an exhibition so creditable from a purely artistic point of view.

XI.

The Dominion of Canada possesses a noble heritage which has descended to us as the result of the achievement of Frenchmen, Englishmen, Scotchmen, and Irishmen, who through centuries of trial and privation, showed an indomitable courage, patience and industry which it is our duty to imitate with the far greater opportunities we now enjoy of developing the latent material and intellectual resources of this fair land.   Possessing a country rich in natural treasures and a population inheriting the institutions, the traditions and qualities of their ancestors, having a remarkable capacity for self-government, enjoying exceptional facilities for the acquisition of knowledge, having before us always the record of difficulties overcome against great odds in endeavouring to establish ourselves on this continent, we may well in the present be animated by the spirit of hope, rather than by that feeling of despair which some despondent thinkers and writers have too frequently on their lips when it is a question of the destiny in store for Canada.   In the course of the coming decades—perhaps in four or five, or less—Canada will probably have determined her destiny—her position among the communities of the world ; and, for one, I have no doubt the results will be far more gratifying to our national pride than the results of even the past thirty years, when we have been laying broad and deep the foundations of our present system of government.   We have reason to believe that the material success of this confederation will be fully equalled by the intellectual efforts of a people who have sprung from nations whose not least enduring fame has been the fact that they have given to the world of letters a Shakespeare, a Molière, a Montesquieu, a Balzac, a Dickens, a Dudevant, a Tennyson, a Victor Hugo, a Longfellow, a Hawthorne, a Théophile Gauthier, and many other names that represent the best literary genius of the English and French races. All the evidence before us now goes to prove that the French language will continue into an indefinite future to be the language of a large and influential section of the population of Canada, and that it must consequently exercise a decided influence on the culture and intellect of the Dominion. It has been within the last four decades that the best intellectual work—both in literature and statesmanship—has been produced in French and English Canada, and the signs of intellectual activity in the same direction do not lessen with the expansion of the Dominion. The history of England from the day the Norman came into the island until he was absorbed in the original Saxon element, is not likely to be soon repeated in Canada, but in all probability the two nationalities will remain side by side for an unknown period to illustrate on the northern half of the continent of America the culture and genius of the two strongest and brightest powers of civilization. As both of these nationalities have vied with each other in the past to build up this confederation on a large and generous basis of national strength and greatness, and have risen time and again superior to those racial antagonisms created by differences of opinion at great crises of our history— antagonisms happily dispelled by the common sense, reason and patriotism of men of both races—so we should in the future hope for that friendly rivalry on the part of the best minds among French and English Canadians which will best stimulate the genius of their people in art, history, poetry and romance. In the meantime, while this confederation is fighting its way out of its political difficulties, and resolving wealth and refinement from the original and rugged elements of a new country, it is for the respective nationalities not to stand aloof from one another, but to unite in every way possible for common intellectual improvement, and give sympathetic encouragement to the study of the two languages and to the mental efforts of each other. It was on this enlightened principle of sympathetic interest that the Royal Society was founded and on which alone it can expect to obtain any permanent measure of success. If the English and

French always endeavour to meet each other on this friendly basis in all the communities where they live side by side as well as on all occasions that demand common thought and action and cultivate that social and intellectual intercourse which may at all events weld them both as one in spirit and aspiration, however different they may continue in language and temperament, many prejudices must be removed, social life must gain in charm, and intellect must be developed by finding strength where it is weak, and grace where it is needed in the mental efforts of the two races   If in addition to this widening of the sympathies of our two national elements, we can see in the Dominion generally less of that provincialism which means a narrowness of mental vision on the part of our literary aspirants, and prevents Canadian authors reaching a larger audience in other countries, then we shall rise superior to those weaknesses of our intellectual character which now impede our mental development, and shall be able to give larger scope to what original and imaginative genius may exist among our people.   So with the expansion of our mental horizon, with the growth of experience and knowledge, with the creation of a wider sympathy for native talent, with the disappearance of that tendency to self-depreciation which is so essentially colonial, and with the encouragement of more self-reliance and confidence in our own intellectual resources, we may look forward with some degree of hopefulness to conditions of higher development, and to the influence on our national character of what can best elevate Canadians and make them even happier and wiser,

" The love of country, soaring far above all party strife ;
The love of learning, art and song,—the crowning grace of life." [65]

BIBLIOGRAPHICAL, ART AND GENERAL NOTES.

LOWELL'S ADDRESSES.

(1) Page 1.—See " Democracy, and Other Addresses," by James Russell Lowell (Boston and New York, 1887) pp. 235-237. The address at the Harvard Anniversary, from which I quote in the commencement of the text, should be carefully read and studied by all those who are interested in education and culture in the Dominion, and do not wish to see the classics superseded by purely scientific and utilitarian theories. " Leave," he said, for instance, " in their traditional pre-eminence those arts that were rightly called liberal ; those studies that kindle the imagination, and through it irradiate the reason : those studies that manumitted the modern mind ; those in which the brains of the finest temper have found alike their stimulus and their repose, taught by them that the power of intellect is heightened in proportion as it is made gracious by measure and symmetry. Give us science, too, but give, first of all and last of all, the science that ennobles life and makes it generous. . . . . . Many-sidedness of culture makes your vision clearer and keener in particulars. For, after all, the noblest definition of Science is that breadth and impartiality of view which liberates the mind from specialties, and enables it to organize whatever we learn, so that it becomes real Knowledge by being brought into true and helpful relation with the rest."

JAMESTOWN, VA.

(2) Page 3.—" Nothing remains of this famous settlement but the ruins of a church tower covered with ivy, and some old tombstones. The tower is crumbling year by year, and the roots of trees have cracked the slabs, making great rifts across the names of the old Armigers and Honourables. The place is desolate with its washing waves and flitting sea-fowl, but possesses a singular attraction. It is one of the few localities which recall the first years of American history ; but it will not recall them much longer. Every distinctive feature of the spot is slowly disappearing. The river encroaches year by year, and the ground occupied by the original huts is already submerged." Cooke's " Virginia" (' American Commonwealths,' 1884), p. 19.

CHAMPLAIN.

(3) Page 6.—Editions of Champlain's works appeared at Paris in 1603, 1613, 1619, 1620, 1627, 1632 and 1640 ; at Quebec in 1830 and 1870. An English translation was published by the Prince Society of Boston in 1878-80. The Abbé Laverdière's edition, in six volumes, 4to., (Quebec, 1870), is the most perfect modern publication of the works. It printed for the first time the text of the voyage of 1599-1601. For bibliographical notes of Champlain's works see Bourinot's " Cape Breton," ' Trans. Roy. Soc. Can.,' vol. ix., Sec. II., App. VIII. (also in separate form, Montreal, 1892) ; Winsor's ' Nar. and Crit. Hist. Am.,' iv., 130-134 ; Harrisse's " Notes sur la bibliographie de la Nouvelle France."

French Canadian writers like Garneau and Ferland have exhausted the language of eulogy in describing the character and life of Samuel Champlain, but no one who follows his career can doubt the truth of this latest tribute to the French colonizer of Canada by Dr. N. E. Dionne in " Samuel Champlain, fondateur de Québec et père de la Nouvelle France : Histoire de sa vie et de ses voyages," Québec, 1891 : " Il possédait à un haut degré le génie colonisateur, et c'est dans ce rôle, si difficile de tout temps, qu'il fit preuve de sagesse et de clairvoyance, et dans le choix des colons, et dans la direction qu'il sut imprimer à leurs premiers efforts. L'intelligence de Champlain se révèle dans de nombreux écrits, où l'observateur judicieux et pénétrant coudoie le savant et le marin aussi hardi qu'expérimenté. Comme cosmographe il a eu l'immense mérite d'avoir surpassé tous ses devanciers, par l'abondance des descriptions et l'agencement heureux des données géographiques. C'est un nouveau titre de gloire que l'on doit ajouter à sa couronne resplendissante de tant de rayons lumineux. Plusieurs historiens, même de ceux qui ne comptent pas parmi les admirateurs des œuvres françaises, lui ont rendu le témoignage d'avoir fait entrer la science cartographique dans une nouvelle ère de progrès. Naturaliste, géographe, marin, cosmographe ; Champlain était tout cela à la fois, et dans une mesure hautement remarquable pour l'epoque où il vivait. . . . . Pas un gouverneur sous l'ancien régime n'a donné d'aussi grands exemples de foi, de piété, et de droiture d'intention."

It is Captain John Smith of Virginia who, among the colonizers of America, can best compare with the founder of Quebec. The following estimate of his character, given by the historian George Bancroft (i., 138-139, ed. of 1866), could be applied in almost every particular to the Frenchman ; all we need do is to read " New France" for " Virginia," " French " for " Saxon," " France " for " England," etc. : " He was the father of Virginia, the true leader who first planted the Saxon race within the borders of the United States. His judgment had ever been clear in the midst of general despondency. He united the highest spirit of adventure with consummate powers of action. His courage and self-possession accomplished what others esteemed desperate. Fruitful in expedients, he was prompt in execution. Though he had been harassed by the persecutions of malignant envy, he never revived the memory of the faults of his enemies. He was accustomed to lead, not to send his men to danger ; would suffer want rather than borrow, and starve sooner than not pay. He had nothing counterfeit in his nature, but was open, honest and sincere. He clearly discerned that it was the true interest of England not to seek in Virginia for gold and hidden wealth, but to enforce regular industry. ' Nothing,' said he, ' is to be expected thence but by labour.' "

LESCARBOT.

(4) Page 6.—Editions of Lescarbot's " Histoire de la Nouvelle France " appeared at Paris in 1609, 1611, 1617 and 1618; but the most complete and available modern copy is that printed by Tross in three volumes (Paris, 1866). For bibliographical notes of Lescarbot's works see ' Nar. and Crit. Hist. Am.,' iv., 149-151 ; Harrisse's " Notes."

CHARLEVOIX.

(5) Page 6.—Editions of Charlevoix's "Histoire et description générale de la Nouvelle France," etc., appeared at Paris in 1744, three volumes, 4to., and six volumes in 12mo., with maps. Dr. Shea's admirable English version and annotations were printed at New York in six handsome volumes, 1866-1872. For bibliographical notes see ' Nar. and Crit. Hist. Am.,' iv., 154, 358.

HUTCHINSON'S HISTORY.

(6) Page 6.—For bibliography of Thomas Hutchinson's excellent "History of Massachusetts Bay" (Boston, 1749, 1767, 1795; London, 1750, 1768, 1828, three volumes), see 'Nar. and Crit. Hist. Am.,' iii., 344. He was royal governor of the province, 1770-72, and died near London in 1789.

SAGARD.

(7) Page 6.—Editions of Sagard's works, "Le Grand Voyage," etc., appeared at Paris in 1632 and 1636, but Tross printed admirable copies at Paris in 1864-66. Charlevoix has not a favourable judgment of Sagard ; but no doubt, while he is diffuse, he gives an excellent insight into Indian life and customs. For bibliographical notes see 'Nar. and Crit. Hist. Am.,' iv., 290-291 ; Harrisse's "Notes."

P. BOUCHER.

(8) Page 6.—Pierre Boucher's "Mœurs et productions de la Nouvelle France" appeared at Paris in 1664 (sm.12mo.), and is described by Charlevoix as a faithful, if superficial, account of Canada. For bibliographical notes, see 'Nar. and Crit. Hist. Am.,' iv., 298 ; Harrisse's "Notes."

JESUIT RELATIONS.

(8) Page 6.—The Canadian Government published at Quebec in 1858, in three large 8vo. volumes, a series of the "Relations," from 1611-1672, and supplemental or complemental issues of allied and later "Relations" were printed through the efforts of Mr. Lenox, Dr. O'Callaghan and Dr. Shea, of New York. For bibliographical notes on these invaluable collections, see 'Nar. and Crit. Hist. Am.,' 290 et seq. ; Harrisse's "Notes."

PÈRE DU CREUX.

(10) Page 6.—Père du Creux or Creuxius published his prolix work, "Historia Canadensis," with map and illustrations, in Latin, at Paris in 1664. For bibliographical notes, see 'Nar. and Crit. Hist. Am.,' iv., 296 ; Harrisse's "Notes." Despite its diffusiveness, it has value for the historical students of his times.

LA POTHERIE.

(11) Page 6.—Bacqueville de la Potherie's "Histoire de l'Amérique Septentrionale depuis 1534 jusqu'à 1701" was published first at Paris in 1722, four volumes, 12mo. ; but a later edition appeared in 1753. Charlevoix's opinion, that it is an undigested and ill-written narrative, is prejudiced, as the work is on the whole a useful and exact account of the French establishments at Quebec, Montreal and Three Rivers, and especially of the condition of the Indians of the time. For bibliographical notes see 'Nar. and Crit. Hist. Am.,' iv., 299, 357-358.

LAFITAU.

(11a) Page 6.—The following note with respect to this able priest's writing is taken from 'Nar. and Crit. Hist. Am.,' iv., 298, 299 : "The Jesuit Lafitau published at Paris in 1724 his 'Mœurs des Sauvages Amériquains' in two volumes, with various plates, which in the main is confined to the natives of Canada, where he had lived long with the Iroquois. Charlevoix said of his book, twenty years later, ' We have nothing so exact on the subject ; ' and Lafitau continues to hold high rank as an original authority, though his book is overlaid with a theory of Tartaric origin of the red race. Mr. Parkman calls him ' the most satisfactory of the elder writers.' " Garneau, ii., 154, mentions that he discovered in 1716 a plant in the Canadian forests which is of the nature of ginseng, which for awhile was a valuable article of export to Canton. Eventually it became valueless in China on account of its being prepared improperly.

C. LE CLERCQ.

(12) Page 6.—Père Chrestien Le Clercq's " Etablissement de la Foy" appeared in two volumes, 12mo., at Paris in 1691, and an excellent translation by Shea at New York in 1881. He also wrote a work, "Nouvelle Relation de la Gaspésie," which was also printed at Paris in 1691. For bibliographical notes see ' Nar. and Crit. Hist. Am.,' iv., 291 ; Harrisse's " Notes."

COTTON MATHER'S "MAGNALIA."

(13) Page 7.—For bibliographical notes on this curious olla podrida of religion and history see ' Nar. and Crit. Hist. Am.' iii., 345; Stevens's " Historical Nuggets," ii., 505.

DR. MICHEL SARRAZIN.

(13a) Page 8.—An interesting account of the life and labours of the eminent pioneer of science in Canada, who came to Quebec in 1685 and died there in 1734, will be found in the fifth volume of the ' Trans. Roy. Soc. Can.' (section IV.), by the Abbé Laflamme. See also Parkman's "Old Regime in Canada," p. 366, n. Also, pp. 390–393 for citations from Kalm and Charlevoix as to social condition of the French colony. Also, pp. 160–163 and notes, for an account and references to authorities on subject of the Seminary.

PETER KALM.

(13b) Page 8.—He was professor of Economy in the University of Aobo, in Swedish Finland, and a member of the Swedish Royal Academy of Sciences. His Travels in North America (" In Risa tel Nord America"), 1748–51, first appeared in Swedish (Stockholm, 1753–61), and subsequently in a translation, with the original somewhat abridged, by John Reinhold Forster (Warrington and London, 1770; 2nd ed., 1772). A translation in French by L. W. Marchand has also been published, and it is from that I quote in the text. (For German and Dutch versions see ' Nar. and Crit. Hist. Am.,' v., 244.) I have since found that Forster, in a note (ii., 185, 2nd ed.) on the remarks of the Swedish savant with respect to the study of science in the Eng lish colonies, calls attention to the fact that " Mr. Kalm has forgotten his own asser tions in the former part of this work." Dr. Colden, Dr. Franklin and Mr. Bartram, he continues, " have been the great promoters and investigators of nature in this country, and how would the inhabitants have gotten the fine collections of North American trees, shrubs and plants, which grow at present almost in every garden, and are as if they were naturalized in old England, had they not been assisted by their friends and by the curious in North America." Forster also refers to the schools, colleges and libraries already existing in the English colonies as evidence that Kalm hardly did justice to the men of culture in those countries. No doubt La Galissonière, Sarrazin, Gauthier, and others created, for a time certainly, much interest in the practical pursuit of science in Canada. The interest, however, must have been necessarily confined to a very small class in the two or three towns and garrisons to which La Galissonière's influence extended. Some of the Jesuit priests like Lafitau (see note 11α) had a taste for natural history, and have left us much information on the subject. But Lafitau, La Galissonière, Gauthier, Sarrazin and others were not native Canadians, though, like Charlevoix and his predecessors who wrote of the country, they have left imperishable memorials connecting their names with the literary and scientific history of New France. On the other hand, Franklin, Bartram, Stith, the Mathers and Beverley, whose names will be always associated with the early culture of science and literature in the old English colonies, were American by birth and education. Still these men represented a very insignificant influence in the practical, money-making population of New England and the middle colonies of which Kalm chiefly spoke. Their influence would be relatively trifling compared with that which was necessarily exercised by a governor like La Galissonière in New France, with its sympathetic officials and priests, and which was necessarily contrasted by Kalm with the indifference of the English colonists. Kalm failed, however, to recognize the public liberty, commercial enterprise and secular education which in New England and other colonial communities gave the people the advantage over the habitans and French Canadians generally. Instead, the spirit of materialism that was a distinguishing feature of the active, enterprising English colonists, must have grated on the susceptibilities of a student like Kalm, and prevented him from doing impartial justice to the strong qualities of a rising nation.

SCHOOLS, 1792—1840.

(14) Page 9.—For accounts of the deplorable condition of the public schools in the rural districts of Upper Canada from 1791 to the union of 1841 see Canniff's "History of the Province of Ontario" (Toronto, 1872). Canniff Haight's "Country Life in Canada Fifty Years Ago" (Toronto, 1885), and Bourinot's "Intellectual Development of the Canadian People" (12mo., Toronto, and 'Canadian Monthly,' 1881). At the present time there are 14 universities and 29 colleges in which a classical education is given ; 6 ladies' colleges, and 5 agricultural colleges and schools of science. The value of their buildings, endowments, etc., is upwards of $12,000,000, and the attendance is about 9,000 students. The classical colleges of Quebec—which make up the greater number of the colleges in Canada—are a combination of school and college attended by both boys and young men. They confer certain degrees and are generally affiliated with Laval University. The effect of the classical studies encouraged in these colleges is very perceptible in the culture of the well educated French Canadian. At present there are in Canada upwards of 17,000 public, high, normal, and model schools, attended by about 1,000,000 pupils, and costing a total annual expenditure of between six and seven millions of dollars. In Ontario (once Upper Canada) there are 16 universities and colleges, including ladies' and agricultural colleges ; about 6,000 schools of all kinds, attended by over 500,000 pupils, and costing annually over $4,000,000. See "The Statistical Year-Book of Canada," Ottawa, 1893.

UPPER CANADA, 1793—1840.

(15) Page 9.—Some interesting details of the early settlement of Ontario will be found in Dr. Canniff's "History of Ontario" (Toronto, 1872). As a local record or annals it is the most valuable yet given to the public by a descendant of the pioneers and U. E. Loyalists. Canniff Haight's "Country Life in Canada Fifty Years Ago" is a readable and sketchy account of old times.

E

CANADIAN JOURNALISM.

(16) Page 10.—A brief historical sketch of Canadian journalism will be found in Bourinot's "Intellectual Development of the Canadian People" (Toronto, 1881) ; also in Dr. Canniff's "History of the Province of Ontario" (Toronto, 1872), and in "Sketch of Canadian Journalism," by E. B. Biggar, "Canadian Newspaper Directory" (Montreal, 1892). Some of the statements in this article appear to require verification. I have now in my possession a copy of the 'York Gazette' printed in July, 1815, though Mr. Biggar states that no paper was published in York after the capture of the town by the American troops and the destruction of the press and type, in 1813, until 1817. The 'York Gazette' was originally the 'Upper Canada Gazette, or American Oracle,' first printed in 1793 at Niagara (Newark), when it was the political capital of Upper Canada after the passage of the Constitutional Act of 1791. It was removed to York (Toronto) in 1800, and became the 'York Gazette' a few years later. At the present time there are in Ontario alone, of daily papers, 47; weekly, 386. In the Dominion there are 98 daily papers, 1,035 weekly, bi-weekly, monthly, etc. In 1838 there were in all British North America not more than 70 papers, of which 38 were in Upper Canada. In 1864 the total was about a quarter of the present number.

HOWE'S SPEECHES.

(17) Page 11.—Joseph Howe's speeches were printed at Boston in 1858, two volumes, 8vo. For bibliographical notes see 'Am. Hist. Ass. Papers, 1892,' p. 396, at end of Bourinot's "Parliamentary Government in Canada."

"SAM SLICK."

(18) Page 11.—Judge Haliburton's famous work has the title, "The Clockmaker; or, Sayings and Doings of Sam Slick of Slickville." London and Halifax, 1st ser. 1837, 2nd ser. 1838, 3rd ser. 1840. Reprinted 1838-1843, three volumes. New edition 1845. Several later cheap English and American editions have appeared from time to time. A bibliography and sketch of the judge's life, written probably by his son, Robert G., appears in the "Bibliotheca Canadensis" (Ottawa, 1872). The humorous sketches, to which he chiefly owes his fame, were contributed anonymously to the 'Nova Scotian,' then edited by Joseph Howe. The paper is still in existence as a weekly edition of the 'Morning Chronicle' of Halifax. The judge was educated in old King's College, Windsor. See *infra*, note 31.

JUDGE HALIBURTON'S HISTORY.

(19) Page 12.—"An Historical and Statistical Account of Nova Scotia," with maps and engravings. Halifax, two volumes, large 8vo. For bibliographical note see Bourinot's "Cape Breton," App. X. A complete copy, with maps and illustrations, is now becoming rare.

W. SMITH'S HISTORY.

(20) Page 12.—"The History of Canada, from its First Discovery to the Peace of 1763; and from the Establishment of the Civil Government in 1764 to the Establishment of the Constitution in 1796." By William Smith, Esquire, Clerk of the Parliament and Master in Chancery of the Province of Lower Canada. "Ne quid falsi dicere audeat, ne quid veri non audeat." In two volumes, large 8vo. (Quebec, 1815.) He was a son of the historian of the province of New York, who after the war of the revolution became chief justice of Canada.

JOSEPH BOUCHETTE.

(21) Page 12.—The works of this eminent Canadian surveyor and hydrographer appeared under the following titles:

1. " A Topographical Description of the Province of Lower Canada, with remarks upon Upper Canada and on the relative connection of both Provinces with the United States of America." London, 1815, royal 8vo., with plates. Also an edition in French.

2. " The British Dominions in North America, or a Topographical and Statistical Description of the Provinces of Upper and Lower Canada, New Brunswick, Nova Scotia, the Islands of Newfoundland, Prince Edward and Cape Breton, including considerations on land-granting and emigration, and a topographical dictionary of Lower Canada; to which is annexed the statistical tables and tables of distances, published with the author's maps of Lower Canada, in consequence of a vote of the Provincial Legislature. Embellished with vignettes, views, landscapes, plans of towns, harbours, etc.; containing also a copious appendix." London, 1831, three volumes, 4to., generally bound in two.

MICHEL BIBAUD'S HISTORICAL WORKS.

(22) Page 12.—" Histoire du Canada sous la Domination Française." Montreal, 1837, 8vo. Do., 1843, 12mo.

" Histoire du Canada sous la Domination Anglaise." Do., 1844. The third volume of the series appeared after the author's death, and was published by his son, J. G. Bibaud, at Montreal, 1878, 12mo.

THOMPSON'S BOOK ON THE WAR OF 1812.

(23) Page 12.—" History of the Late War between Great Britain and the United States of America, with a retrospective view of the causes from which it originated, collected from the most authentic sources; to which is added an appendix containing public documents, etc., relating to the subject." By David Thompson, late of the Royal Scots. Niagara, U. C. Printed by T. Sewell, printer, bookbinder and stationer, Market Square, 1832, 12mo., pp. 300. This was for some time believed to be the first book printed in Upper Canada, but Dr. Kingsford, F.R.S.C., in " The Early Bibliography of the Province of Ontario " (Toronto and Montreal, 1892), enumerates a list of some thirty-three publications that antedated it, and Mr. Charles Lindsey, a bibliophilist and *littérateur* of Toronto, adds a number of others. See Toronto ' Week,' Dec. 9, 1892, Dr. Kingsford's rejoinder, *ib.*, Dec. 30, and another article on same subject by Mr. Lindsey, *ib.*, Jan. 13, 1893. All these bibliographical notes are interesting, and show how insignificant in point of intellectual and original ability was the literature of Ontario for fifty years previous to 1841.

BELKNAP'S HISTORY.

(24) Page 13.—Mr. Jeremy Belknap's "History of New Hampshire " was published in Philadelphia and Boston in 1784-92, three volumes. See Bourinot's " Cape Breton," in ' Trans., Roy. Soc. Can.,' vol. ix., p. 315, and p. 147 in the separate volume (Montreal, 1892).

THE POET CRÉMAZIE.

(25) Page 17.—Octave Crémazie was one of the *vrai sang* of French Canada, and a bookseller without the least aptitude for business. He left Quebec after his failure, and lived under an assumed name in France, where he died in poverty. His life was most unfortunate, and in the gloomy days of his later French career he never

realized the expectations which his literary efforts in Canada raised among his ardent friends. His poems appeared at first in the 'Soirées Canadiennes' and French Canadian journals, but his works were published in full at Montreal, in 1882, under the patronage of the Institut Canadien of Quebec, of which he was one of the founders. The Abbé Casgrain has given the introduction for this edition, and added some of the letters written to him by Crémazie from Paris. Crémazie, and indeed many of his friends, considered the "Trois Morts" as the best effort of his poetic genius ; but the Abbé truly says : "Crémazie has never really been original except in his patriotic poems; in them must be sought the secret of his popularity and his strongest claim to fame." And he goes on to say : "The old mother-country has so far given a warm welcome to only one of our poets. She has acknowledged Fréchette as the most emphatically French of our poetic aspirants ; but the time is not far distant when she will recognize in Crémazie the most thoroughly Canadian of them all. His verses have not the exquisite workmanship that is so much admired in Fréchette, but it is full of a patriotic inspiration that is not so often found in the author of 'Fleurs Boréales.' Despite his inequalities and imperfections, Crémazie must live among us as the father of our national poetry." The patriotic poem which has touched most deeply the hearts of his countrymen is "Le Drapeau de Carillon," in which he recalls the military achievements of the days of Lévis and Montcalm—

> " Les jours de Carillon,
> Où, sur le drapeau blanc attachant la victoire,
> Nos pères se couvraient d'un immortel renom
> Et traçaient de leur glaive une héroïque histoire.

> " O radieux débris d'une grande épopée !
> Héroïque bannière au naufrage échappée !
> Tu restes sur nos bords comme un témoin vivant
> Des glorieux exploits d'une race guerrière;
> Et, sur les jours passés, répandant ta lumière,
> Tu viens rendre à son nom un hommage éclatant.

> " Ah ! bientôt puissions-nous, ô drapeau de nos pères !
> Voir tous les Canadiens, unis comme des frères,
> Comme au jour du combat se serrer près de toi !
> Puisse des souvenirs la tradition sainte,
> En régnant dans leur cœur, garder de toute atteinte,
> Et leur langue et leur foi."

When we hear aspirations whispered nowadays that there may be only one language in Canada, it is well to consider the influence of such nervous poetic French on the national feelings of the large population in the province of Quebec. The French language is likely to be deeply seated for some generations yet while there are French Canadian poets.

CHAUVEAU AS A POET.

(26) Page 17.—Hon. Mr. Chauveau's poems appeared at different times in the 'Canadien' of Quebec, 'Le Répertoire National,' 'Les Soirées Canadiennes,' 'La Revue Canadienne,' and in other papers and publications from 1838 until the year of his death, 1890. One of his latest poems, "Le Sacré Cœur," was printed in the second volume of the 'Trans. Roy. Soc. Can.,' Sec. I. A valuable paper by the same

littérateur, " Etude sur les commencements de la poésie française au Canada," appeared in the first volume of the ' Trans.,' Sec. I., p. 65. In "Songs of the Dominion" (London, 1889), App., pp. 455-448) the editor gives an illustration of his spirited style by citing "Donnacona" at length.

HOWE'S POEMS.

(27) Page 17.—These were collected by his son after his death, and printed in a little volume with the title "Poems and Essays." Montreal, 1874, 12mo.

THE POETS SANGSTER AND McLACHLAN.

(28) Page 17.—Charles Sangster was a native of Kingston, and consequently a native Canadian like the others mentioned in the text. His principal poems appeared in the following books : "The St. Lawrence and the Saguenay, and Other Poems." Kingston and New York, 1856, 8vo. " Hesperus and Other Poems and Lyrics." Montreal, 1860, 8vo. Oliver Wendell Holmes, Bayard Taylor and Jean Inglelow wrote of his verse in terms of eulogy. See " Bibliotheca Canadensis," p. 337.

Alexander McLachlan was a poet contemporary with Sangster, and imbued with much poetic fervour and Canadian sentiment, but he was born and educated in Scotland, and came to Canada when a young man. His "Emigrant and Other Poems" (Toronto, 1861) merited the praise it received , though this, like his other poetic efforts, are now rarely cited, and no new edition of his works has appeared of recent years.

CHARLES HEAVYSEGE'S WORKS.

(29) Page 18.—"Saul: a Drama in Three Parts." Montreal, 1857, 8vo. 2nd ed., 1859.

"Count Filippo; or, The Unequal Marriage: a Drama in Five Acts." Montreal, 1860.

" Jephthah's Daughter." London and Montreal, 1865, 12mo.

" The Advocate: a Novel." Montreal, 1865, 8vo. This was a decided failure.

TODD'S WORKS.

(30) Page 18.—The first edition of Todd's "Parliamentary Government in England" appeared at London in 1867-68, two volumes, 8vo., and the second after his death in 1887. An abridged edition, by Spencer Walpole, an English writer, was printed in 1893, two volumes, 12mo. For bibliographical notes of this and other Canadian constitutional works see the Appendix to Bourinot's " Parliamentary Government in Canada : an Historical and Constitutional Study," 'Am. Hist. Ass. Papers,' Washington, 1892.

CHRISTIE'S HISTORY.

(31) Page 18.—Mr. Christie's "History of Lower Canada" embraced the period from the commencement of its political history as a British dependency until it was reunited with Upper Canada in 1840 by act of the imperial parliament. It appeared in Quebec and Montreal from 1849 to 1855, when the sixth volume, a collection of valuable documents, completed the work. Previously the author had published several memoirs and reviews of political events and administrations, which were all finally embraced in the history. For bibliographical notes see ' Am. Hist. Ass. Papers,' 1891, p. 393 ; "Bibliotheca Canadensis," art. " Christie." It is noteworthy

that Mr. Christie was, like Judge Haliburton, born and educated in Windsor, Nova Scotia, where old King's College still pursues its calm academic studies amid its sheltering and ancestral elms. In 1890 this venerable and interesting institution celebrated the centenary of its foundation. See Hind's " University of King's College, Windsor, N.S., 1790-1890," New York, " The Church Review Co.," 1890. But Robert Christie could not in those times be educated in King's, as he was not a member of the Church of England like the Judge.

GARNEAU.

(32) Page 18.—The first volume of François Xavier Garneau's " Histoire du Canada depuis sa découverte jusqu'à nos jours" appeared at Quebec in 1845 ; the second in 1846 ; and the third, bringing the history down to the establishment of constitutional government in 1791, was printed in 1848. A second edition completed the work to the union of the Canadas in 1841, and was published in 1852 at Montreal by Mr. Lovell, the well-known publisher. A third edition appeared at Quebec in 1859, and a somewhat slovenly translation was made by Mr. Andrew Bell and printed at Montreal in 1860. The fourth edition appeared in four volumes after the historian's death. It is the third edition, as originally written by Mr. Garneau. The fourth volume of this edition contains an eulogistic review of the author's life by Mr. Chauveau, a poem by Mr. Louis Fréchette on " Notre Histoire "—also printed in ' Trans. Roy. Soc. Can.,' vol. i., Sec. I.,—and an analytical table by Mr. B. Sulte. A portrait of Mr. Garneau is the frontispiece to the same volume. The ' Trans. Roy. Soc. Can.,' vol. i., Sec. I., has a paper by Abbé Casgrain on Garneau and Ferland, "Notre Passé Littéraire, et nos deux historiens." In the same volume appears a paper by Mr. J. M. LeMoine on "Nos quatre historiens modernes, Bibaud, Garneau, Ferland, Faillon," which, like the preceding essay, certainly does not fail in the way of eulogy. French Canada assuredly is proud and not often too critical of her eminent writers.

FERLAND AND FAILLON.

(33) Page 18.—"Cours d'Histoire du Canada. Première partie, 1534-1663." Par J. B. A. Ferland, prêtre, professeur d'histoire à l'Université Laval. Québec, 1861, 8vo. Seconde partie, 1663-1759 ; do., 1865, 8vo. The second volume was going through the press at the time of the author's death, and subsequently appeared under the careful supervision of his friend the Abbé Laverdière, to whose historical labours Canada is deeply indebted. Indeed French Canada owes much to Laval, with its able teachers, historians and scientists.

The Abbé Faillon, a Sulpician, who wrote a "Histoire de la Colonie Française en Canada" (Paris, 1865) in four 4to. volumes, was not a Canadian by birth and education like Ferland and Garneau, but came to Canada in 1854 and, after residing there for over ten years, returned to his native country, where he published his well known and valuable work.

DENT'S WORKS.

(34) Page 19.—John Charles Dent was an English journalist, who subsequently became connected with the Toronto press. He wrote the two following works : " The Last Forty Years : Canada since the Union of 1841," Toronto, 1881, two volumes, sm.4to. ; " The Story of the Upper Canada Rebellion," Toronto, 1885-86, two volumes, sm.4to. He also edited the " Canadian Portrait Gallery," Toronto, 1880-81. Although not a Canadian by birth or education, he identified himself thoroughly with Canadian thought and sentiment, and was made a Fellow of the Royal Society of Canada

before his too sudden death. A criticism of his work on "Canada since the Union" by the Abbé Casgrain ('Trans. Roy. Soc. Can.,' vol. iii., Sec. I.) indicated that his opinions did not always meet with the warm approval of the French Canadians of a very pronounced type.

LOUIS TURCOTTE'S HISTORY.

(35) Page 20.—This work appeared at Quebec in two 12mo. volumes in 1871. Mr. Turcotte was a French Canadian by birth and education, and connected with the legislative library at Quebec when he died. See a favourable review of his literary work by Mr. Faucher de Saint-Maurice, F.R.S.C., in 'Trans. Roy. Soc. Can.,' vol. i., Sec. I.

B. SULTE.

(36) Page 20.—"Histoire des Canadiens-Français, 1608-1880. Origine, Histoire, Religion, Guerres, Découvertes, Colonisation, Coutumes, Vie domestique et politique, Développement, Avenir. Par Benjamin Sulte. Ouvrage orné de portraits et de plans." Eight volumes, 4to., Montreal, 1882-1884. Mr. Sulte is also the author of several poems, (See Note 40) and numerous essays and monographs of much literary merit and historic value. He is one of the most industrious members of the Royal Society of Canada.

ABBÉ CASGRAIN.

(37) Page 20.—The Abbé H. R. Casgrain's best known works are the following :
"Légendes Canadiennes." Quebec, 1861, 12mo. New ed., Montreal, 1884.
"Histoire de la Mère Marie de l'Incarnation, première supérieure des Ursulines de la Nouvelle France. Précédée d'une esquisse sur l'histoire religieuse des premiers temps de cette colonie." Quebec, 1864, 8vo. New ed., Montreal, 1886.
"Guerre du Canada, 1756-1760. Montcalm et Lévis." Quebec, 1891, two volumes, 8vo.
The Abbé has been a most industrious historical student, and to enumerate all his literary efforts would be to occupy much space. He has been a principal contributor to the 'Trans. Roy. Soc. Can.' His monographs, "Un pèlerinage au pays d'Evangeline" (vol. iv.) and "Les Acadiens après leur dispersion" (vol. v.), are particularly interesting, and the former has been crowned by the French Academy, and appeared in book form at Quebec. He is very much imbued with the national spirit and fervour of his countrymen.

KINGSFORD'S AND OTHER HISTORICAL WORKS.

(38) Page 20.—Six volumes of Dr. Kingsford's "History of Canada" have appeared since 1887. Volume i. embraces the period from 1608 to 1682 ; vol. ii., 1679-1725 ; vol. iii., 1726-1756 ; vol. iv., 1756-1763 ; vol. v., 1763-1775 ; vol. vi., 1776-1779. Toronto and London, 8vo. For bibliographical notes on various works relating to the political and general history of Canada see Bourinot's "Parliamentary Government in Canada," 'Am. Hist. Ass. Papers,' 1891, App. References are there made to McMullen, Withrow, Murdoch, Campbell, Hincks, etc. Also 'Nar. and Crit. Hist. Am.,' viii., 171-189. As usual, the learned editor, Dr. Winsor, supplies by his notes many deficiencies in the text. Also, Edmond Lareau's "Histoire de la Littérature Canadienne" (Montreal), c. 4, and Mr. J. C. Dent's "Last Forty Years ; or, Canada since the Union of 1841," c. 42, on "Literature and Journalism." Among the later French Canadian writers who are doing excellent historical work is Dr. N. E. Dionne, F.R.S.C., author of several books on Cartier and his successors and Champlain. Mr. Hannay

of St. John has written a "History of Acadia," which has been well received (St. John, N.B., 1879, 8vo.)   The Abbé Auguste Gosselin is another industrious French Canadian writer.   Mr. Joseph Tassé, whose "Canadiens de l'Ouest" (Montreal, 1878, two volumes) was distinguished by much research and literary skill, has of late years devoted himself mainly to politics and journalism, though he has found time to write several essays for the 'Trans. Roy. Soc. Can.,' and a small volume, "38ᵐᵉ Fauteuil, ou Souvenirs Parlementaires" (Montreal, 1891), a series of political sketches, written in excellent French.   A monumental work is the "Dictionnaire Généalogique des familles canadiennes" by Mgr. Tanguay, F.R.S.C., invaluable to students of French Canadian history and ethnography.

CANADIAN BIBLIOGRAPHY.

(39) Page 20.—A bibliography of the members of the Royal Society, on the plan of one given in the sixth volume (1892) of the 'Papers of the American Historical Association,' is now being prepared for the eleventh volume of the 'Transactions.' It will be much fuller necessarily than the bibliographical notes that appear in this monograph.

LATER CANADIAN POETS, 1867–1893.

(40) Page 20.—Dr. Louis Fréchette's poems are admitted to be the most finished illustrations of French poetic art yet produced in the Dominion ; and one who reads them can easily understand that "Les Fleurs Boréales" and "Les Oiseaux de Neige" (now in the third edition, Montreal) should have been crowned by the French Academy in 1880, and that he should have been accorded the Monthyon prize as a matter of course.   His other volumes of poems are these : "Mes Loisirs," Quebec, 1863; "La Voix d'un Exilé," Quebec, 1869; "Pêle-Mêle," Montreal, 1877; "Les Oubliés" and "Voix d'Outre-Mer," Montreal, 1886 ; and "Feuilles Volantes," Montreal, 1891.   His poem on the discovery of the Mississippi is probably his best sustained effort on the whole.   A number of his poems have appeared in the 'Trans. Roy. Soc. Can.,' vols. i., ii., iii., iv.   He has published some dramas and comedies (see 'Am. Cyclopædia of Biography,' vol. ii., p. 539), which have not been as successful as his purely poetic essays.   He has also written several essays of merit in 'Harper's Monthly' and other periodicals of the day, as well as in the 'Trans. Roy. Soc. Can. The following is an extract from his poem on "La Découverte du Mississippi":

> " Tantôt je croyais voir, sous les vertes arcades,
> Du fatal De Soto passer les cavalcades
> En jetant au désert un défi solennel ;
> Tantôt c'était Marquette errant dans la prairie,
> Impatient d'offrir un monde à sa patrie,
> Et des âmes à l'Eternel.

> " Parfois, sous les taillis, ma prunelle trompée,
> Croyait voir de La Salle étinceler l'épée,
> Et parfois, groupe informe allant je ne sais où,
> Devant une humble croix—ô puissance magique !—
> De farouches guerriers à l'œil sombre et tragique
> Passer en pliant le genou !

> " Et puis, berçant mon âme aux rêves des poètes,
> J'entrevoyais aussi de blanches silhouettes,
> Doux fantômes flottant dans le vague des nuits :
> Atala, Gabriel, Chactas, Evangeline,
> Et l'ombre de René, debout sur la colline,
> Pleurant ses immortels ennuis.

" Et j'endormais ainsi mes souvenirs moroses . . . .
Mais de ces visions poétiques et roses
Celle qui plus souvent venait frapper mon œil,
C'était, passant au loin dans un reflet de gloire,
Ce hardi pionnier dont notre jeune histoire
    Redit le nom avec orgueil.

" Jolliet ! Jolliet ! deux siècles de conquêtes,
Deux siècles sans rivaux ont passé sur nos têtes,
Depuis l'heure sublime où, de ta propre main,
Tu jetas d'un seul trait sur la carte du monde
Ces vastes régions, zone immense et féconde,
    Futur grenier du genre humain !

" Oui, deux siècles ont fui ! La solitude vierge
N'est plus là ! Du progrès le flot montant submerge
Les vestiges derniers d'un passé qui finit.
Où le désert dormait, grandit la métropole ;
Et le fleuve asservi courbe sa large épaule
    Sous l'arche aux piles de granit.

" Plus de forêts sans fin : la vapeur les silonne !
L'astre des jours nouveaux sur tous les points rayonne ;
L'enfant de la nature est évangélisé ;
Le soc du laboureur fertilise la plaine ;
Et le surplus doré de sa gerbe trop pleine
    Nourrit le vieux monde épuisé.

Mr. Pamphile LeMay, one of the best known French Canadian poets, has published the following : " Essais Poétiques," Que bec, 1865 ; " La Découverte du Canada," Quebec, 1867 ; " Poèmes Couronnés," Quebec, 1870 ; " Les Vengeances," Quebec, 1875, 1876 and 1888 (also dramatized) ; " Une Gerbe," Quebec, 1879. He has also written " Fables Canadiennes," Quebec, 1882. A number of his poems have appeared in the 'Trans. Roy. Soc. Can.,' vols i.,. iii., v., vi., ix. He has also written several stories of Canadian life : " L'Affaire Sougraine," Quebec, 1884 ; " Le Pèlerin de Sainte-Anne," new ed., Montreal, 1893 ; and " Rouge et Bleu," comedy. One of his best works was a translation of Longfellow's " Evangeline."

The following is a list of other Canadian books of poems, of varying merit, which have appeared within a quarter of a century :

" The Songs of a Wanderer." By Carroll Ryan. Ottawa, 1867. Indicated much poetic taste, but the poet has been submerged in the busy journalist.

"Songs of Life." By Rev. E. H. Dewart. Toronto, 1867. He was author of the first collection of Canadian poems made in this country. See infra.

" The Prophecy of Merlin and other Poems." By John Reade. Montreal, 1870. In many respects the best sustained poems written by a Canadian can be read in this book.

" Les Laurentiennes." By Benjamin Sulte. Montreal, 1870.

" Les Chants Nouveaux." By the same. Ottawa, 1880.

" The Legend of the Rose." By Samuel J. Watson. Toronto, 1876. Mr. Watson was a writer of promise who died in the maturity of his power.

" The Feast of St. Anne, and other Poems." By P. S. Hamilton. Montreal, 1878 ; 2nd ed. 1890. Has some interest from its description of the ceremonies at the feast of Sainte-Anne du Canada—the tutelary saint of the Canadian aborigines—which is held by the Micmacs on the 26th day of July in each year on Chapel Island,

in the beautiful Bras d'Or Lake of Cape Breton. See Bourinot's "Cape Breton."
"Waifs in Verse." (Ottawa, ed. in 1878, 1887 and 1891.) By G. W. Wicksteed,
Q.C., for fifty years the able law clerk of the Canadian Commons.

"A Collection of Poems." By Miss Williams of Grenville, P.Q., 1879.

"The Coming of the Princess, and Other Poems." By Kate Seymour Maclean of
Kingston. 1880.

"Lyrics, Songs and Sonnets." By A. H. Chandler and C. Pelham Mulvany.
Toronto, 1880.

"The Times, and Other Poems." By J. R. Newell of Woodstock. 1880.

"The Consolation." By George Gerrard. Montreal, 1880.

"Poems of the Heart and Home." By Mrs. J. C. Yule. Toronto, 1880.

"Poems, Songs and Odes." By Archibald McAlpine Taylor. Toronto, 1881.

"The New Song, and Other Poems." By Mrs. W. H. Clarke. Toronto, 1883.

"Zenobia. A Poem in Rhymed Heroics." By Rev. Æ. McD. Dawson, F.R.S.C.
1883.

"The Mission of Love, and Other Poems." By Caris Sima. 1883.

"Lorenzo, and Other Poems." By J. R. Pollock of Keswick, Ont. 1883.

"Caprices Poétiques et Chansons Satiriques." Par Rémi Tremblay.
Montréal, 1883.

"Les Echos." Par J. B. Routhier. Québec, 1883, 12mo. Judge Routhier is a
member of the Royal Society of Canada, in whose 'Trans.' (vol. iv., Sec. I.) appeared
"Lettre d'un Volontaire du 9ieme Voltigeurs campé à Calgary." His literary reputation stands high among his countrymen.

"Old Spookse's Pass, and Other Poems." By Isabella Valancy Crawford. Toronto, 1884.

"Marguerite, and Other Poems." By George Martin. 1886.

"Laura Secord : a Ballad of 1812." By Mrs. Curzon. Toronto, 1886.

"Songs, Sonnets and Miscellaneous Poems." By J. Imrie. Toronto, 1886.

"Dreamland, and Other Poems" (Ottawa, 1868), and "Tecumseh : a Drama"
(Toronto and London, 1886). By Charles Mair, a poet of original talent, and descriptive power, who is now a resident of the North-west Territories.

"Orion, and Other Poems" (Philadelphia, 1880), and "In Divers Tones" (Montreal, 1887). By Prof. C. G. D. Roberts, who is the best known abroad of all Canadian
poets, and represents that Canadian or national spirit which has been slowly rising
from the birth of Confederation. Since the days of Crémazie—over thirty years ago
—there are other poets who recognize the existence of a Canadian people in a large
sense—a Canadian people of two races, born and educated in the country, and having
common aspirations for a united, not an isolated, future. Prof. Roberts is now
bringing out a new volume of poems in London.

The poetic taste of the Archbishop of Halifax, the Most Rev. C. O'Brien, F.R.S.C.,
is well illustrated in the following volume : "Aminta : a Modern Life Drama," New
York, 1890. The Archbishop is also the author of a novel, "After Weary Years,"
(Baltimore and New York, 1885), the scenes of which are laid in Rome and Canada,
and are described with much power of invention and fervour. As the author himself
says, "historic places and events are accurately described." He has, it will be seen
from his preface, great confidence in the future national greatness of the Dominion.

"A Gate of Flowers." By T. O'Hagan. Toronto, 1887. He has another volume
in press.

"The Masque of Minstrels, and Other Pieces, chiefly in verse." By B. W. and
A. J. Lockhart. Bangor, Me., 1887. These two brothers are Nova Scotians by birth
and education, who lived their youth in the land of Evangeline. The Gaspéreaux and
Grand Pré are naturally the constant theme of their pleasing verse.

"Among the Millet, and Other Poems." By Archibald Lampman. Ottawa, 1888. Some of Mr. Lampman's most finished sonnets have appeared in the best American periodicals, to which he is still a frequent contributor; his work shows the true poetic instinct. He holds a position in the Civil Service at Ottawa.

"The Water Lily. An Oriental Fairy Tale." By Frank Waters. Ottawa, 1888.

"De Roberval : a Drama. Also the Emigration of the Fairies, and the Triumph of Constancy : a Romaunt." By John Hunter Duvar. St. John, N.B., 1888. Mr. Duvar, who has fine literary tastes, has been a resident of Prince Edward Island for some years.

"The Epic of the Dawn, and Other Poems." By Nicholas Flood Davin. Regina, N.W.T., 1889. Mr. Davin is the clever "Irishman in Canada," and while the most pretentious of his poems in this little book were written across the ocean, others are the product of Canadian thought and sentiment.

"Lake Lyrics, and Other Poems." By W. Wilfred Campbell. St. John, N.B., 1889. Mr. Campbell, who was originally a clergyman of the Church of England, is now in the public service at Ottawa, and has written some of his best poems for American magazines. One on "The Mother," in 'Harper's Monthly' is full of poetic thought and deep pathos, and should be better known by Canadians than it appears to be. At this time of writing his new volume of poems entitled "The Dread Voyage" (Toronto, 1893), has appeared ; it sustains his reputation, though one can hardly encourage his effort to imitate Tennyson in such poems as "Sir Lancelot." Canadian poets too frequently are imitative rather than original. Mr. Campbell's verses on the varied scenery of the lakes of the West show the artistic temperament.

For instance :

> "Domed with the azure of heaven,
>   Floored with a pavement of pearl,
> Clothed all about with a brightness
>   Soft as the eyes of a girl.

> "Girt with a magical girdle,
>   Rimmed with a vapour of rest—
> These are the inland waters,
>   These are the Lakes of the West."

ON THE LEDGE.

> "I lie out here on a ledge, with the surf on the rocks below me,
>   The hazy sunlight above and the whispering forest behind ;
> I lie and listen, O lake, to the legends and songs you throw me,
>   Out of the murmurous moods of your multitudinous mind.

> "I lie and listen, a sound like voices of distant thunder,
>   The roar and throb of your life in your rock-wall's mighty cells ;
> Then after a softer voice that comes from the beaches under,
>   A chiming of waves on rocks, a laughter of silver bells.

> "A glimmer of bird-like boats, that loom from the far horizon ;
>   That scud and tack and dip under the gray and the blue ;
> A single gull that floats and skims the waters, and flies on,
>   Till she is lost like a dream in the haze of the distance, too.

> " A steamer that rises a smoke, then after a tall, dark funnel,
> That moves like a shadow across your water and sky's gray edge ;
> A dull, hard beat of a wave that diggeth himself a tunnel,
> Down in the crevices dark under my limestone ledge.

> " And here I lie on my ledge, and listen the songs you sing me,
> Songs of vapour and blue, songs of island and shore ;
> And strange and glad are the hopes and sweet are the thoughts you
>   bring me
> Out of the throbbing depths and wells of your heart's great store."

"Pine, Rose and Fleur-de-Lis." By S. Frances Harrison (" Seranus "). Toronto, 1891.

"Songs, Lyrical and Dramatic." By John Henry Brown. Ottawa, 1892, 12mo. The New York ' Nation' truly says of this new poetic aspirant that he has Walt Whitman's tendencies, but nevertheless he "writes in a generous spirit, and may yet have thoughts and expression all his own." The fact is, I repeat, most Canadian poets are too imitative and too rarely original.

"Tendres Choses. Poésies Canadiennes." By Dr. R. Chevrier. Montreal, 1892, 12mo. That an author unknown to fame should give us his portrait, as in this case, is perplexing. Still the verse is frequently melodious, though it represents what is a feature of French poetry, melodious rhythm, rather than strength and thought.

"This Canada of Ours, and Other Poems." By J. D. Edgar, M.P., Toronto, 1893. This little volume contains "The White Stone Canoe : a Legend of the Ottawas," which had been published in separate form some years previously. His French and Latin translations are full of taste.

"Les Perce-Neige, premières poésies." By Napoléon Legendre. Montreal, 12mo. He is a member of the Royal Society of Canada, and constant contributor (generally in prose) to its 'Transactions.'

"Mes Rimes." By Elzéar Labelle. Montreal, 1886, 8vo.

Selections of Canadian poems have appeared of recent years in the following publications :

1. "Selections from Canadian Poets : with occasional critical and biographical notes and an introductory essay on Canadian poetry." By the Rev. E. H. Dewart. Montreal, 1864, 8vo.

2. "Songs of the Great Dominion : Voices from the Forests and Waters, the Settlements and Cities of Canada." Selected and edited by W. D. Lighthall, M.A., of Montreal. London, 1889, 12mo.

3. "Younger American Poets, 1830-1890." Edited by Douglas Sladen, B.A., Oxon. With an Appendix of Younger Canadian Poets. Edited by G. B. Roberts of St. John, N.B. New York, 1891, 12mo.

4. "Later Canadian Poems." Edited by J. E. Wetherell, B.A. Toronto, 1893.

In the first mentioned work, which is judiciously edited, the poets until 1864 obtain a place. In the three other books we have selections from John Reade, Geo. Frederick Cameron, Prof. Roberts, Bliss Carman (now a resident of the United States), A. H. Chandler, Isabella Valancy Crawford, Mrs. Leprohon, Hereward K. Cockin, John Hunter Duvar, Rev. A. W. H. Eaton, Louis Fréchette, James Hannay, Sophie M. Hensley, Charles Sangster, M. Richey Knight, Archibald Lampman, W. D. Lighthall, A. J. Lockhart, B. W. Lockhart, Agnes Maude Machar (" Fidelis "), W. McLennan, Charles Mair, Mary Morgan (" Gowan Lea"), Charles P. Mulvany, Rev. F. G. Scott, Philip Stewart, H. R. A. Pocock, Barry Stratton, A. Weir, Mary

Barry Smith, John T. Lespérance ("Laclède"), W. Wye Smith, Ethelwyn Wetherald, John E. Logan ("Barry Dane"), George Martin, Mrs. Harrison ("Seranus"), D. Campbell Scott, James D. Edgar, E. Pauline Johnson, George Murray, William Kirby, Annie Rothwell, W. A. Sherwood, Isidore G. Ascher, P. J. O. Chauveau, B. Sulte, P. LeMay, and others. I enumerate these names to show how many Canadians have ventured upon the field of poesy despite the practical realities of life in this relatively new country. The selections in the second of these works would have been more valuable had they contained "Our Fathers" by Joseph Howe—the most spirited poem in some respects ever written by a native Canadian. To the names of poetic aspirants, too, must be added those of M. J. Katzmann and of M. J. Griffin, whose fugitive pieces have attracted notice. Mr. Griffin has fine literary tastes and his few poems, only the relaxation of leisure hours, show he might win fame in this delightful department of letters. The reader will obtain some idea of the standard of Canadian poetry by reading the selections, and should not be carried away by the too obvious enthusiasm that has at times stifled the critical faculty in the editors. The poetic genius of Canadians is to be stimulated, not by sentimental gush, but by a judicious criticism that is not sufficiently cultivated by our writers who review the efforts of our poets, historians and essayists. These remarks also apply to such articles as that by the late Mr. Lespérance on "The Poets of Canada" in 'Trans. Roy. Soc. Can.,' vol. ii., Sec. II.

Mr. Evan McColl, F.R.S.C., is the Gaelic poet of Canada. Three editions have appeared of the "Clàrsach nam Beann," which was printed as far back as 1838 in Glasgow. The same was also published in English in the same year, under the title of "The Mountain Minstrel," of which six editions have been printed. In 1883 he published in Toronto "Poems and Songs chiefly written in Canada." Mr. McColl is a great favourite among his Scotch countrymen everywhere; but his decidedly original poetic genius, rude and wild as it is at times, is not a Canadian product, for he was born at Kenmore, Lochfyne-Side, Scotland, in 1808, and it was not until he was forty years of age that he made Canada his home. He is now a resident of Toronto, and still comes to the annual meetings of the Royal Society, of which he was one of the original members.

(41) Page 21.— "IN MY HEART." By John Reade.

" In my heart are many chambers through which I wander free ;
    Some are furnished, some are empty, some are sombre, some are light ;
    Some are open to all comers, and of some I keep the key,
    And I enter in the stillness of the night.

" But there's one I never enter—it is closed to even me !
    Only once its door was opened, and it shut for evermore ;
    And though sounds of many voices gather round it like a sea,
    It is silent, ever silent, as the shore.

" In that chamber, long ago, my love's casket was concealed,
    And the jewel that it sheltered I knew only one could win :
    And my soul foreboded sorrow, should that jewel be revealed,
    And I almost hoped that none might enter in.

" Yet day and night I lingered by that fatal chamber door,
    Till—she came at last my darling one, of all the earth my own ;
    And she entered—then she vanished with my jewel which she wore ;
    And the door was closed—and I was left alone.

" She gave me back no jewel, but the spirit of her eyes
    Shone with tenderness a moment, as she closed that chamber door,
    And the memory of that moment is all I have to prize—
    But *that*, *at least*, is mine for evermore.

" Was she conscious, when she took it, that the jewel was my love ?
    Did she think it but a bauble she might wear or toss aside ?
    I know not, I accuse not, but I hope that it may prove
    A blessing, though she spurn it in her pride."

LAURA SECORD'S WARNING.

(41*a*) Page 24.—In Mrs. Edgar's excellent annotations to the Ridout Letters in
" Ten Years of Upper Canada in Peace and War, 1805-1815," (Toronto, 1890), appears
the following account of a courageous woman's exploit which brought disaster to
the Americans soon after their defeat at Stoney Creek :

" At a place called Beaver Dams, or Beechwoods, (about twelve miles in a direct
road from Queenstown), where is now the town of Thorold, was a depot for provi-
sions for the Canadian troops, guarded by a detachment of thirty of the 49th regiment under Lieutenant Fitzgibbon with some Indians and militia, in all about 200
men. In order to surprise and dislodge this outpost, an American force of 500 men,
with fifty cavalry and two field-pieces, under Colonel Boerstler, set out from Fort
George (Niagara) on the 23rd of June [1813]. A surprise was meditated, in retaliation,
no doubt, for the affair of Stoney Creek. Laura Secord, wife of a Canadian farmer,
who had been wounded in the battle of Queenstown Heights, accidentally heard of
the designs of the Americans, and determined to give the outpost timely warning.
She set out alone before day-break, on the 23rd June, from her house at Queenstown,
and arrived at Fitzgibbon's headquarters, a stone house known as DeCew's, near the
Beaver Dams, at sunset of the same day. On account of the American sentries and
outposts, she had to avoid the high roads and beaten paths, thus making her toilsome journey nearly twice as long. In spite of weakness and fatigue, this heroic
woman went on her way through pathless woods, over hill and dale and unbridged
streams, till she reached her destination. Her warning came just in time. Lieutenant Fitzgibbon disposed of his little force to the best advantage possible, placing
them in ambush on both sides of the road, and taking every precaution to make it
appear that he had a large force in reserve. Between eight and nine in the morning
of the 24th June, the advance guard of the American riflemen appeared. A volley
from the woods received them and emptied their saddles. Soon firing came from all
directions, and bugle calls, and Indian yells. The bewildered Americans imagined
themselves in the presence of a much superior force. Finding that his men were
losing heavily from the fire of the unseen foe, and that they were suffering from
fatigue and heat, he consented to surrender. By the capitulation 542 men, 2 field-
pieces, some ammunition waggons, and the colours of the 14th U. S. regiment were
delivered over to the Canadians. For this brilliant achievement Lieutenant Fitzgibbon [afterwards a military knight of Windsor] received his Company and a Captain's commission. As to Laura Secord, her reward has come to her in fame. The
heroine lived until the year 1868, and sleeps now in that old cemetery at Drummond-
ville, where lie so many of our brave soldiers. There is no ' Decoration Day ' in
Canada, but if there were, surely this woman is entitled to the laurel wreath."
Pp. 198-201.

AUSTRALIAN POETS AND NOVELISTS.

(42) Page 25.—The Canadian reader can profitably and easily compare his own poets with those of Australia by reading Slade's "Australian Poets, 1788–1883, being a selection of poems upon all subjects written in Australia and New Zealand during the first century of the British colonization, with brief notes on their authors, etc." (London and Sydney, 1889.) It will be seen, however, that nearly all the so-called "Australian" poets are English born, while with one or two exceptions, those of Canada best known to fame are the product of Canadian life and thought. Henry Clarence Kendall, "the poet of New South Wales," was born at Ulladulla, on the coast of that colony, in 1842. He is the one Australian poet of reputation, except his forerunner, Charles Harpur, who was actually born under the Southern Cross. Kendall's verses on "Coogee," a striking natural feature of Australian scenery, show true poetic instinct and rhythmical ease:

" Sing the song of wave-worn Coogee—Coogee in the distance white,
With its jags and points disrupted, gaps and fractures fringed with light ;
Haunt of gledes and restless plovers of the melancholy wail,
Ever lending deeper pathos to the melancholy gale.
There, my brothers, down the fissures, chasms deep and wan and wild,
Grows the sea-bloom, one that blushes like a shrinking, fair, blind child,
And amongst the oozing forelands many a glad green rockvine runs,
Getting ease on earthy ledges sheltered from December suns."

But among the many spirited poems written in Australia since its settlement not one can equal the "Sick Stock-rider," by Adam Lindsay Gordon, who came to South Australia in his early manhood, and attempted sheep-farming, with the result of "owning nothing but a love for horsemanship and a head full of Browning and Shelley." This is a quotation from an introduction to his book by Marcus Clarke, himself a novelist and poet. One can see in the mind's eye the scenes described in the following verses, so full of real life and genuine poetry :

" 'Twas merry in the glowing morn, among the gleaming grass,
To wander as we've wandered many a mile,
And blow the cool tobacco cloud and watch the white wreaths pass,
Sitting loosely in the saddle all the while ;
'Twas merry 'mid the backwoods, when we spied the station roofs,
To wheel the wild scrub cattle at the yard,
With a running fire of stockwhips and a fiery run of hoofs.
Oh ! the hardest day was never then too hard !

" Aye ! we had a glorious gallop after 'Starlight' and his gang,
When they bolted from Sylvester's on the flat ;
How the sun-dried reed-beds crackled, how the flint-strewn ranges rang
To the strokes of 'Mountaineer' and 'Acrobat' ;
Hard behind them in the timber, harder still across the heath,
Close behind them through the tea-tree scrub we dashed ;
And the golden-tinted fern-leaves, how they rustled underneath !
And the honeysuckle osiers, how they crash'd ! "

The best known novels of Australian life are these : " For the Term of His Natural Life," by Marcus Clarke, who was an Englishman born and educated ; "The Miner's Right," "The Squatter's Dream," "A Colonial Reformer," and "Robbery Under Arms," by Thomas A. Browne ("Rolf Boldrewood"), who was also English born :

" Uncle Piper of Piper's Hill," by Madame Couvreur (" Tasma "), who is of Belgian descent, and is now a resident of Belgium, though she was born in Australia and there studied its social conditions; "The Australian Girl " and " A Silent Sea," by Mrs. Alick McLeod. Mrs. Campbell Praed, who is colonial born, has, in addition to several novels, written "Australian Life," which is described by Sir Charles Dilke ("Problems of Greater Britain," i., 374) as "a vivid autobiographical picture of the early days of Queensland." Copies of these and other Australian books the writer owes to the thoughtfulness of Chief Justice Way, D.C.L., Oxon., of Adelaide, South Australia. For many years he has been the recipient of these graceful attentions from friends in that fair land of the Southern Cross, and though it looks very much as if he will never meet some of them face to face—for the time is passing rapidly with us all—he takes this opportunity of now sending them his thanks across the seas.

HOWE'S " FLAG OF OLD ENGLAND."

(43) Page 26.—This spirited song was written for the one hundreth anniversary of the landing of Lord Cornwallis at Halifax. As many persons in old Canada do not know it—for it is not reproduced in recent collections of Canadian poems—I give it in full for the benefit of the youth of this Dominion, on whom the future destiny of the country depends :

> " All hail to the day when the Britons came over,
>> And planted their standard with sea foam still wet,
> Around and above us their spirits will hover,
>> Rejoicing to mark how we honour it yet.
> Beneath it the emblems they cherished are waving,
>> The Rose of Old England the roadside perfumes ;
> The Shamrock and Thistle the north winds are braving,
>> Securely the Mayflower blushes and blooms.

CHORUS.
> " Hail to the day when the Britons came over,
>> And planted their standard with sea-foam still wet,
> Around and above us their spirits will hover,
>> Rejoicing to mark how we honour it yet.
>> We'll honour it yet, we'll honour it yet,
>> The flag of Old England ! we'll honour it yet.

> " In the temples they founded their faith is maintained,
>> Every foot of the soil they bequeathed is still ours,
> The graves where they moulder no foe has profaned,
>> But we wreathe them with verdure, and strew them with flowers !
> The blood of no brother, in civil strife pour'd,
>> In this hour of rejoicing, encumbers our souls !
> The frontier's the field for the Patriot's sword,
>> And cursed be the weapon that Faction controls !

> CHORUS—" Hail to the day, etc.

> " Then hail to the day ! 'tis with memories crowded,
>> Delightful to trace 'midst the mists of the past,
> Like the features of Beauty, bewitchingly shrouded,
>> They shine through the shadows Time o'er them has cast.

As travellers track to its source in the mountains
The stream which, far swelling, expands o'er the plains,
Our hearts, on this day, fondly turn to the fountains
Whence flow the warm currents that bound in our veins.

CHORUS—" Hail to the day, etc.

" And proudly we trace them : no warrior flying
From city assaulted, and fanes overthrown,
With the last of his race on the battlements dying,
And weary with wandering, founded our own.
From the Queen of the Islands, then famous in story,
A century since, our brave forefathers came,
And our kindred yet fill the wide world with her glory,
Enlarging her Empire and spreading her name.

CHORUS—" Hail to the day, etc.

" Ev'ry flash of her genius our pathway enlightens—
Ev'ry field she explores we are beckoned to tread—
Each laurel she gathers our future day brightens—
We joy with her living, and mourn for her dead.
Then hail to the day when the Britons came over,
And planted their standard, with sea-foam still wet,
Above and around us their spirits shall hover,
Rejoicing to mark how we honour it yet.

CHORUS—" Hail to the day," etc.

ESSAYISTS.

(44) Page 27.—The principal contributors to the English and American periodical press of late years have been George Stewart of Quebec, Principal Grant, J. G. Bourinot, Martin J. Griffin, W. D. LeSueur, G. M. Dawson, S. E. Dawson, Arnold Haultain, John Reade, J. M. Oxley and Sir W. Dawson. Dr. Stewart of Quebec, despite the demands of journalism, has been always a most earnest literary worker, foremost by his own contributions and by his efforts to encourage the labours of others in the too indifferent little Canadian world. Goldwin Smith has always been a contributor of note, but he is rather an English than a Canadian writer. Among the names of the French Canadian general writers are those of Fréchette, Sulte, Marmette, Faucher de Saint-Maurice, J. Tassé, DeCelles, Dionne, Casgrain and LeMoine ; but their efforts have been confined as a rule to the numerous French Canadian periodicals which have appeared for the last thirty years, and after a short career died for want of adequate support. In the numerous periodicals of England and the United States English Canadian writers have great advantages over French Canadians, who are practically limited to their own country, since France offers few opportunities for such literary work.

WILLIAM KIRBY'S WORKS AND OTHER ROMANCES BY CANADIANS.

(45) Page 27.—" The Golden Dog : a Legend of Quebec." New York and Montreal, 1877, 8vo. Also translated by Pamphile LeMay, the French Canadian poet, Montreal, 1884. Mr. Kirby is also the author of several poems of merit : " The U. E. : a Tale of Upper Canada. A Poem in XII. Cantos." Niagara, 1859, 12mo.

F

"Canadian Idylls," Toronto, 1878, etc. He was born in England in 1817, but came to Canada at the early age of fifteen. He was one of the original members of the Royal Society of Canada.

Mr. Lespérance, F.R.S.C., was the author of the "Bastonnais" and other historical romances of some ability, but not of that high order of merit which gives a permanent reputation. The Hon. L. Seth Huntington, long known in Canadian political life, was the author of a semi-political novel, "Professor Conant " (Toronto, 1884), which had its merits, but it fell practically still-born from the press. Many other efforts have been made in the same branch of literature, but the performance, as stated in the text, has not been equal to the ambition that prompted the experiment.

MAJOR RICHARDSON.

(45a) Page 27.—Major Richardson was born at Niagara Falls in 1797, and educated at Amherstburg, U.C., where some of the scenes of " Wacousta " are laid. He served in the war of 1812, in the West Indies and in Spain, where he belonged to the British legion. He came back to Canada in 1838, and was for years connected with the press. He wrote a number of novels and short histories of Canadian events, but they are now all forgotten. His historical narrative is not generally trustworthy, while his later romances never even came up to the merit of "Wacousta." He died in obscurity some time after 1854—I cannot find the exact year—in the United States, where he attempted to continue a career of literature.

MARMETTE.

(46) Page 27.—Mr. Joseph Marmette, F.R.S.C., is the author of several works of fiction, viz. :

"François de Bienville. Roman historique." 1ere ed., Québec, 1870 ; 2e ed., Montréal, 1882.

"L'Intendant Bigot. Roman historique." Montréal, 1872.

"Le Chevalier de Mornac. Roman historique." Montréal, 1873.

"La Fiancée du Rebelle. Roman historique." Published in 'La Revue Canadienne,' Montreal, 1875.

DE GASPÉ'S WORKS.

(47) Page 27.—" Les Anciens Canadiens." By Philippe Aubert de Gaspé. Quebec, 1863, 8vo.

Several translations have appeared since 1863. That by Prof. Roberts (New York, Appleton & Co., 1890) omits the notes and addenda, which, if not interesting to the general reader, have much value for the historical student. Sulte's " Histoire des Canadiens," vol. vi., contains a portrait of the old French Canadian novelist. He also wrote "Mémoires" (Ottawa, 1886, 8vo.), which have also much historic value on account of their fidelity and simplicity of narrative.

MRS. CATHERWOOD.

(48) Page 28.—Mrs. Mary Hartwell Catherwood, whose home is in Hoopeston, Ill., has so far written and published the following admirable romances of the old days of New France and Acadie :

"The Romance of Dollard." Illustrated. New York, 1889, 12mo.

"The Story of Tonty." Illustrated. Chicago, 1890, 16mo.

"The Lady of Fort St. John." Boston and New York, 1891, 16mo.

"Old Kaskaskia : An Historical Novel of Early Illinois." Boston and New York, 1893, 16mo.

She has now commenced in ' The Century ' Magazine a new romance with the title, " The White Islander," a story of old Fort Michillimackinac, and in ' The Atlantic Monthly' another story, " The Chase of Saint Castin." Her romances are never long, but bear the impress of close study of the subject and of much careful writing.

GILBERT PARKER.

(49) Page 28.—He is a most industrious worker in various branches of literature in London. After a residence of a few years in Australia, where he was connected with the Sydney press, he went to England, where he wrote many sketches of Australian life which were well received. Recently he has been studying the interesting phases of French Canadian and Northwest life, and has produced, among other stories, " The Chief Factor," the principal scenes of which are laid in the great territories of the Dominion before they were opened up to the farmer, the rancher and the railway.

DE MILLE'S WORKS.

(50) Page 29.—James De Mille was a native of New Brunswick, and a professor in Dalhousie College, N. S., at the time of his death. His first work of fiction was " Helena's Household : a Tale of Rome in the First Century " (New York, 1858). His most popular works, " The Dodge Club Abroad " (1866), " Cord and Creese " (1867), " The Cryptogram " (1871), and " A Castle in Spain " (1883), first appeared in ' Harper's Monthly.' A strange, imaginative work, " A Curious MS. Found in a Copper Cylinder," was published in New York in 1888, and is understood to have been written by him. It was not until Rider Haggard's fiction became popular that the New York publishers ventured to print a book which so severely taxes the credulity of the reader. As a work of pure invention it is in some respects superior to those of the English author. Mr. De Mille died in 1880, at the age of 43, when much was expected of him. See Appleton's " Cyclo. Am. Biogr.," ii., 138, for a list of his published works except the one just mentioned.

SARA JEANNETTE DUNCAN.

(51) Page 29.—She is the author of three books. " A Social Departure " and " An American Girl in London " have had many readers and are full of promise. Miss Duncan, in company with another young lady, in 1889-90, went around the world, and made numerous contributions to the press of Canada during that tour, but its noteworthy result is the first mentioned volume. She is now married and a resident of India, whose striking aspects of social life she is studying and portraying in print. Her latest story, or rather sketch, of Indian customs, " The Simple Adventures of a Memsahib" (New York, 1893), has many touches of quiet humour. One must regret that her talent has not been directed to the incidents of Canadian life.

MATTHEW ARNOLD ON LITERATURE AND SCIENCE.

(52) Page 31.—The extract given in the text is taken from " Literature and Science," one of Mr. Matthew Arnold's " Discourses in America," published in book form in London, 1885. See pp. 90-92.

PRINCIPAL GRANT'S ADDRESS.

(53) Page 32.—This address to the Royal Society of Canada, to which reference is made in the text, is given in the ninth volume of the ' Transactions,' pp. xxxix-xl. Dr. Grant could never be uninteresting, but the address shows his ideas can now

and then be a little chaotic or enigmatic.　It is quite evident he has never studied with much care the volumes of the 'Transactions,' or comprehended the useful work the Society is doing in its own way.　Never an active member himself, he has not done adequate justice to those who have been at all events conscientious labourers in the vineyard where he has planted no seed.

SIR J. W. DAWSON.

(54) Page 32.—This distinguished scientific man is a Nova Scotian by birth, who, before he became so closely identified with the prosperity of McGill College at Montreal as its principal, was superintendent of education in his native province.　His scientific works are numerous, but the one which first brought him fame was his "Acadian Geology: an Account of the Geological Structure and Mineral Resources of Nova Scotia and Portions of the Neighbouring Provinces of British America" (Edinburgh and London, 1855, 8vo.), which has run through many editions, and is now a very large volume compared with the little modest book that first ventured into the world of literature nearly forty years ago.

MR. BILLINGS.

(55) Page 33.—He was born on his father's farm, in the township of Gloucester, near Ottawa.　A bibliography, evidently prepared by his own hand, is to be found in "Bibliotheca Canadensis," pp. 31-34.　His most important memoirs are on the third and fourth Decades and the Palæozoic fossils of the Canadian Geological Survey, in which nearly all the genera and species of the fossils there described were discovered by himself.

ORIGIN OF THE ROYAL SOCIETY OF CANADA.

(56) Page 33.—The first volume of the 'Trans. Roy. Soc. Can.' (1882-83), pp. i-lxxiv., contains an account of the proceedings before and after the foundation of the Society, with the addresses in full of the Marquess of Lorne and of the first President and Vice-President of the body.　On the occasion of the Montreal meeting, 1891, a handbook was largely circulated by the Citizens' Committee with the view of giving information of the object and work of the Society.　It was written by Mr. John Reade, F.R.S.C., and contains a succinct history of the origin and operations of the body until May, 1891.　It contains plans of McGill College grounds and of Montreal in 1759, and sketches of the old Seminary towers, St. Gabriel-street church, St. Ann's, besides some interesting facts relating to Montreal's historic places.

SIR D. WILSON, T. S. HUNT AND MR. CHAUVEAU.

(57) Page 34.—Dr. Kingsford has given a paper, "In Memoriam, on Sir Daniel Wilson" ('Trans. Roy. Soc. Can.,' vol. xi.) in which he briefly reviews the excellent literary work and the wide culture of that eminent man.　In volume ix. of the 'Trans.,' Sec. I., pp. 53-58, there is a well-written paper on the late Mr. Chauveau, by his successor, Mr. L. O. David of Montreal.　The presidential address of Abbé Laflamme in 1892 (see 'Trans.,' vol. x.) was devoted to a review of the scientific attainments of Dr. T. Sterry Hunt.

CANADIAN SOCIETIES.

(58) Page 34.—At the present time there are over twenty Canadian scientific and literary societies associated with the Royal Society in its work.　Mr. John Reade, in the "Montreal Handbook of 1891" (see Note 56), gives the following list of societies

established before 1867 : Literary and Historical Society of Quebec, 1824 ; Natural History Society of Montreal, 1827—act of incorporation five years later ; Institut Canadien, Quebec, 1846; Canadian Institute, Toronto, 1851 ; Institut Canadien, Ottawa, 1852; Hamilton Association, 1856; Société Historique, Montréal, 1858 : Nova Scotia Institute of Natural Science, 1862 ; Natural History Society, St. John, N.B., 1862 ; Numismatic and Antiquarian Society, Montreal, 1862 ; Entomological Society of Ontario, 1863.

THE EARL OF DERBY AND THE ROYAL SOCIETY OF CANADA.

(58a) Page 42.—Four years ago you were good enough, in offering me the position of your honorary president, to ask the sympathy and encouragement which the governor-general, as Her Majesty's representative, might rightly be asked to manifest towards the representatives of science and of the liberal arts. I am afraid that my contributions to literature and science have been few. I do not know they are such as would have merited the notice of the Royal Society, but I can assure you that none of the members of your body take a deeper interest in all that concerns the welfare of your Society than he who is now laying down the office of honorary president. (Cheers.) There were some persons who considered that in a comparatively new country like Canada it was ambitious on her part when the foundations of the Royal Society were laid, but there must be a beginning of all things, and I think I may appeal to the work which has been and is being done by the different branches of the Society as evidence that its establishment was in no sense premature, but that it was fittingly determined that the progress of science and literature should take place coincidently with that of the country. In a new country like this—I think you have touched upon it in your address—there is a great tendency to further one's material wants, to promote trade and commerce, and to put aside, as it were, literature and the sciences ; but here the Royal Society has stepped in and done good work by uniting those who were scattered by distance and who find in the meetings of our Society a convenient opportunity of coming together for the exchanging of ideas and renewing of those friendships which, though perhaps only yearly meetings permit, are nevertheless enduring. If we look back we shall best see what good work is being done. If we could imagine the existence of such a society as this in the older countries in olden times, what a mine of wealth of information would have been afforded us ! We see that from the very first, whether in literature, which forms so important a part in our Society ; whether it be in the constitutional studies, in which our President is such an adept—and I was glad to see his authority has been quoted on the other side of the Atlantic as well as on this—whether it be in the literature of the chivalrous pioneers of France, who first led the way into the unbroken wilderness, or whether it be in the latter days of constitutional progress of this country and its relations both to the old world and the country growing up alongside of us.

In literature, history and poetry, also, the Society will from the first have its stamp, as we trust, upon the future of the Canadian race. (Cheers.) That science and the arts to an equal extent may find a place here is our earnest wish, in order that by sentiment and feeling we may bind together in the closest ties that by which she must achieve a great and enduring success. I must not detain you from your other duties, but I could not refrain from saying in a few words how heartily and truly I appreciate and believe in the work of the Royal Society. At your next meeting, as you truly say, I fear I shall not be amongst you ; but though the Atlantic may roll between us, you may be certain that in spirit, at least, I hope to be present at your meeting, and shall follow with the liveliest and deepest interest any record you

may be good enough to send me of what takes place on that occasion. * * * * *
I appeal not the less to my French colleagues than to my English ones in all matters
which relate to the welfare of the Society. Science, art and literature, it is true, are
cosmopolitan, but they are well knit together in this Society. We who have experienced in Canada the hospitality of its people are grateful for it. We have admired
the greatness of the resources of this country, and we look forward to a society like
this as having ample work to do in the future. As in every respect Canada seems to
be disposed always to take a forward part, so I hope the Royal Society will ever
press on to a higher and higher goal ; and, gentlemen, I can wish to the Royal
Society, to all my friends and brothers of the Society, to whom I once more tender
my hearty thanks, no greater blessing than, like Canada itself, that they may be
happy, united and prosperous. (Loud and prolonged cheers.)

S. E. DAWSON ON TENNYSON.

(59) Page 40.—" A Study, with Critical and Explanatory Notes, of Lord Tennyson's Poem, The Princess." By S. E. Dawson. Montreal, 1882, 12mo. 2nd ed. 1884.
The preface contains a long and interesting letter from the poet, which " throws
some light upon some important literary questions regarding the manner and
method of the poet's working." Tennyson describes the "Study " truly as an "able
and thoughtful essay."

THE OLD 'CANADIAN MONTHLY.'

(60) Page 40.—It first appeared in Toronto in 1872 (Adam Stevenson & Co.), soon
after Prof. Goldwin Smith took up his permanent residence in that western city.
Much of its reputation for years necessarily depended on the contributions of a
writer who, if he has failed to identify himself of late with the national or Canadian
sentiment of the people, has at all events done something in the past to improve the
style of Canadian *littérateurs* and to elevate the tone of journalism. The ' Monthly'
was the ablest successor of a long list of literary aspirants in the same field, the majority of which had a still shorter existence. See Bourinot's "Intellectual Development of the Canadian People " (Toronto, 1881), chap. iv. and ' Canadian Monthly,'
March, 1881.

FORM OF ROYAL SOCIETY 'TRANSACTIONS.'

(61) Page 42.—Since the delivery of the presidential address the Royal Society
decided by a considerable majority—chiefly made up of the two scientific sections—
to continue the quarto form for the present. Under these circumstances the com-
promise suggested may be adopted—that of printing separate editions of important
monographs and works from time to time by some understanding with the author.

THE STUDY OF THE CLASSICS.

(62) Page 49.—The following is a fuller quotation from Prof. Goldwin Smith's
very apposite remarks delivered before the Classical Association of Ontario (see
' The Week,' April 28th, 1893) : " No age has stood more in need of humanizing
culture than this, in which physical culture reigns. One of the newspapers the
other day invited us to take part in a symposium the subject of which was ' How
to Produce a Perfect Man.' The problem was large, but one help to its solution
might have been a reminder to keep the balance. A romantic age stands in need of

science, a scientific and utilitarian age stands in need of the humanities. Darwin avows that poetry gave him no pleasure whatever. This surely was a loss, unless the whole side of things which poetry denotes is dead and gone, nothing but dry science being left us ; in which case the generations that are coming may have some reason, with all their increase of knowledge and power, to wish that they had lived nearer the youth of the world." See *supra*, Note 1, for Mr. Lowell's remarks on the same subject.

CANADIAN LIBRARIES.

(63) Page 53.—Some interesting facts as to the evolution of libraries in the Dominion can be gathered by reference to Bourinot's " Intellectual Development in Canada" (Toronto, 1881) ; Canniff Haight's " Country Life in Canada Fifty Years Ago " ; Dr. Canniff's " History of Ontario" ; and Dr. Kingsford's " Early Bibliography of Ontario. " The principal results of the Ontario law providing for the establishment of free libraries by votes of ratepayers in a community have been the opening of two excellent libraries in Hamilton and Toronto—the latter under the judicious superintendence of Mr. James Bain.

CANADIAN ARTISTS.

(64) Page 54.—An Art Society was founded in Upper Canada as far back as 1841, but its exhibitions were necessarily representative of British works of art. The present Art Association was founded in Montreal in 1860, and the Ontario School of Arts, which is doing excellent work, twelve years later, with its headquarters in Toronto. The Royal Canadian Academy, mentioned in the text, was established in 1880. The influence of these and two or three minor institutions in Canada has been on the whole in the direction of stimulating art, but their efforts are not adequately encouraged by government or people in the provinces.

The following is a list of the painters in oils and water colours whose pictures now make the principal features of the annual exhibitions in Ontario and Quebec, and the majority of whom were inadequately represented at Chicago : F. A. Verner, whose Indian and Canadian scenes are excellent ; H. M. Matthews, who has made a high reputation for his Rocky Mountain paintings ; L. R. O'Brien, essentially the most finished painter of picturesque Canada ; T. Mower Martin, an industrious painter of wild sports and Canadian scenery ; E. Wyley Grier, who has done some good work in portraits and natural scenery ; W. Brymner, one of the most promising younger painters of Canadian scenes : George Reid, whose " Foreclosure of the Mortgage " is one of the best pictures produced in the Dominion ; John Hammond of St. John, N.B., a painter of water life ; Percy Woodcock, whose efforts at sketches of Canadian rural life are praiseworthy : F. M. Bell-Smith, who has a decided artistic faculty for the portraiture of our noblest scenery ; Homer Watson, a favourite for his rustic landscapes and romantic pastorals ; J. W. L. Forster, in some respects the best figure painter, but also capable of good landscapes ; G. Bruenech, a careful artist of scenery ; Ernest Thompson, who has made some good efforts at prairie subjects ; J. C. Forbes, who painted Mr. Gladstone's portrait, and is one of the best artists of the class that Canada has so far known ; W. Raphael and O. R. Jacobi, two of the oldest and best known painters of Canadian landscape. To these we must add Miss Minnie A. Bell, A. Watson, Miss Sidney S. Tully, Mrs. M. H. Reid, J. T. Rolph, R. F. Gagen, T. C. McGillivray Knowles, Forshaw Day, L. Huot, Mlle. Colombier, E. Dyonnet, C. Macdonald Manly, D. P. MacKillsan, J. W. Morrice, A. D. Patterson,

Miss G. F. Spurr, F. S. Challener, Paul J. Wickson, Mrs. M. B. Screiber, W. Revell, D. Fowler, Miss E. May Martin, Miss Laura Muntz, Miss F. M. Bell-Smith, Miss Florence Carlyle, Miss I. M. F. Adams, Owen P. Staples, Mrs. M. E. Dignam, Charles Alexander, W. E. Atkinson, J. C. Mills, J. A. Fraser (in New York), Carl Ahrens, W. A. Sherwood, Miss Fannie Sutherland, T. C. V. Ede, H. Sandham (in New York), Mr. Harvey, Mr. Cruickshank, Mr. Seavey, A. Cox, Miss Edwards, J. Griffith, Colin Scott, J. Wilson, James Smith, C. J. Way, F. Brownell, A. P. Coleman, R. Harris, Miss Holden and Miss Houghton. Many of these artists, whose merits, of course, vary much, are not native Canadians. One of the strongest landscape painters, Mr. Matthews, is an Englishman, who has now, after some years, thoroughly understood the light and colour of Canadian scenery. O'Brien, Brymner, L. Huot, Forbes, Forster, Pinhey, Sidney Tully, G. Harris, Gagen, Knowles, Watson, Alexander, A. D. Patterson, C. M. Manly, E. May Martin and George Reid are Canadians. G. T. Berthon, who died recently in Toronto at an advanced age, and was known as a painter of numerous portraits, the best of which are to be seen in Osgoode Hall, was of French origin and education. Raphael is German by birth and education. Jacobi is a painter of the Dusseldorf school, and was at one time employed in the court of the King of Bavaria. Bruenech is a native, I understand, of Denmark, though educated in Canada. E. W. Grier is an Englishman by birth and education, with a knowledge of French art derived from study in Paris. So is Ernest Thompson, who also studied in Paris. Mower Martin is an Englishman, educated in that country and in Canada, with whose scenery he has been always enamoured. Carl Ahrens was born and educated in the United States. Miss Minnie Bell and Miss Laura Muntz are among the most promising younger artists of Canada. Both were born and received their elementary education in Canada. Miss Bell, after studying in Paris, is now in Montreal. Miss Muntz is still studying in Paris. Robert Harris is a native of Prince Edward Island. Mr. N. Bourassa, who is a French Canadian artist, has of late years devoted himself to ecclesiastical decoration. His best work is to be seen in the architecture and decoration of the churches of Notre Dame de Nazareth and Notre Dame de Lourdes, in Montreal, and he has the credit of having first applied probably in America " the art of painting to the adornment of Christian churches in the broad and thorough manner so common at one period in central Italy." (See Dr. S. E. Dawson's "Handbook of Canada," Montreal, 1888, pp. 183, 184.) The influence of the French schools of painting can be seen in the best works of Paul Peel (now dead), Forster, Harris, Geo. Reid and John Pinhey (born at Ottawa), all of whom have had success at the salons. At the present time there are some twenty five Canadians, more or less, studying in Paris, and the majority are French Canadians. In fact, the French schools draw students from Canada as well as from the United States, and England is relatively ignored. The artistic temperament is more stimulated by the *ateliers* and the student life of Paris than among the more business-like and cold surroundings of a student in London. In sculpture the names are very few, Hamilton McCarthy, Hébert and Dunbar having alone done meritorious work, but of these three Hébert is the only native Canadian. One of the very first painters to draw attention, years ago, to Canadian scenery, especially to the wonderfuly vivid tints of autumn, was Krieghoff, whose pictures have been so much copied that it is difficult now to tell the originals from the reproductions. He was, however, not a native Canadian but a Swiss painter from the German-speaking cantons, I believe. The name of Paul Kane (born in Toronto) will be always identified with Indian life and customs, and as the pioneer of art in Canada. A fine collection of his paintings is in the possession of Hon. G. W. Allan, who has always taken an active interest in the development of art in the city of which he has been so long an honoured citizen.

Among other Canadian artists who laboured in the commencement of art studies in this country may be mentioned the following: Dulongpré, Samuel Berczy, Audy, William Berczy, Vincent Zacharie Thelariolin (Indian of Lorette, 1812-1886), Hamel, Carey, T. H. Burnett, J. J. Girouard, P. Leber—many of whose artistic efforts are already forgotten though their work was meritorious. With respect to Berthon, the following note by Col. G. T. Denison, F.R.S.C., of Toronto, which I have received since writing of the artist above, will be of interest: " His father was a court painter under the great Napoleon, and several of his pictures are now in Versailles. He was a Frenchman, and I think was in Vienna when his son, my old friend, was born; for I am under the impression Berthon told me he was born in Vienna. I think he was brought up in France, and went to London when comparatively young, and there set up as a portrait painter. He was induced to come out to Canada about the year 1843 or 1844, and settled in Toronto soon after, where he died about a year ago, over eighty years of age He was certainly, when in his prime, the best portrait painter we ever had in Canada, and in my opinion was better than most of the men of great celebrity in London to-day."

The successful artists at the World's Fair, where 113 works in all were presented from Canada, were the following: Mr. G. Reid, whose great picture mentioned above could not fail to attract much notice, Mr. Harris, Mr. Ede, Miss Holden and Mr. J. A. Fraser. This is satisfactory in view of the fact that the best work of the majority of leading Canadian artists was not represented in the exhibition. Apart from Mr. Reid's painting, the pictures that were signalled out for special notice were not equal in some respects to other efforts of the same artists that have been seen in our annual exhibitions.

In closing this note I cannot do better than give the following judicious remarks on art in Canada, delivered before the Canadian Institute, by an able Canadian artist, J. W. L. Forster: " The art of Canada to-day is a mingling of elements. . . . The influence of the old world may be seen in the work of many who cherish still the precepts of their masters. Yet it is due to those who have adopted Canada as their home to say they are as Canadian in the faithful reproduction of the pure glories of our climate as those who first saw the sun in our own sky. Our native artists who have studied abroad are much inclined to paint a Canadian sky with the haze of Western Europe, and our verdure, too, as though it grew upon foreign soil. Our art is not Canadian. . . . Material is certainly not wanting, nor *motif* of the grander order. The first requisite is for a stronger national spirit. Events are slowly developing this; and the signs are full of promise in this direction. The second great need is for a museum equipped with well-chosen specimens of the world's art. Our government and citizens are establishing schools of industrial and fine art, yet when we would point our pupils to examples of pure art, lo! there are none; and when we would know what art has been, in order to discover what art may be, we must go as exiles and pilgrims to foreign cities. A museum that gives the best of their art history and achievement will greatly strengthen our hope and give rein to our ambition. A third need is for capable and generous criticism. There are many men whose discernment and sympathies fit them eminently for the roll of art critic; but as yet journalism has not opened wide the door to advancement in such a specialty."

ARCHITECTURAL ART.

(64a) Page 57.—While Canadian architecture is generally wanting in originality of conception, yet it affords many good illustrations of the effective adaptation of the best art of Europe to the principal edifices of the large cities. These are the most noteworthy public buildings :

In *Ottawa.*—The parliament and departmental buildings, admirable examples of Italian Gothic of the 13th century, with a fine central tower, the effect of which has been marred by a later tower in the western block out of harmony with the general design of an otherwise perfect group.

In *Quebec.*—The legislative building in the French style of the 17th century, noteworthy for its niches containing statues of men famous in French Canadian history.

In *Montreal.*—The parish church of Notre Dame, on the Place d'Armes, of a simple Gothic style, attractive for its stateliness and massiveness.

Christ Church Cathedral, on St. Catherine street, worthy of study as an admirable specimen of the early English style of ecclesiastical architecture, exhibiting unity of design and correctness of proportions.

Notre Dame de Lourdes, whose interior has been already spoken of (see preceding note) ; a good example of the Byzantine order, combined with effects of the Italian Renaissance recalling Venetian architecture.

The Montreal Bank, on St. James street, an artistic illustration of the Corinthian order, with an interior interesting for the artistic effort to illustrate on the walls remarkable scenes in Canadian history.

The Canadian Pacific Station, on Windsor street, a fine example of an adaptation of old Norman architecture to modern necessities.

In *Toronto.*—The University, perhaps the best example in America of a modern conception of Norman architecture, with a tower of much beauty.

Trinity University, whose graceful Tudor-Gothic design, in which the tower is a conspicuous feature, is marred by the clumsy projection of a later chapel building, entirely out of harmony with the admirable front.

Osgoode Hall, of the Ionic order, modified by additions of the Italian Renaissance.

St. Andrew's Church, a combination of the Norman and Byzantine orders, more suitable for a great library or a hall than an ecclesiastical edifice. As a specimen of architecture, apart from its purpose, it is harmonious and artistic.

The new legislative buildings, which are the most pretentious in Canada after the Ottawa parliament house, are a praiseworthy effort to illustrate the Romanesque, with details of the Celtic and Indo-Germanic schools.

The Methodist Metropolitan Church, a judicious example of a modern form of the Gothic style which distinguished the 13th century in France. It is at once simple and harmonious in its general design, and has a massive tower which adds to the general effect of the whole structure.

St. James's Church, often cited as a good example of ecclesiastical Gothic, with a graceful and well-proportioned tower and steeple, conspicuous from all points of view.

In *Hamilton.*—The court-house is in some respects the best designed of its kind in Canada. The head office of the Canada Life Assurance Company is noteworthy for its graceful simplicity, in its way not equalled in Canada.

In *Fredericton.*—The Church of England Cathedral, a perfect specimen, on a small scale, of pure early English Gothic on the Continent.

The new library building which McGill University owes to the public spirit of Mr. Redpath, of Montreal, is distinguished by the graceful simplicity of its external form, and the conveniences of its beautiful interior. Apart from this fine edifice, however, and the parliamentary library at Ottawa, whose external design is harmonious and whose internal fittings illustrate the effectiveness of our natural woods, Canada has no such libraries—in special buildings I mean—noteworthy for beauty of architecture and convenience of arrangements as we find among our neighbours, illustrating their public and private spirit. Neither have we an art gallery of special architectural features, for the building at Montreal is simple in the extreme. Such as it is, however, it is an object of imitation to other cities in Canada.

" FIDELIS."

(65) Page 60.—The poetic citation which closes the presidential address is taken from Miss Machar's (" Fidelis ") verses on " Dominion Day," which appear in " Songs of the Great Dominion," pp. 15-17, and merit a wide audience for their patriotic spirit and poetic taste.

INDEX

G

'English-Canadian Literature'

THOMAS GUTHRIE MARQUIS

ENGLISH-CANADIAN LITERATURE

ENGLISH-CANADIAN LITERATURE

I

INTRODUCTORY

HAS Canada a voice of her own in literature distinct from that of England ? This question has attracted a good deal of attention in Canada and has been the subject of numerous discussions in home magazines and reviews. In Great Britain, however, the critical periodicals apparently have not yet recognized a purely Canadian[1] literature. While these periodicals have frequently reviewed the literatures of Norway, Sweden, Russia, the United States, Spain, Italy and other countries, no British critic so far seems to have thought Canadian literary achievement of sufficient importance to treat it seriously as a whole or to look for its distinctive note.

The United States has a literature fine and forceful, and though the language is the language of England the voice is her own : her writers have a vigorous national note, and narrate and sing the achievements of their ancestors and contemporaries in a manner characteristic of a nation that in so short a time has attained a giant's proportions. Has Canada such a voice ? The answer is that she has—not one of great volume, it is true ; but, as we shall see, in poetry at least, the Canadian note is clear and distinct and the performance is of good quality and of permanent value.

[1] To avoid repetition of the awkward and inexact expression English-Canadian, Canadian is used throughout this article to designate literature produced by writers using the English language. For a survey of French-Canadian literature see p. 435 *et seq.*

But, if we except such isolated writers as Richardson, Haliburton and Sangster, we shall find very little Canadian literature worthy of consideration that is not the product of the last fifty years. This should not be a source of surprise. Canada as a British country is only about one hundred and fifty years old. During the first thirty or forty years of the British régime few English people settled in the new colony, and these, for the most part, were of the official and military class, and scorned things colonial. They brought with them British traditions and British ideas, and remained satisfied with the literary productions of the Old World and treated lightly any attempt at literary achievement in the New. The Canadian-born as a force did not appear on the scene until near the close of the eighteenth or the beginning of the nineteenth century. When he did arrive he had but little leisure or inclination for literature. He had pioneer work to do—forests to cut down, stubborn lands to till, homes to build and roads to construct. It is only necessary to read the narratives of English travellers in Canada to appreciate how impossible it was for Canadians in the early days of British rule to turn their minds to creative effort, or indeed to devote much of their time to study. Moreover, until the first quarter of the nineteenth century had passed, there were no educational institutions in the country of a character likely to fit the inhabitants to interpret nature or life adequately, or to express their views in artistic form. King's College at Windsor, Nova Scotia, was the one striking exception. Its influence was early felt; it made Haliburton possible and gave him a small audience in his native province capable of appreciating his work.

During one hundred and fifty years before Canadians began to express themselves in prose and in verse, literature had been cultivated in the American colonies, and writers of such power as Benjamin Franklin had appeared to give models to the young nation. The people of the United States had, too, almost from the beginning of their colonial history, exceptionally fine educational institutions. Harvard and Yale were renowned centres of culture long before English settlers ventured in numbers into the unbroken wilderness of Upper Canada or to the rugged shores of the Maritime Provinces.

It is not surprising, then, to find that nearly all the noteworthy literature of Canada is of recent origin. We must expect, too, that the quantity, compared with that of older nations, will be small ; and yet if quantity were the only test Canada might be said to have a significant literature. In verse alone she has had from three hundred to four hundred singers, who have piped their lays in every province from the Atlantic to the Pacific. But, as might be expected, most of this verse is crude and commonplace, and it is unfortunate that some compilers have seen fit to include such work in Canadian anthologies, and that pseudo-critics have given words of the highest praise to what are clearly very inferior performances. The time has arrived when the writers of Canada should be studied as English and American writers are studied ; for in spite of its youthfulness, in spite of the disadvantages under which its people have laboured, the Dominion may lay claim to a creditable body of good prose and good verse. It is no longer necessary to pad out a review with encomiums of backwoods poets, or to claim, as Canadian, men and women of English or American birth and training who were mere 'birds of passage' in Canada, and whom Canada has no more right to claim than has the United States to claim Roberts, Carman and Duncan. Some of these 'birds of passage,' it is true, had a profound influence on Canadian writers, and early showed the wealth of material that lay at hand for the sons and daughters of Canada when they should arrive at maturity and take pride in their country and its builders. Any survey of Canadian literature should therefore include references to a number of non-indigenous authors who received their inspiration and did their work in Canada ; but a distinction should be made between such writers and those who may properly be considered as native Canadians.

It is proposed to deal with Canadian literature in the following order : history, biography, travels and explorations, general literature, fiction and poetry. In some instances, as in the case of Haliburton and of Roberts, an author will be found in several of these classes, but the main study of his work will be given in the class where he has won peculiar distinction.[1]

II

HISTORY

CANADA is exceedingly rich in material for historical literature, yet no Canadian so far has produced a great history in the sense in which the works of Macaulay, Green, Prescott and Motley are great. The richest field, that of the old régime, was invaded by an American historian, Francis Parkman, whose histories have been an influence for growth and a storehouse on which hundreds of writers have drawn ; short stories, studies innumerable, and many able novels have had as their inspiration incidents strikingly presented by Parkman ; but his narratives ended with the conspiracy of Pontiac, and he left untouched all the later history of Canada. The chronicles of the pioneers of Upper Canada and of the Eastern Townships, the stirring events of that nation-making conflict, the War of 1812, and the annals of a long struggle for political freedom still await a Canadian historian of knowledge and constructive genius.

The first noteworthy Canadian historian writing in English was George Heriot (1766-1844). Heriot was born in the island of Jersey, but early in life he came to Canada, where he occupied a number of important government positions. He was deputy postmaster-general of British North America from 1799 until 1816. He served through the War of 1812 and was with Morrison and Harvey at the gallant fight of Chrystler's Farm. Heriot published in 1804 in London, England, the first volume of his *History of Canada*. The work was never completed, and was little more than a well-written digest of the *Histoire Générale de la Nouvelle France* by Charlevoix. Heriot is much better known to the

---

[1] No attempt has been made to give a complete list of Canadian writers and their works. The aim has been to select for study those who appear to be most representative of the country and its people.

student of Canadian affairs by his *Travels Through the Canadas*, published in 1807—a work that admirably describes the country and the hard conditions under which the pioneer laboured.

More important and far-reaching in his influence as a historian was William Smith, the son of an eminent New York lawyer. William Smith was born in New York. His father was a pronounced loyalist, and after the independence of the revolting colonies was recognized he moved with his family to Quebec. Shortly after his arrival in Canada he was appointed chief justice. His son took up the study of law and was clerk of the legislative assembly in Lower Canada and later master in Chancery. In 1814 he was appointed an executive councillor. For many years during his official life he had been making careful notes on Canadian history for his own use. He appears to have had no thought of publishing these, but was persuaded to do so by his friends. His *History of Canada, from its First Discovery to the Year 1791*, although printed in 1815, did not reach the public until 1826. These two volumes do not make interesting reading. The style is heavy and there is but little literary ease shown in telling the thrilling story of early Canada. The work is, however, very valuable. Smith had access to much first-hand material, and his appendices and notes add greatly to the usefulness of his history.

Robert Christie (1788-1856) had the honour of being the first Canadian-born English-speaking historian to do any important work. Christie was a native of Windsor, Nova Scotia, and studied law in Quebec. Shortly after beginning the practice of law he was elected to the assembly for Gaspe. In the stormy period prior to the Rebellion of 1837 he threw the weight of his influence on the governor's side and was on three different occasions expelled from the house by the popular party. On each occasion he was re-elected by his constituents, and he had the honour of being Gaspe's representative in the first parliament after the Union. He is now remembered solely by his *History of Canada*, a work in six volumes. The title-page of the first volume gives a very complete description of the contents of his history.

It is *A History of the late province of Lower Canada, Parliamentary and Political, from the commencement to the close of its existence as a separate province, embracing a period of fifty years, that is to say, from the erection of the province in 1791 to the extinguishment thereof in 1841, and its re-union with Upper Canada by Act of the Imperial Parliament,* etc. The title-page is characteristic of the work. The style is dull, involved, almost unreadable ; but Christie, though no stylist, was a conscientious workman and collected every available document bearing on the period, and studied and assiduously examined contemporary publications for historical material. This, added to the fact that he lived in Canada during the years covered by his history and played an active part in the events leading up to the Union, makes his work essential to any person desirous of gaining a true knowledge of the political struggle that took place in the Province of Quebec during the first half of the nineteenth century. Before producing his *magnum opus* Christie had published, in 1818, *Memoirs of the Craig and Prevost Administration, 1807-1815,* and, later, a study of Lord Dalhousie's administration. These he incorporated in his larger work.

John Charles Dent (1841-88) was a native of England ; but he was brought as an infant to Canada, and he took such an active interest in Canadian affairs, and studied Canadian questions to such purpose, that it is not unfitting to place him among purely Canadian writers. Dent received his early education in Canada, and studied and practised law for a time in Ontario, but later went to London, England, and took up journalism. In 1867 he returned to America and worked at journalism in Boston for three years, coming to Canada in 1870 to join the staff of the Toronto *Globe*. Dent produced two notable Canadian histories—*The Last Forty Years* (1841-81) and *The Story of the Upper Canadian Rebellion,* both of which, from a literary and historical point of view, show a great advance on any previous Canadian historical work. Besides these two comprehensive works he edited and for the most part wrote *The Canadian Portrait Gallery,* an invaluable source of information regarding the important leaders in social and political life in Canada. Dent was conscientious, painstaking and fearless, though not always without bias. He had an attractive literary style—lucid, smooth-flowing and vigorous—and much of Macaulay's power without Macaulay's rhetorical or, better perhaps, oratorical exaggeration. Some of his characterizations of public men are particularly good ; exceptions are noted in the case of William Lyon Mackenzie and of John Rolph in *The Upper Canadian Rebellion.* Dent, like many others, had a deep-seated dislike of Mackenzie, who was battling by fair means and foul that the old order might give place to the new, and an undue admiration for Rolph, Mackenzie's more timid associate in the struggle ; and accordingly his narration of the events of the rebellion appears strained and, in some degree, untrue.

William Canniff (1830-1910), an eminent Ontario physician, found in his busy life time to devote to the writing of Canadian studies of an important character. Canniff was of United Empire Loyalist descent, and was born near Belleville, Upper Canada. He received his general education at Victoria University, Cobourg, and his medical training in Toronto and New York. Before beginning the practice of medicine in Canada he gained experience as an army surgeon in the Crimean War. He also acted in the same capacity with the army of the North during the Civil War in the United States. Canniff was not a literary artist, but his *History of the Settlement of Upper Canada,* his *Sketch of the County of York,* and his *Upper Canadian Rebellion, 1837,* afford a storehouse of facts that future historians will find exceedingly useful.

The most remarkable history so far produced in the Dominion is *The History of Canada* by William Kingsford (1819-98). Kingsford was born and educated in England, but came to Canada in 1837, when a mere boy, with the 1st Dragoon Guards, in which he had enlisted. He obtained his discharge in 1841 and took up engineering as a profession. He devoted much of his time to literary work, and wrote numerous essays and pamphlets on engineering and other questions. He was long impressed with the possibilities of a voluminous history of Canada, and when sixty-five years old he began the Herculean task of writing the story of the country from its discovery to the Union of 1841. He toiled laboriously at his vast undertaking for over thirteen years, and had the satisfaction of completing it shortly before his death. His ten massive volumes are a monument to individual industry. On account of the heaviness of his style his work can never become popular. No student of Canadian history can afford to ignore it, but it has to be used cautiously. When Kingsford had made up his mind on any question, he often seemed unable to recognize the value of evidence contrary to his view. His effort to prove that Champlain was a Huguenot is an excellent example of his historical method. While he was diligent to examine historical documents he does not seem to have been careful in making his notes, and his volumes bristle with errors of detail.

In 1901-2 there appeared a work in six large volumes entitled *The Siege of Quebec*. This work was the joint production of Arthur G. Doughty and George W. Parmelee. It stands by itself as a comprehensive study of a special period. Everything pertaining to the great siege of the battle-scarred city was examined, and documents and letters bearing on the period were faithfully reproduced. The authors had the advantage of working on the spot where the events narrated occurred. They were able, with the historical documents before them, to trace accurately the movements of the vessels and the troops taking part in the siege.

Doughty followed up this work with his shorter books, *Quebec under Two Flags*, *The Fortress of Quebec* and *The Cradle of New France*. In these there is true literary history; ' fancy, the one-fact more,' has coloured and given life to material that in the hands of many other historians would have made ' dry as dust ' reading. Before undertaking these historical works, Doughty, in his *Rose Leaves* and *Song Story of Francesca and Beatrice*, had won distinction as a graceful poet.

William Wood of Quebec has produced a most able book, *The Fight for Canada*, wherein he covers the same ground dealt with by Parkman in *Wolfe and Montcalm*, and does not suffer by comparison. He has thrown much new light on the struggle between France and England for imperial control in North America, and his style is vigorous, swift and pictorial. His characterizations of Montcalm and Vaudreuil and the men surrounding them, of Wolfe and his officers and men show insight and judgment. In *The Fight for Canada* Wood emphasizes the importance of sea power. He shows most convincingly that without the wooden walls of England France could never have been driven from the American continent. In 1912 two little biographies, *Wolfe* and *Montcalm*, appeared from his pen. These were intended mainly for young readers, but they are so vigorous in treatment that any mature man or woman should enjoy them.

Thomas Chandler Haliburton as a force in literature is pre-eminent among Canadian writers. Haliburton, as we shall see later, was essentially a humorist, but he began his literary career with history, and his *Historical and Statistical Account of Nova Scotia*, published in 1829, gave evidence of a master hand. Notwithstanding the title of his book, Haliburton was a historian of the romantic school. He examined such documents as were at hand, but the story interested him more than statistical detail or documentary evidence. He does not seem to have recognized that the discussions in popular assemblies, the commonplaces of political endeavour, have a human interest that is as entertaining and instructive, if properly handled, as the struggles between nations for empire. Two other works of a historical nature were produced by Haliburton, *The Bubbles of Canada* (1837) and *Rule and Misrule of the English in America* (1851).

Nova Scotia has produced several other important historians, such as Beamish Murdoch and Duncan Campbell. Both these men were little more than compilers, but tried honestly to do useful patriotic work. Campbell in his *History of Nova Scotia* and his *History of Prince Edward Island* showed greater historical accuracy than did Haliburton, but Campbell had nothing of Haliburton's illuminating personality or of the breadth and vigour of his outlook.

Closely allied to Murdoch's *History of Nova Scotia* is James Hannay's *The History of Acadia from its First Discovery to its Surrender to England by the Treaty of Paris.* Hannay's work has vigour, but he was a man of strong prejudices and in his history is not always accurate or just. He had little sympathy with the Acadians or their leaders, and he had such a rooted dislike of the New Englanders who came in contact with them that he is not always fair to these sturdy colonists.

No event in Canadian history has received greater attention and study than the War of 1812. David Thompson (1796-1868) was one of the first to deal with this nation-making struggle. His *War of 1812* gives, as far as he was able to do so, an accurate and unprejudiced account of the contest. Thompson's book is of peculiar value in that the author had a knowledge of military affairs—having been a soldier of the Royal Scots—and a personal acquaintance with the first seat of the war—having for a time taught school at Niagara. But, as might have been expected in a country where there was practically no reading public, the book was a financial failure. Thompson was unable to pay his printers' bills, and thus the first historian of the War of 1812 spent a term in gaol as a debtor as a result of his efforts to enlighten Canadians on their country's past.

Lieutenant-Colonel William F. Coffin (1808-78) published in Montreal in 1864, *1812: The War and its Moral; a Canadian Chronicle.* Colonel Coffin's account is of little value, as it is exceedingly inaccurate. The material is badly organized and the numerous digressions detract from the narrative.

Gilbert Auchinleck's *History of the War* is more valuable, on account of the wealth of official documents it contains, but the writer, who was one of the editors of the *Anglo-American Magazine*, in which his history made its appearance serially, was possessed of an antagonism to the Americans that mars many of his chapters.

James Hannay (1842-1910), already referred to with regard to his *History of Acadia*, also wrote a comprehensive account of the War of 1812. Hannay was a journalist and had a facile pen and a trenchant style. His *War of 1812* is a very readable book, but, for the average reader, a dangerous one. He had a hatred of the United States and its institutions, and as a consequence his judgment was sadly warped. The works of such writers as Coffin, Auchinleck and Hannay are chiefly significant as an antidote to the violently partisan histories of this period published in the United States.

In many ways the most important Canadian history of the War of 1812 is that by Major John Richardson. Richardson fought through the campaign from the capture of Detroit until he was taken prisoner at the battle of Moravian Town. It was his purpose to write a history of the entire war, but so apathetic was the public that he became discouraged and left his task unfinished. His history was a somewhat hurried performance, undertaken with the hope of increasing the circulation of his newspaper, *The New Era*, in which it appeared serially. But Richardson was a trained writer and soldier, and the events of the war during the years 1812 and 1813 were strongly presented. His characterizations of such men as Brock, Procter and Tecumseh are excellent. In 1902 his *War of 1812* was brought out in a well-edited new edition by Alexander Clark Casselman. The full bibliography, the excellent biography, and the copious notes on men and incidents touched on in the work make this edition of Richardson's *War of 1812* one of the valuable books published in the Dominion. Major Richardson likewise wrote *Eight Years in Canada*, a historical narrative covering the Durham, Sydenham and Metcalfe administrations.

While Eastern Canada has had its historians the West has not been neglected. Alexander Ross produced several works which, both as history and literature, rank high. Ross was for a time a clerk in the service of the North-West Company. He joined Astor's Pacific Fur Company in 1810, but returned to the service of the North-West Company in 1814. At the time of the union of the fur companies in 1821 he entered the service of the Hudson's Bay Company and settled in the Red River colony. He consequently knew the West at first hand, and his *Fur Hunters of the Far West*, his *Adventures on the Columbia* and his *Red River Settlement* depict the struggles of the Western pioneer fur traders and settlers. The *Red River Settlement* is a particularly strong book. The description of the fight of the first inhabitants against flood, famine, the rigours of the western winter, and human enemies, if at times rough and crude in style, is graphic and impressive.

Alexander Begg (1840-98) published several histories of the North-West and a controversial work entitled *The Creation of Manitoba*. Begg lived in Manitoba during the formative period of the province, and his account of the causes and course of the first Riel rebellion is valuable. He had very little literary power, and his books are useful only for the information they contain.

Another Alexander Begg (1824-1904) of Victoria, British Columbia, wrote the *History of British Columbia from its Earliest Discovery to the Present Time*. Other works of importance on the West are: Sir W. F. Butler's *Great Lone Land*, J. C. Hamilton's *The Prairie Province*, R. G. Macbeth's *The Selkirk Settlers* and *The Making of the Canadian West*, G. M. Adam's *The North-West*, Donald Gunn's *The Province of Manitoba*, Captain Huyshe's *Red River Expedition*, Alexander Morris's *The Treaties of Canada with the Indians of Manitoba and the North-West Territories*, John Macoun's *Manitoba and the North-West*, and George Bryce's *Manitoba ; Its Infancy, Growth and Present Condition, Lord Selkirk's Colonists* and *The Remarkable History of Hudson's Bay Company*.

Agnes Laut has done more than any living writer to make the work of the pioneer explorers and traders of Canada known to the world. Her books, *The Conquest of the Great North-West, Pathfinders of the West*, and *Vikings of the Pacific*, prepared after conscientious research in the archives of the Old World and the New, and after the author had personally traced the wanderings of many of the explorers, give illuminating accounts of the heroic days of Canadian history.

Not the least among Canadian writers was Adolphus Egerton Ryerson (1803-82). Ryerson won a wide reputation as a controversial writer and played an important part in moulding public opinion in the struggle leading up to Confederation. When over seventy years old he undertook to write a history of the *Loyalists of America and Their Times.* His work contains valuable information, but the vigour he displayed in his early literary work is lacking.

There have been many short popular histories of Canada ; among the best of these are : John Mercier Mᶜ Mullen's *History of Canada,* George Bryce's *Short History of the Canadian People,* Henry H. Miles's *History of Canada under the French Régime,* W. H. Withrow's *Popular History of Canada,* J. Castell Hopkins's *Story of the Dominion,* Sir John George Bourinot's *Story of Canada,* Charles G. D. Roberts's *History of Canada,* and W. H. P. Clement's *History of the Dominion of Canada.*

The histories by Roberts and Bourinot have literary qualities of a high order, but, like all the writers of popular histories, these authors have not paid sufficient attention to their sources, and have relied too much on books and too little on documentary evidence for their facts.

There are, besides, a number of works dealing with special phases of Canadian affairs. Useful books are : John Hamilton Gray's *Confederation*—an unfinished production, Nicholas Flood Davin's *The Irishman in Canada,* W. J. Rattray's *The Scot in British North America,* George Stewart's *Canada under the Administration of the Earl of Dufferin,* Joseph Edmund Collins's *Canada under the Administration of Lord Lorne,* A. G. Morice's *The History of the Northern Interior of British Columbia* and *The Great Déné Race,* W. O. Raymond's *The History of the River St John, 1604-1784,* and W. R. Harris's *The Catholic Church in the Niagara Peninsula.* Gray's book is of peculiar value, coming as it does from the pen of a man who played an essential part in the Confederation movement. Rattray's and Stewart's books show a distinct advance in style and treatment on previous Canadian histories.

There are, too, numerous local histories that have great value for the general historian. There is scarcely a district, in old Canada at any rate, that has not had its historian : James Croil's *Historical Sketch of Dundas,* H.

Scadding's *Toronto of Old*, T. W. H. Leavitt's *Counties of Leeds and Grenville*, J. Ross Robertson's *Landmarks of Toronto*, E. A. Owen's *Pioneer Sketches of Long Point Settlement*, Calnek and Savary's *History of Annapolis County*, James Young's *History of Galt and Dumfries*, Mrs C. M. Day's *The Eastern Townships*, R. Cooney's *History of Northern New Brunswick*, and many others, should be studied by the historian to enable him to grasp the details of the story of the making of the Dominion.

All Canadian historians, however, have worked at a disadvantage. Until recently original sources were in a large measure unavailable to the general public, and writers had to depend for the most part on second-hand evidence. Thus errors have been repeated and multiplied. Now, fortunately, the Dominion Archives and several of the provincial archives have been placed on a sound basis, and the future historian will have the material at his hand to enable him to deal with any period fully and accurately.

III

BIOGRAPHY

THE subject of biography is one that is quite as interesting and important in any nation's development as the mere narration of the facts and incidents of history. The movements of troops in battle, the passing of acts in assemblies, are simply manifestations of the personalities of the strategists and tacticians who inspire the forces in the field, and of the statesmen and politicians who mould the opinions and fashion the ideals of the nation.

The writing of Canadian biography has been too often left to personal friends or pronounced partisans with no literary training ; and in many instances the result has been collections of excerpts from diaries, of extracts from letters and political speeches, strung together by a thin and commonplace thread of narrative.

William Hamilton Merritt was one of the most important figures in early British-Canadian history. He was a veteran of the War of 1812, a pioneer of Upper Canada, a man high in the councils of his country, and the chief force in carrying to completion the construction of the fine system of canals that connect the Great Lakes with the ocean. The preparation of his biography was entrusted to a relative, who threw together a mere compilation of bald facts, badly arranged. The biographer forestalled criticism by remarking in his preface that ' No efforts have been made to render the work attractive by sensationalism, or to introduce the finer arts known to those who write for effect.' It is never necessary to be sensational, but to produce a book of any permanent value it is essential that the author should know his art. Books are written that they may be read, and only literature that appeals at once to the heart and to the mind can ever find a wide audience. Unfortunately the majority of Canadian biographers, like the author of the *Life of William Hamilton Merritt*, have been inadequately equipped for the work they undertook.

To the same class belongs *The Life and Speeches of the Honourable George Brown*, by the Hon. Alexander Mackenzie, a former prime minister of Canada and an honest, conscientious statesman. But fighting political battles and administering the affairs of a nation do not peculiarly fit a man for literary work, and Mackenzie's biography of George Brown is not a strong book. An excellent contrast is afforded in the recently published *George Brown* by John Lewis, an experienced writer and a close student of the political development of Canada. The author of this book shows a thorough grasp of national events and a sympathetic insight into the character of the distinguished statesman and the men, both friends and foes, who surrounded him.

A book that stands out with peculiar prominence in Canadian biographical literature is *The Life and Times of William Lyon Mackenzie*, by his son-in-law, Charles Lindsey. Lindsey, if not the outstanding Canadian writer of his time, at least occupied a particularly high place as a littérateur. Although closely related to Mackenzie, he did not agree with all his political tenets, and having his historical conscience highly developed, he was able to produce a work of the very greatest value. The matter is well arranged, the style is vigorous and in keeping with the subject, and the important political and social questions touched on are skilfully handled. This biography was republished in 1908 with a valuable introduction, numerous notes, and some additions by G. G. S. Lindsey.

John Fennings Taylor (1820-82) did much to perpetuate the memory of eminent Canadians. Taylor was born in London, England, but came to Canada when nineteen years old. He held several clerical offices in the assembly and council of Canada under the Union, and was deputy-clerk of the Dominion Senate after Confederation. He wrote numerous essays and reviews and three notable biographical works: *Portraits of British Americans*, *The Last Three Bishops appointed by the Crown in British North America* and *The Life and Death of the Honourable Thomas D'Arcy McGee*.

David Breckenridge Read, a lawyer by profession, devoted much of his life to presenting to his countrymen the lives of their notable men. He has enriched Canadian biographical literature by his *The Lives of the Judges of Upper Canada*, *The Life and Times of General John Graves Simcoe*, *The Life and Times of Major-General Sir Isaac Brock* and *The Lives of the Lieutenant-Governors of Upper Canada and Ontario*. He likewise wrote a careful account of the Rebellion of 1837. Read was painstaking, but many of his pages have but little direct bearing on the subject under treatment. His *Life of Brock* often looks as though he deliberately took up side issues for the purpose of padding his book.

The *Life of James Fitzgibbon*, by Mary Agnes Fitzgibbon, is valuable both for its subject-matter and the manner in which this is presented. Fitzgibbon was one of the most picturesque figures in the early history of Canada, and he is admirably drawn in this biography. He was a veteran of the War of 1812, and in studying the character and conduct of Fitzgibbon the author has thrown much new light on that nation-making period of Canadian history.

Sir John A. Macdonald, the most striking figure that has appeared on the political stage of British North America, naturally attracted biographical writers. J. Edmund Collins, G. Mercer Adam, J. P. Macpherson, George R. Parkin and Sir Joseph Pope have all written extended biographies of the great statesman. Sir Joseph Pope's is the standard, and is indeed probably the best example of biographical writing that has been produced in Canada, its only weakness being that the writer is not always just to Macdonald's great opponent, George Brown. Pope was for ten years Sir John's private secretary, and having had the confidence of Sir John and of Sir John's friends, he was well equipped to give a full and accurate account of the early life and of the political struggles of the foremost of the Fathers of Confederation. In two large volumes the political story, extending over forty years, is told with truth, fulness and vigour ; and in all discussions the central figure, Macdonald, stands out prominently— the author never losing touch with the main subject of his work.

A companion production to Pope's *Memoirs of the Right Honourable Sir John Alexander Macdonald* is Sir John Stephen Willison's *Sir Wilfrid Laurier and the Liberal Party.* Willison, through his journalistic experiences in the press gallery of the House of Commons in Ottawa and his thorough training on the Toronto *Globe*, of which he ultimately became editor-in-chief, was well fitted to deal with the distinguished leader who has latterly controlled the destinies of the Liberal party, and, until very recently, of Canada. Willison was handicapped in that he was writing the life-story of a man still living. It is difficult to view a contemporary with proper historical perspective or to judge of contemporary questions without some bias. The work, however, is re-markably free from prejudice, and the style is at once graceful and elevated. Pope's *Sir John Alexander Macdonald* and Willison's *Sir Wilfrid Laurier* give an excellent insight into the political history of Canada during the latter half of the nineteenth century. The one supplements the other, and they should be read together.

There is no adequate study of the life of Joseph Howe, the great Nova Scotian. Though lacking in the practical wisdom of Macdonald or Laurier, Howe is perhaps the only

Canadian-born parliamentarian who in intellectual power and breadth of view may be classed with the great men of the British Isles—Cobden, Bright and Gladstone. George E. Fenety has given a chatty anecdotal life of Howe, but it has little literary or historical value. Principal Grant's *Joseph Howe* is brilliant, brief and sketchy, a bit of hero-worship, and leaves much to be said ; but when Grant speaks of Howe as ' Nova Scotia incarnate ' he sums up in a compelling phrase the secret of Howe's influence in his native province. He was not merely the leader of the popular party ; he *was* the popular party. Judge Longley, in his *Joseph Howe*, has given an interesting and vigorous account of the orator, poet and statesman, but this work is inadequate—a sketch that requires much filling in.

Edward Manning Saunders in his *Three Premiers of Nova Scotia* has given a graphic account of the lives of the three most notable politicians of his native province—J. W. Johnstone, Joseph Howe and Sir Charles Tupper. Edward Ermatinger wrote a readable biography of that most picturesque of pioneers in Upper Canada, Colonel Talbot. A. N. Bethune gave a commonplace and somewhat biased study of Bishop Strachan. George M. Wrong's *Life of Lord Elgin* is one of the latest and best of Canadian biographical productions. J. Castell Hopkins is a voluminous writer on Canadian questions, and, judging by the circulation of his books, a very popular one. His work usually shows traces of hurried preparation, but his *Life and Work of Mr Gladstone* and his *Life and Work of Sir John Thompson* indicate superior gifts for biographical and historical narrative.

George Monro Grant, by his son, William Lawson Grant, in collaboration with Charles Frederick Hamilton, is in every way a worthy presentation of the career of the eminent divine, publicist and educationist.

Any one who desires an intimate acquaintance with a number of strong men who played important parts in the drama of nation-making in Canada will find the following works of non-Canadian authors valuable : Stone's *Life of Joseph Brant* (Thayendanegea) and *Life of Sir William Johnson*, Scrope's *Life of Lord Sydenham*, Kaye's *Life of*

Lord Metcalfe, and Walrond's *Life and Letters of Lord Elgin.* These books, written by men born and trained under other skies, are free from the provincialism and local prejudice that mar many of the biographies by Canadian-born writers.

At the beginning of the twentieth century an important series of Canadian biographies, *The Makers of Canada,* began to make its appearance. Many of the books in this series are good, and some are of exceptionally high quality. Jean N. McIlwraith's *Sir Frederick Haldimand* gives an excellent insight into the character of that early governor of Canada, and is peculiarly valuable for the sidelights it throws on life in Canada in the period immediately after the Revolutionary War. In Duncan Campbell Scott's *John Graves Simcoe* is found the best modern study of the pioneer life of the loyalists in Upper Canada. Adam Shortt's *Lord Sydenham* is a scholarly study of the man who, by consummating the Union, paved the way for responsible government and Confederation. W. D. Le Sueur's *Frontenac* is a sympathetic treatment of the history of the greatest of the governors of New France. It is sober in judgment and has a literary finish and a historical accuracy that make it at once entertaining and instructive.

While *The Makers of Canada* series and the works of Pope and Willison have done much to elevate the tone of Canadian biographical literature, there yet remains room for improvement in this field. The public will in the future demand of Canadian biographers a high standard and will not be satisfied, as they apparently have been in the past, with compilations pitchforked together regardless of workmanship or historical truth.

IV

TRAVELS AND EXPLORATION

THE possibilities of stirring adventure tempted many daring spirits to penetrate the vaguely known region stretching from Hudson Bay and the Great Lakes to the Pacific and the Arctic. Traders in search of beaver skins, travellers lured on through curiosity, explorers eager to extend geographical and scientific knowledge, invaded in numbers the mighty rivers of the east and west and north, and the plains and mountain regions haunted by buffalo, grizzly bears and savages. Journals were kept, and many, such as those of Samuel Hearne, of Thomas Simpson and of Daniel Williams Harmon, are of great interest. Even though these journals have small literary value, they are storehouses of information and observation on which the trained writer can draw. But there are a few books of Canadian exploration that rank high, in passages at least, as literature.

One of these explorers, Alexander Henry the elder (1739-1824), produced a remarkable book. Henry was born in New Jersey. After many years spent as a fur trader in the region of the Great Lakes, he settled as a merchant in Montreal. He occupied his leisure time writing an account of his explorations, under the title *Travels and Adventures in Canada and the Indian Territories*. This book was published in New York in 1809, and nearly a century later, in 1901, a new edition with an adequate biography and copious notes was brought out under the editorship of James Bain of Toronto. Henry was a man of great powers of observation. He was more than a mere trader, and he gives much valuable information about the regions he visited. The flora and fauna of the country and the savage tribes are all carefully described by him. He traded in the West during the time of Pontiac's War, and his thrilling experiences at Michilimackinac, where he was at the time the massacre of the garrison took place, are related with the skill of a literary artist. Henry's powerful pen-picture of Minavavana, the Ojibwa chief, and his painted warriors, the dramatic report of the chief's speech defending the attitude of the Indians towards the English, are in the manner and have some of the force of the father of history, Herodotus. So good was Henry's narrative that Francis Parkman, who usually clothed the accounts of traders and historians in his own glowing language, saw fit, when dealing with the massacre of Michilimackinac in his *Conspiracy of Pontiac*, to quote at great length from Henry's book, and there is nothing finer in Parkman's works than the passage of thrilling narrative taken from Henry's *Travels and Adventures*.

Sir Alexander Mackenzie (1755-1820) was another trader and explorer who had literary power in a high degree. Mackenzie was born at Stornoway, Island of Lewis, Scotland. He came as a young man to Canada and joined the North-West Company. In its service he soon rose to high rank; but with him the fur trade was chiefly a means to an end. The north and west of the American continent were still unexplored, and his great aim was to penetrate to the farthest north and to the Pacific Ocean. Both of these feats he ultimately accomplished, reaching the Arctic in 1789 and the Pacific in 1793. On his return from his last great exploring expedition he wrote his *Voyages from Montreal through the Continent of North America, 1789-1793*. This work was published in London, England, in 1801. His narrative is the simple direct relation of a man of action. The hardships he endured in his great undertakings, the determination not to be overcome, make stimulating reading. Like Henry he was a keen observer. The awe-inspiring and sublime scenes that he passed through on his way to the Arctic, down the lordly river that has since borne his name, and that met him on every hand as he courageously toiled through the hitherto impenetrable Rocky Mountains, are depicted with wonderful clearness and strength. The wanderings of the heroic Ulysses are commonplace compared with the travels of this Scottish explorer who was his own Homer. Mackenzie's account of the Peace River country and his pen-picture of the Methye Portage and of the Rockies rank with the best descriptive literature. For his eminent achievements he was honoured with knighthood shortly after the publication of his *Voyages*.

In the first half of the nineteenth century a number of travellers, some of them of exceptional literary ability, visited Canada and embodied their impressions of the country and its people in books. While these books are not to be classed as Canadian literature, they are of such importance to those who desire to know the early struggles of the pioneers and the conditions of the formative period

of Canada, that they cannot be passed by without a word
of comment.

John Howison visited Canada in 1819-20, and published
in 1821 his *Sketches of Upper Canada*. Howison's travel
sketches are of 'a domestic and personal nature.' His
journey through Upper Canada was made shortly after the
War of 1812, and shows in a convincing manner the results
of the war on the growth of the country and on the character of the people. The picture he gives is not a pleasing
one ; but it is undoubtedly a true one. Ignorance and
poverty abounded, and hardship was the common lot.
Howison wrote with a vigorous pen, and many of his descriptive touches are very fine. His account of Niagara Falls
gives one of the earliest pictures we have of that stupendous
cataract, and it still ranks among the best.

Anna Brownell Jameson (1794-1860), who had already
won a high place in British literature, spent a part of 1836-37
in Upper Canada, and in 1838 published in London, England,
three volumes entitled *Winter Studies and Summer Rambles
in Canada*. She was in ill-health ; the hard conditions
and lack of genial companionship in Toronto made her lot
during the first period of her sojourn far from a happy one,
and her mental and physical condition coloured her work.
She saw little beauty in the settled part of the country,
and sought escape from ennui in studying masterpieces of
modern literature. No finer appreciative criticism has been
written in Canada than that in her 'winter studies.' But she
is at her best in her 'summer rambles.' She was a brave
woman, who courageously endured the rude conditions in
the primitive inns and the rough journeys over forest roads
in her eagerness to know at first hand the character of this,
at that time, out-of-the-way and sadly neglected corner of
the British Empire. Every page of her three volumes is
delightful, and her nature sketches and her characterizations
are incomparable. Mrs Jameson completely shakes off her
depression when she is once in the presence of primeval nature
in the vast forests and by the broad sea-like lakes. She has an
artist's eye for nature and a fine sympathy with the pioneers
in their toil and isolation. Her descriptions, too, of the

Indians and their customs throw much light on the aboriginal tribes inhabiting the Great Lakes region, and on their relationship to the Canadian government. Her journey through Western Canada from Toronto to Sault Ste Marie and return was a rapid one ; but every point of interest is described with a graphic pen and a trained observer's insight.

Sir R. H. Bonnycastle (1791-1848) wrote two books on Canada—*The Canadas in 1841* and *Canada and the Canadians* (1846). Bonnycastle spent a number of years in Canada and was familiar with the country from the Labrador coast ' to the far solitudes of Lake Huron.' He had visited ' the homes of the hard-working pioneers in the vast forests ' and the wigwams ' of the wandering and savage Indians.' He was a lieutenant-colonel in the Royal Engineers and had served as a lieutenant-colonel of militia in Upper Canada during the Rebellion of 1837. His work has therefore the double interest of being that of an observer of this outpost of empire and of one who had helped to hold it true to British connection in a time of storm and stress. He had a genuine love of the country. His descriptions are all inspired by affection, and his characterizations of the people are done with sympathy. His portrayal of the French-Canadian boatmen who managed the boats in which he ascended the St Lawrence from Montreal to Kingston is particularly good, and his books are of exceeding interest for the sidelights they throw on Canadian social and political conditions.

A somewhat remarkable book was published in London in 1853. It was entitled *Pine Forests and Hacmatack Clearings*. From the title one would naturally expect to find an account of the forest wealth and the lumbering industry of Canada ; but there is little in it about either. It is a story of ' travel, life and adventure,' in which the pine forests and hacmatack clearings occasionally appear incidentally. This book was written by Lieutenant-Colonel Sleigh, who, as an officer of the 77th Regiment, had seen service in Nova Scotia, in Cape Breton and in Lower Canada. He later served as a field-officer of militia, a lieutenant-colonel commanding a regiment, and a justice of the peace. His military and official career in British North America, together with extensive travel in Nova Scotia, New Brunswick, Prince Edward Island and the Canadas, enabled him to speak with more or less authority on the country and its people. He was, moreover, one of the proprietors of Prince Edward Island, and a pioneer steamship owner in British North America, for he had a steamer, the *Albatross*, of 1100 tons burden, which ran between New York and the ocean ports of the Maritime Provinces and Canada. Sleigh was a man of strong views, and his account of the movement for reciprocity, which he vehemently opposed, shows the opposition that Lord Elgin had to contend with in consummating that important trade measure. But it is not as a soldier, landed proprietor, steamship owner or political writer that Sleigh is interesting; it is as an observer of conditions in Canada in the middle of the nineteenth century. His graphic account of the ice-passage of the Straits of Northumberland, his scathing remarks on the 'anti-renters' and the council of Prince Edward Island, his chatty accounts of manners and conditions in primitive Cape Breton, and his appreciation of work done by French Canadians on behalf of Great Britain in 1775 and again in 1812, all make an excellent contribution to Canadian history.

There are many other works somewhat similar, in whole or in part dealing with Canada and Canadians, by travellers and sojourners in the country, that are important to the student of Canadian literature and history. Historians generally lay stress on war and exploration, on parliaments and legislators. This is essential; but the people at their meetings, in their homes and workships, on the farms and in the inns should be studied and understood; and the Canadian writer who wishes to make his history, poetry or romance a living thing must draw largely on the literary productions of the men and women who wrote from personal observation of pioneer life in the provinces of British North America.

In 1859 Paul Kane (1810-71), the celebrated Canadian artist, whose career as a painter is dealt with elsewhere in this volume,[1] published in London, England, his *Wanderings of an Artist among the Indian Tribes of North America*. His

[1] See p. 602.

literary effort proved to be no less interesting than the
important series of paintings produced as a result of his
three years' wanderings among the western tribes.   The
trained eye of the artist is seen on every page.   The habits,
customs and mode of life of the savages of the plains and
of the Pacific slope are faithfully delineated.   The picturesque
scenery of the Far North and West—the towering mountains,
the tumbling streams and the broad plains—is portrayed
with a 'great painter's clear and exact vision.'   His account
of British Columbia in the forties made that country for
the first time familiar to the world.

In the summer of 1872 Sandford (afterwards Sir Sandford) Fleming, engineer-in-chief of the Dominion government, made an overland journey to the Pacific to study
the country in the interests of the projected railway, which
was to be a physical bond of union between old Canada
and the western provinces.   On this expedition he took
with him as his private secretary the Rev. George Monro
Grant (1835-1902).   The literary result of this journey was
Grant's book *Ocean to Ocean*.   Principal Grant (as he was
afterwards known) was born at Albion Mines, Nova Scotia,
and was educated for the ministry of the Presbyterian
Church at the University of Glasgow.   In 1877 he was
chosen principal of Queen's University, Kingston ; and, by
his organizing ability and his indefatigable industry, he made
that institution one of the notable seats of learning in the
Dominion.   He was an ardent Canadian and a pronounced
imperialist, and wrote much in the interests of Canada and
the Empire.   His busy public life prevented him from
devoting his energies to creative literary work, but his
Ocean to Ocean shows that he might easily have won as
high a place in letters as he achieved as an educationist,
publicist, and platform and pulpit orator.   *Ocean to Ocean*
is in the form of a journal.   It was written from day to
day at hotels, by camp fires and in trading posts.   It
abounds in humour and pathos.   Breadth of judgment and
keenness of observation illuminate its pages ; and in the
presence of nature—vast, rugged and inspiring—Grant had
a lyrical force and fire that make many of his pages read like

prose poems. One of his touches of description, dealing with the Rocky Mountains, will serve as an example of his power :

We had come inside the range, and it was no longer an amphitheatre of hills, but a valley ever opening and at each turn revealing new forms, that was now before us. Roche Ronde was to our right, its stratification as distinct as the leaves of a half-opened book. The mass of the rock was limestone, and what at a distance had been only peculiarly bold and rugged outlines, were now seen to be different angles and contortions of the strata. And such contortions ! One high mass twisting up the sides in serpentine folds ; another pent in great waving lines, like petrified billows. The colouring, too, was all that artist could desire. Not only the dark green of the spruce in the corries, which turn into black when far up, but autumn tints of red and gold, as high as vegetation had climbed on the hillside ; and above that, streaks and patches of yellow, green, rusty red and black, relieving the grey mass of limestone ; while up the valley every shade of blue came out according as the hills were near or far away, and summits hoary with snow-bounded horizon.

George Monro Grant was deeply impressed with the richness and possibilities of the Dominion, and his book did much to awaken thinking Canadians to the potential greatness of their country. In *Ocean to Ocean* he foretold with prophetic insight the Great West of to-day, with its broad cultivated plains, its great cities, and its hundreds of towns and villages.

One of the most entertaining and instructive books of exploration written by a Canadian is J. W. Tyrrell's *Across the Sub-Arctics of Canada*. The author made three journeys (in 1885, 1893 and 1900) through the wilderness region west of Hudson Bay. The narrative of his trip in 1893 is as thrilling as Mackenzie's account of his overland journey to the Pacific. The plunge into the unknown wilderness, the hunting of cariboo and musk-ox, adventures with polar bears and the wild leap down the unfamiliar rapids make stirring reading.

Samuel Edward Dawson is a Canadian author who has

done good work in several fields, but is best known by his writings dealing with discovery and exploration. His voluminous work, entitled *The St Lawrence Basin and its Border-Lands*, is the result of many years of historical investigation. In it there is given an exhaustive account of ' the discovery and exploration of the north-east coast of North America and of the great transverse valley of the St Lawrence which searches the continent to its very heart.' It was intended to be mainly a contribution to geographical literature, but the ground traversed is full of ' historic interest and abounds with romantic adventure'; and Dawson, while handling his subject with scientific exactness, is never dull. The pages are illuminated with glowing touches of description, and he occasionally pauses in his narrative to depict the characters of the explorers and colonizers. With a stroke of his pen such a man as Champlain is revealed : ' Champlain, while practical and efficient in his daily duties, aimed at establishing a settled industrial colony which should hold for France the gateway of the golden East. With unflagging perseverance and with imperturbable patience he devoted his whole life to this patriotic task—the most single-hearted and single-eyed servant France ever possessed.' *The St Lawrence Basin and its Border-Lands*, both by its exact information and its literary finish, will doubtless long hold an unrivalled place as an authoritative work on the early exploration of what are now the eastern provinces of British North America.

In 1908 Lawrence J. Burpee published his *The Search for the Western Sea*. This is in many ways the ablest historical account of the work done by explorers of the Great West and North from the days of Henry Hudson to those of Simon Fraser, David Thompson and Sir John Franklin. There is in Burpee's book little effort after rhetorical effect. The work is admirably organized. The multiplicity of detail is given with the care and accuracy of a skilled investigator, and the personalities of the explorers are presented with sympathy and fidelity. *The Search for the Western Sea* is an essential book to the student of the early history of the great North-West.

In the matter of travels and exploration the reports of scientists working in the interests of the Canadian government, such as Henry Youle Hind, J. B. Tyrrell, Robert Bell and A. P. Low, will be found to be of interest, from both a scientific and a literary point of view. The army of workers sent out by the government year by year to the ends of the great Dominion bring back with them notes that, when thrown into the form of an official report, serve in many instances as excellent raw material for literature. Indeed there are at times in these reports passages that are in themselves true literature.

V

GENERAL LITERATURE

BRITISH NORTH AMERICA had as its first settlers men from the British Isles and from the thirteen colonies. In the Old World, during the latter half of the eighteenth century, agitations for reform were in the air and the battle for the freedom of the Press was being waged. Magazines and newspapers were beginning to make their influence felt. In the thirteen colonies education was highly valued, and American inquisitiveness was making the newspaper a necessity in the homes of the settlers. It thus happened that when the English-speaking people began to pour into the provinces by the sea and along the St Lawrence and Great Lakes, printing presses were soon at work in their midst.

Three years after the founding of Halifax the *Halifax Gazette* made its appearance. It was published 'at the printing office in Grafton Street' by John Bushnell, and was first issued on March 23, 1752. It had a hard struggle for existence; it suspended publication after several months, and did not appear regularly until late in the year 1760. The first number of the *Quebec Gazette* was printed on June 21, 1764; for seventy-eight years this paper was published in both French and English, and for thirty-two years longer was continued as an English newspaper. In 1783, the year of the great migration of the United Empire Loyalists to St John, and before the Province of New Brunswick was organized, the *Royal St John Gazette and Nova Scotia Intelligencer* was issued. The name was changed in the following year to that of *Royal Gazette and New Brunswick Advertiser*. Montreal had a newspaper, the *Gazette*, in 1785, Charlottetown one in 1791, Newark (Niagara) one in 1793, Fredericton one in 1806, and Kingston one in 1810. The papers of the widest influence in the early part of the nineteenth century were the Montreal *Herald*, the *Nova Scotian* at Halifax, and the *Colonial Advocate* at Toronto.

The establishment of these newspapers had the good effect of widely disseminating a desire for education. Every man was ambitious to get at first-hand news and politics—particularly the latter. The times were rough, and the style of the writers for the most part was in keeping with the conditions of life. From the beginning of the nineteenth century until the establishment of responsible government there was in the Canadas and in the Maritime Provinces a sharp line drawn between the party favouring executive control of affairs and its opponents, and the papers supporting either of these factions presented their views with a fanatical vigour and a vituperative force that often descended to the coarsest Billingsgate. The general reading public of British North America may be said to have been cradled in satire and abuse, exaggeration and party vindictiveness. But there were a number of early writers who rose to a higher plane. Some of the letters to the Press have been preserved in book form, and show their authors to have been men of seriousness, insight and lofty powers of expression. The letters of three of these writers are of great value for the light they throw on the times in which they were written. They are *Nerva* (1815), *The Letters of Veritas* (1815) and *The Lower Canadian Watchman* (1825).

The first magazine published in Canada was the *Nova Scotia Magazine* in 1789. This was followed by the *Quebec Magazine* published by Samuel Neilson, of which the first number was issued on August 1, 1792. With few exceptions Canadian magazines have been short-lived. The reading population of Canada—that is, the population that cares for serious reading—has been, until recent years, comparatively small. Moreover, British and American magazines have been available at small cost, and it has been difficult for a Canadian publisher to compete with them. But several of the magazines while they lasted gave the public substantial reading. Chief among those published in the Canadas were the *Canadian Magazine* (1823-24), the *Canadian Review* (1824-26), the *Anglo-American Magazine* (1852-55), the *British American Review* and the *Literary Garland* (1838-51), the last having as contributors such able writers as William Dunlop, Charles Sangster, Susanna Moodie and Catharine Parr Traill. Later in the century George Stewart for five years (1867-72) conducted at St John *Stewart's Quarterly*, in which the articles were of a high order. The *Canadian Monthly* (1872-82) and *Belford's Magazine* (1876-79) were high-class magazines that had a wide influence in their day. These early magazines had among their contributors a number of well-known writers who had received their training in Great Britain, and many of their articles compare favourably with those appearing at the same period in the British reviews. In the *Bystander* [1] Goldwin Smith gave the public brilliant studies of current events. In the *Week* (1884-96), promoted and, at any rate in its first year, largely maintained by him, he fostered the literary spirit, and placed the paper in the front rank of Canadian literary journals. But the public demand was insufficient, and, like every similar venture, the *Week*, after a few years' battling, was forced to cease publication.

Latterly Canadian magazines have been in lighter vein, aiming to please rather than to instruct. Caught by the spirit of the time, publishers now devote more of their attention to the pictorial than to the literary side of their

---

[1] The *Bystander* was begun in January 1880 and appeared monthly for eighteen months. It was revived as a quarterly in January 1883, and continued for one year; again revived as a monthly in October 1889 and continued to September 1900.

publications. In a commercial age, too, business and finance occupy much attention, and many of the leading periodicals give more space to the literature of the dollar than to anything else. Reviews that appeal to the serious-minded are, however, still published in Canada. The *University Magazine*—brilliantly edited by Andrew Macphail at Montreal—and *Queen's Quarterly*—conducted by a group of able men at Kingston—are worthy exponents and interpreters of current investigation and opinion.

There are several other important Canadian works that should properly come under the head of periodical literature. Since 1896 the *Review of Historical Publications Relating to Canada*, edited by George M. Wrong and H. H. Langton and published annually by the University of Toronto, has been giving excellent criticism by specialists on books relating to the Dominion. The *Canadian Annual Review of Public Affairs*, founded in 1901 by J. Castell Hopkins, and written wholly by him, is an exceedingly valuable work. It is a yearly register of current Canadian history, but, unlike other annuals or year-books, it is written in so broad a spirit and with so fluent a pen that interest is given to the very commonplaces of political, social and business life.

Two large Canadian publications of the 'monumental' kind should be mentioned. The first, *Picturesque Canada*, was edited by Principal Grant. The magnificent and diversified scenery of the Dominion from ocean to ocean, the varied types of life, the romantic interest that surrounds the birth and growth of the provinces and hallows such spots as Annapolis Royal, Quebec, Niagara, Winnipeg, and the Pacific coast give writers and artists admirable opportunities for creative work. It is doubtful if *Picturesque Canada* is or ever was much read, but the reader who turns to it will find a number of descriptive passages well worthy of perusal. The second, *Canada: an Encyclopædia of the Country*, edited by J. Castell Hopkins, covers a great variety of topics and contains much valuable information. Many of the contributions are well written, others are faulty and immature, and the whole shows evidence of hasty compilation. The editor gives numerous valuable notes on Canadian affairs ; but even here the hurried workmanship leaves much to be desired.

Canada presents a rich field for scientific writers. The sea-fretted provinces, the polar world, the prairie region, the tumbled hills, have all attracted Canadian writers of exact scientific knowledge and no small degree of literary skill. Four at least have won a world-wide reputation by their studies—Sir William Logan, Henry Youle Hind, Sir Daniel Wilson and Sir John William Dawson.

Sir William Logan (1798-1875) was born in Montreal and was of United Empire Loyalist descent. He was educated in the Royal Grammar School in his native city, and at Edinburgh High School and University. In 1829, after completing his university studies, he returned to Canada and remained for a brief period, but he went back to Great Britain and laboured in a scientific capacity in Swansea, Wales. He again returned to North America in 1841, and after investigating the coal-fields of Nova Scotia and Pennsylvania he accepted the position of first director of the Geological Survey of Canada. He wrote extensively on science, his articles appearing chiefly in technical journals and in the proceedings of scientific societies. The *Geology of Canada* was his chief literary-scientific work, and has been the basis for the studies of all subsequent geological investigators.

Henry Youle Hind was born in England in 1823 and came to Canada in 1847. He occupied important positions as teacher of science in the Toronto Normal School and Trinity College, and he conducted important exploring expeditions in the prairie country drained by the Red and Saskatchewan Rivers. Hind wrote a number of works of a scientific character, chief among which are—*Narrative of the Canadian Red River Exploring Expedition of 1857, The Assiniboine and Saskatchewan Expedition of 1858, Sketch of the Overland Route to British Columbia* and *Explorations of the Interior of the Labrador Peninsula*. Between the years 1852 and 1855 he edited the *Canadian Journal*, a periodical in the interests of science and art, and in 1864 brought out an ambitiously planned work entitled *Eighty Years' Progress of*

British North America, 1781-1861. This work contains a number of articles by Hind and by such other eminent authorities of the day as T. C. Keefer, J. C. Hodgins and the Rev. William Murray. Its statistics on transportation, resources, education and population are very valuable. All that Hind touched he made interesting, and he did much to make Canada known to the world. He possessed a ready pen, and by his literary skill and scientific insight made the driest facts attractive.

Sir Daniel Wilson (1816-92) was a Scotsman whose influence as a scientist, littérateur and educationist was felt in every part of the Dominion. He came to Canada in 1853, and his most valuable scientific production, *Prehistoric Man,* was published in 1862. While he was a prolific writer on scientific subjects, he devoted much of his time to general literature. His *Chatterton, a Biographical Study* (1869) gives an illuminating and sympathetic account of the life of the half-mad boy poet. *The Missing Link* (1871) is an entertaining venture into the Shakespearian field. His scientific labours did not dull his imagination, and he found time for poetry, and his *Spring Wild Flowers* (1873) is a volume of graceful verse. But Sir Daniel is chiefly remembered as an educationist. He occupied for many years the chair of English Literature in University College, Toronto, and in 1887 became president of the University of Toronto. For his work as a scientist, educationist and littérateur he was knighted by the queen in 1888.

Sir John William Dawson (1820-99) holds easily the first place among native Canadian scientific writers. Dawson was born in Pictou, Nova Scotia, and received his early training in Pictou Academy. After leaving the Academy he went to Edinburgh, and in that city devoted himself to the study of science. He early attracted the attention of Sir Charles Lyell, and while a student and after graduation assisted that eminent scientist in his explorations in Nova Scotia. In 1850 Dawson was appointed superintendent of education for Nova Scotia and did much to put on a sound basis the educational system of the province. In 1855 he was chosen principal of McGill University, Montreal, and for thirty-eight years remained at the head of that institution. Under him, and largely by his work, it became one of the most conspicuous seats of learning in the British Empire. Although absorbed in educational work, he found time to continue his scientific studies and investigations and to produce a number of able books on geology and palæontology. While he handled his subjects with scientific exactness, he had a facile pen, and he breathed the breath of life into the driest scientific themes. Among his chief works are *Acadian Geology, Story of the Earth and Man, Science of the Bible, Dawn of Life, Origin of the World, Egypt and Assyria, The Meeting-Place of Geology and History* and *The Ethics of Primeval Life.* He was an uncompromising opponent of the more advanced school of scientific writers represented by such men as Darwin, Wallace, Huxley and Haeckel, and although somewhat narrow in his views he commanded the respect of the scientific world to the end of his career, and was highly esteemed both at home and abroad. When the Royal Society of Canada was organized Dawson was chosen as its first president ; and in 1884 he was knighted by Queen Victoria for his achievements in education and science.

Some of the best literary work done in Canada has been in nature studies. This northern land, teeming with animal life, has proved a rich field for a number of nature writers, chief among whom are Ernest Thompson Seton and Charles G. D. Roberts. There is a similarity in the respective attitudes of the writers just mentioned towards the brute world, and yet between them there is a difference. Thompson Seton is the more scientific of the two and has the trained eye of the specialist. His *Lives of the Hunted, The Biography of a Grizzly, The Biography of a Silver Fox* and *Krag, the Kootenay Ram* show him at his best, combining as they do the exact knowledge of the scientific observer with a fine sympathy for the lives of the hunted who always have, in his phrase, ' a tragic end.' His point of view is admirably stated in *Wild Animals I Have Known* : ' We and the beasts are kin. Man has nothing that the animals have not at least a vestige of ; the animals have nothing that man does not in some degree share. Since, then, the animals are creatures with wants and feelings differing in degree only from our own, they surely have their rights. This fact, now beginning to be recognized by the Caucasian world, was first proclaimed by Moses and was emphasized by the Buddhist over two thousand years ago.'

Even more valuable than his romantic studies of animal life are his purely scientific studies : *Mammals of Manitoba, Birds of Manitoba, Art Anatomy of Animals* and *The Life History of North America. The Arctic Prairies of Canada* is a travel book dealing with every phase of nature in the Far North of the Dominion, and is an admirable and useful study of the region drained by the Peace and Mackenzie Rivers. The geology of the country, and plant and animal life are all described in this work in minute detail.

Ernest Thompson Seton was born in South Shields, England, on August 14, 1860, but as he came to Canada when five years old, and spent ten years of his life in the backwoods of the country and was trained in Canadian schools, it is proper to claim him as an exclusively Canadian writer, even though, like many other recent Canadian littérateurs, he has been drawn away from the country of his adoption to the United States. But so long has he lived with Canadian nature in the mountain regions of the West and in the vast prairie country, so saturated is his mind with Canadian life, colour and atmosphere, that he can never be anything but a Canadian.

Charles G. D. Roberts, who, as we shall see later, has gained high rank as a poet, is a prolific writer of animal stories. In *Earth's Enigmas* (1896) he first appealed to the public in this rôle, and since that time he has won wide popularity with such books as *The Heart of the Ancient Wood, The Kindred of the Wild, Watchers of the Trail, Red Fox* and *Haunters of the Silences.* Roberts lacks the scientific exactness with regard to nature of Thompson Seton, but he has the same general point of view towards the animal kingdom ; to him ' we and the beasts are kin.' His studies of the life-habits of birds, animals and fishes are written with knowledge and sympathy. *Red Fox* is his most perfect animal story, but *Earth's Enigmas* contains a number of animal stories that are typical of all his work. The stories in this volume, 'Do Seek their Meat from God,' 'The Young Ravens that call upon Him,' dealing with the mystery of the struggle for existence in the animal world, and the powerful piece of word-painting, 'Strayed,' touch upon enigmas that appeal to all thoughtful minds. In these the writer is finely serious ; he is in the presence of the mysteries of life, and he handles them as only a man with a poet's imagination and creative genius could. In his workmanship, too, he shows the same characteristics that mark his poetical productions. His artistic conscience never slumbers, and he carves and chisels his stories with the care of a Daudet or a de Maupassant. Nothing could be finer than his drawing of the ewe wildly rushing after the eagle that is fleeing to its rocky eyrie with the ewe's young lamb ; 'the lamb hung limp from his talons, and with piteous cries the ewe ran beneath, gazing upward and stumbling over the hillocks and juniper bushes.'

The main fault with the nature stories of Thompson Seton, Roberts and indeed the great majority of writers who make studies of animal life is that their animals are too human. Landseer in his masterpieces of animal life put a human eye in every animal he painted, and Roberts and Thompson Seton and their fellow-writers put a human brain in their animals : but their work is salutary; it creates sympathy with nature and refines the human heart.

Margaret Marshall Saunders of Halifax has written many short stories and a number of excellent novels, but her chief strength is as a student of domestic animal life. Her *Beautiful Joe* is already a classic and has had the distinction of being translated into many foreign languages.

These are the best known of Canadian popular students of nature, but there are many others. No country is richer in this kind of work, and in all the leading journals articles and stories dealing with nature frequently appear and are widely appreciated.

Literary criticism has little place in a young country, and quite naturally there has been a dearth of critical writers in Canada. Until very recent years criticism was done in a very haphazard manner, but there are now, mainly in the universities, a number of men who are exerting a wide influence by giving sound critical standards and thus elevating literary taste in the Dominion. One of the strongest of these is James Cappon of Queen's University, Kingston. Cappon is a Scotsman, educated in the universities of his native land, of England and of the Continent. He has been in Canada since 1888 and has shown an appreciation of Canadian effort. Before coming to the Dominion he published an exhaustive study of Victor Hugo entitled *Victor Hugo: a Study and Memoir*. He found at least one Canadian author worthy of the most serious examination, and in his *Roberts, and the Influence of His Times* has pointed the way for Canadian critics. This work is scholarly, sympathetic and discerning. It is to be regretted that Cappon stopped with Roberts. Lampman, Carman, Campbell and Isabella Valancy Crawford are worthy of similar treatment, and an adequate presentation of their strength and weakness would tend to shape the character of Canadian letters; and no one seems to be so well fitted to give this presentation as is James Cappon.

W. J. Alexander in his *Introduction to the Poetry of Robert Browning* shows insight into that 'subtlest asserter of the soul in song.' Archibald MacMechan by his editing of Carlyle's *Sartor Resartus* and *Heroes and Hero-Worship* has achieved excellent critical work. He has likewise done much by his appreciative studies of James de Mille's prose and verse to make that distinguished Nova Scotian known to a large public. Andrew Macphail of McGill University is an essayist of power. Pelham Edgar and Theodore Arnold Haultain have both done excellent work in the field of the essay and review. George M. Wrong and H. H. Langton and their associates in the *Review of Historical Publications*, already mentioned, have contributed not a little to the elevation of literary standards in Canada. For some years Martin Griffin has contributed an excellent column of literary comment and criticism, 'At Dodsley's,' to the Montreal *Gazette*. George Murray was long the most forceful critic in Montreal, and John Reade of the same city has devoted much of his literary skill and mature judgment to appreciative criticism of Canadian work. Recently several able articles on Canadian poetry have been contributed by J. D. Logan to the *Canadian Magazine*. These show good critical judgment. Criticism is needed. Authors and publishers would both be the better for it. Until Canada has literary standards of judgment, born of criticism, the trivial, commonplace, melodramatic and even vulgar will continue to usurp the place of serious, dignified, artistic literature.

Canadians, like all northern people, take life seriously. There is a marked lack of humour in poets, novelists and dramatists—and without humour there can be no true greatness. Haliburton, indeed, has it to a pre-eminent degree, but since the day of Haliburton Canadian literature has been woefully deficient in humour. Among the poets William Henry Drummond, and among the novelists Sara Jeannette Duncan, both of whom will be dealt with later, have a keen sense of humour, but they are exceptions. Since the death of Haliburton, for some sixty odd years, Canadian literary work has had a very sober tinge. Recently a humorist has arrived in the person of Stephen Leacock. Leacock is an Englishman by birth, but as he came to Canada when only seven years old, Canadians can claim him, if not as a product of the soil, at least as a graft on the Canadian literary tree. While writing such sober biography as his *Baldwin, La Fontaine and Hincks*, and such dry economics as his *Elements of Political Science*, he has found time to write three purely humorous works—*Literary Lapses, Nonsense Novels* and *Sunshine Sketches of a Little Town*. But Leacock is not so much a humorist as a wit. It is not the atmosphere of his work but the absurd situations and incidents that attract us. He is purely of the American school of humorists, and while enjoying his ' nonsense '—to use his own word—a sentence of that celebrated critic Sainte-Beuve is worth reflecting upon : ' The first consideration is not whether we are amused and pleased, but whether we were right in being amused and in applauding it.' Leacock is one of the most promising of Canadian writers. He has a graphic and brilliant style, and is a close observer of character.

Several Canadian writers have won a high place by their studies of constitutional history and parliamentary institutions. Two stand out with peculiar prominence—Alpheus Todd and Sir John George Bourinot. Alpheus Todd (1821-1884) was one of the most scholarly, painstaking and exact writers of Canada. He was born in England but came to America when a boy. He early entered the service of the legislative assembly of Upper Canada, and after the Union was assistant librarian and later librarian. At Confederation he became Dominion librarian and held this important office till his death. His works, *The Practice and Privileges of the Two Houses of Parliament*, *A Treatise on Parliamentary Government in England: its Origin, Development and Practical Operation* and *Parliamentary Government in the British Colonies* are largely technical in nature, but are written in a masterly style and are most highly valued as exhaustive treatises on their subjects.

Sir John George Bourinot (1837-1902) occupied for many years a leading place in Canadian letters. He was born in Nova Scotia and was educated in that province and at Trinity College, Toronto, Ontario. This dual training gave him a broad national attitude free from provincialism. He was at once a historian, a biographer, an essayist and a writer of works of a more or less technical character, but his fame rests chiefly on his exhaustive studies of Canadian parliamentary practice and procedure and of the constitution of Canada. In *Canada Under British Rule*, *Builders of Nova Scotia*, *The Story of Canada* and *Lord Elgin* he presents Canadian affairs with strength and with not a little grace of style. Among his best efforts were his *Intellectual Development of the Canadian People* and *Canada's Strength and Weakness*. As clerk of the House of Commons, Ottawa, a position which he held for thirty-two years, he had ample opportunities to study Canadian national affairs and men, and he made full use of them. He was a man of sympathetic nature, discriminating judgment and wide learning.

The life and political career of Joseph Howe (1804-73) will be fully dealt with in the section of this work on the Atlantic provinces. But that eminent statesman cannot be passed by without notice in this general review of Canadian literature. Howe was a journalist who for many years was without a peer in his native province, Nova Scotia. He moulded popular opinion and created a literary taste that has had its influence to the present day. As an orator he was without an equal in British North America, and some of his orations, inspired by passing events and local conditions, have still power to thrill the reader, even though the man with the flash of eye and telling gesture that mean so much in oratory, that ephemeral art, is absent. Howe's speeches and letters, edited by his friend William Annand and first published in 1858, hold a place by themselves in Canadian literature. In the two volumes are included his letters to Lord John Russell written in 1839. These letters have a vigour and a dignity, a temperate tone and a literary finish, a statesmanlike grasp of provincial and imperial questions, that place Howe in a class by himself among eminent Canadian parliamentarians. They are, too, models of style that might advantageously be studied by every Canadian student of national and imperial questions. His lectures are somewhat too rhetorical, and to be appreciated must be read in the light of the times in which they were uttered.

But for his busy political and journalistic life Howe might have won distinction as a poet. A volume of his poems and essays was published in Montreal in 1874, one year after his death; and while these poems lack finish and are for the most part echoes of the music of such masters as Scott, Byron and Moore, they are the spontaneous utterance of a full heart and have a fine singing quality and abundant humour. Among Howe's other literary efforts were a tale, *The Locksmith of Philadelphia*, and a political lampoon, *The Lord of the Bedchamber*. Howe did much to foster Canadian letters, and to him is due the honour of having, through the columns of his paper, introduced Thomas Chandler Haliburton to the public.

William Henry Withrow (1839-1908) was a theological writer of power and a historian capable of presenting the driest facts in a pleasing manner, but in this latter rôle he depended too much on secondary sources for his information.

He was born in Ontario and was educated at Victoria College, Cobourg, and University College, Toronto, and entered the ministry of the Methodist Church. His grasp of living questions and his literary ability were soon recognized, and he was appointed editor of the *Canadian Methodist Review*. As an editor his tolerant pen was a force for Christian unity. He wrote one exceptionally scholarly work, *The Catacombs of Rome and Their Testimony Relative to Primitive Christianity*. The catacombs of Rome have attracted many writers, but Withrow's study of them has never been surpassed.

Goldwin Smith (1823-1910), to whom reference has already been made, spent the last thirty-nine years of his life in Canada, but he lived apart from Canadians, and never came thoroughly into touch with Canadian ideals. He is in no sense of the word a Canadian author, but he had a wide influence on Canadian opinion and Canadian literature. Through the *Bystander*, the *Week*, the *Farmer's Sun* and other papers in which he was interested, he did much to cultivate a higher taste in journalism, and even his most bitter antagonists (and he won the dislike of not a few men) acknowledged his pre-eminence as a writer. He encouraged Canadian literature while contending that, from its situation and traditions, Canada could never have a literature separate from that of the United States or of Great Britain. He had in the beginning hoped otherwise, and there is a pathos in the words given in his *Reminiscences* at the close of his career: ' My Oxford dreams of literary achievement never were or could be fulfilled in Canada.'

But Canada is awakening, and there is a growing national sentiment that demands national expression ; and when Canadians have learned that money-making is not the most important thing in life, native writers may find a fit audience in their homeland and may not be forced to go to the markets of the United States or of Great Britain to win distinction before they receive recognition at home.

VI

FICTION

THE novel has been to the modern world for over one hundred years what the drama was to the Elizabethan age. The average reader desires knowledge with a sugar coating, and, as a result, men and women of imaginative bent of mind and literary skill find the story the best means of giving pleasure and instruction. History, politics, manners and customs, psychology, pathology, science and even theology have all been served up with the sauce of fiction.

The novel, as we know it, had its origin about the middle of the eighteenth century. Samuel Richardson, when he published his *Pamela ; or, Virtue Rewarded* in 1740, disclosed a new field for English literary talent. *Pamela* was in the form of letters, connected by plot interest, and to this form Richardson adhered in his other works. His style was widely imitated, and one of the ablest of his followers was Mrs Frances Brooke, the wife of the Rev. John Brooke, a chaplain of the forces at Quebec in the days of Guy Carleton.

Mrs Brooke, before coming to Canada, had published a romance entitled *Lady Julia Mandeville*, and while a resident of the Province of Quebec she wrote the first Canadian novel, *The History of Emily Montague*. This story was dedicated to Guy Carleton 'to whose probity and enlightened attention the colony owes its happiness, and individuals that tranquillity of mind, without which there can be no exertion of the powers of either the understanding or the imagination.' Mrs Brooke was a bird of passage in Canada, but her romance faithfully depicts Canadian life and glowingly pictures Canadian scenes, and it is essential that every student of Canadian literature should have some acquaintance with it.

Emily Montague was first published in 1769, and so popular was it that a second edition, at least, was issued in four volumes in 1777. The story is told, after the manner of Richardson, in the form of letters, which are so skilfully presented that a pleasing and uninterrupted plot is woven throughout. The letters are full of enthusiasm for Canada, a country where ' one sees not only the *beautiful* but the *great sublime* to an amazing degree.' The descriptions of wild nature, of the glories of such cataracts as Montmorency, are well done, while with a rapid pen the *beau monde* of Quebec—the officers and noblesse—and the Canadians, ' gay, coquettish and sprightly,' are faithfully reproduced. In the letters the characters of the writers are admirably revealed. Emily Montague, the typical fair maiden of early English fiction, and Edward Rivers, an ideal English gentleman, the heroine and hero of the piece ; Arabella Fermor, a vivacious, sprightly coquette, and her father Captain William Fermor, a serious-minded, thoughtful officer ; Major Melmoth and Captain Fitzgerald ; Madame des Roches, a French lady of noble type ; and Sir George Clayton, a conceited cox-comb—are all distinct personalities. Arabella Fermor is as finely drawn as any character in eighteenth-century fiction, while her lover, Fitzgerald, is as good as the best of Lever's gallant Irish soldiers. In an age when literature was broad, when vulgar jests often marred the written page, the first Canadian novel made its appearance—a strong, clean, healthy romance.

During the next fifty years no Canadian novel of importance was published. In 1832 the publication of *Wacousta*, by Major John Richardson, marked the true beginning of Canadian fiction. There were, it is true, such books as *Comparison for Caraboo* (1817) by Walter Bates (1760-1842), sheriff of King's County, New Brunswick ; and Mrs Julia Catharine Hart's (1796-1867) *St Ursula's Convent ; or, the Nun of Canada* (1824), the first book printed in Upper Canada,—but these were not true novels and are scarcely worthy of notice in a literary review. Major Richardson is, therefore, entitled to be called the first Canadian novelist.

John Richardson was the son of Robert Richardson, a Scottish surgeon in the Queen's Rangers stationed at Niagara.

In 1793 the young surgeon married Madeline Askin, daughter of Colonel John Askin, a wealthy merchant of Detroit. In 1796 their son John was born. From 1801 until the outbreak of the War of 1812 young Richardson lived in the vicinity of Detroit. This was a historical spot, the scene of many Indian combats, and replete with grim, ghastly and heroic events. Richardson's grandmother, who vividly recalled the Pontiac siege, entertained her imaginative grandson with thrilling stories of the romantic and tragic days of her youth. These tales had a twofold impulse ; they created the martial spirit in the boy and impelled him, when his mind was mature, to give the world stories of his country's heroic past.

When the Americans declared war against Britain and marched their soldiers across the Canadian border, Richardson was one of the first to enlist in Brock's army. With the 41st Regiment he was present at the capture of Detroit, and he was in every important fight with the right division of the army until the fatal battle of the Thames (Moravian Town), when he was taken prisoner and held captive for nearly a year in a United States prison. After the war ended he received a commission in the 8th (King's) Regiment, and sailed from Quebec, hoping to play a part in the European struggle in which England was engaged against Napoleon; but before his vessel reached Europe Wellington and Napoleon had met at Waterloo, and the great European war was at an end.

In 1816 Richardson went to the Barbados with the 2nd (Queen's) Regiment, but the climate so affected his health that he returned invalided to England within two years. For some ten years he lived in London on his half-pay, supplemented by what he could earn with his pen. He seems to have written mainly on Canadian and West Indian subjects. It was at this period that he wrote the only poem by him that has come down to us, *Tecumseh*, a correct but somewhat stilted performance. In 1828 his first important novel appeared, *Ecarté ; or, The Salons of Paris*. This story was so severely and unjustly criticized that Richardson lost heart, and for several years attempted no sustained literary work. *Ecarté* is in some ways a striking book, depicting in lurid colours the evils of gambling.

Wacousta ; or, The Prophecy is the novel by which Richardson is best known. In this story he deals with a heroic theme. It is based on the tales he had heard while living near Detroit and on his own knowledge of the region where the events he describes are supposed to have taken place. In *Wacousta* we have characters similar to those that move through Cooper's romantic pages. It has been said that Richardson is a mere imitator of Cooper, and his own statement, that he had 'absolutely devoured three times' *The Last of the Mohicans*, would seem to show that he had been influenced by the popular American novelist. But Richardson's Indians are his own and are in many ways more natural than Cooper's ' noble red men.' Richardson knew Indians at first-hand, and had fought side by side with such warriors as Tecumseh in the War of 1812. *Wacousta* has a well-woven plot and is packed with thrilling incidents. British soldiers, fur traders, habitants and Indians figure in it and are all distinctly drawn. True, it has much that is melodramatic, and the language at times is utterly out of keeping with the position and circumstances of the speakers ; but *Wacousta* has lived and can still be read with interest.

Richardson spent a part of 1835-36 in Spain with the British Auxiliary Legion. His experiences in Spain were the occasion for two interesting works : *Movements of the British Legion* and *Personal Memoirs of Major Richardson.*

When the Rebellion of 1837 threatened to disrupt the Empire, Richardson hurried to Canada to give his military experience to his country, but all danger was passed before his arrival. The writing impulse once more possessed him, and he set to work on a new story—this time dealing with events and characters with which he had become familiar in the War of 1812. *The Canadian Brothers; or, The Prophecy Fulfilled* was published in Montreal in 1840. It was not a profitable venture, and eleven years later Richardson wrote of it as a book ' I published in Canada—I might as well have done so in Kamschatka.' But Canada was hardly to be censured for not consuming a large edition ;

it had then a very limited reading population, and this population was engaged in hewing down the forests and breaking soil and had little time for novels. *The Canadian Brothers* is weakly constructed. In the story Richardson introduces historical figures under their own names, and takes unwarranted liberties with historical facts. Some years later *The Canadian Brothers* was published in the United States under the title *Matilda Montgomery*.

During the next ten years Richardson was engaged largely in journalism and in the writing of historical works, but he went back to fiction in 1850, and in that year published *Hard Scrabble ; or, The Fall of Chicago*, and in 1852 *Wannangee ; or, The Massacre of Chicago*. Several years after his death *The Monk Knight of St John : a Tale of the Crusade* and *Westbrook ; or, The Outlaw* appeared with his name on their title-pages. These novels were written in New York city, to which Richardson had moved in 1848 or 1849. The close of his life was a most unhappy one. He was an exile from the land he loved, and had a hard struggle in New York city against disease and extreme poverty. He died in 1852 and lies buried in an unknown grave. There is something pathetic in the fate of this first Canadian novelist who ended his days seeking to earn his bread among a people against whom he had valiantly fought.

While Richardson was engaged in historical studies and fiction in England and in Upper Canada, down by the sea in Nova Scotia a much greater genius was at work. Thomas Chandler Haliburton (1796-1865) occupies a unique place in Canadian literature, and stands undoubtedly as the foremost writer of British North America. Haliburton was the son of Henry Otis Haliburton, a judge of the Inferior Court of Common Pleas. He was born in Windsor, Nova Scotia, and was educated at King's College in that place, from which institution he graduated in 1815. He was called to the Bar in 1820 and practised law in the historic old town of Annapolis (Port Royal). He had a pleasing personality and in early life a fine gift of oratory. This won him a seat in the legislative assembly, but he remained in the assembly for only three years, and seemed to take much to heart a reprimand he received from the council for calling that venerable body 'twelve dignified, deep-read, pensioned old ladies, but filled with prejudices and whims like all other antiquated spinsters.' In 1829 he was appointed to the judgeship formerly held by his father, and moved from Annapolis to Windsor. Here, with leisure and an ideal spot for a creative genius, he began his literary work. In 1841 he became a judge of the Supreme Court. This office he resigned in 1856 and went to England, where he was to spend the rest of his life. In 1859 he entered the British House of Commons as representative for Launceston. It was a time when the Little England idea held a place in parliament ; colonies were looked on as a burden and many of the statesmen deemed that it would be wise to let them shift for themselves. Haliburton, an ardent imperialist, battled against this doctrine to the end of his parliamentary career, and did much to keep alive the imperial idea in both Great Britain and Canada.

Haliburton as a historian has already been noticed in reference to his history of Nova Scotia. The *Bubbles of Canada* and *Rule and Misrule of the English in America* show him to have been able to illuminate the past and to throw much light on contemporary political problems. An aristocrat by training and bent of mind, he feared mob rule, and was strongly opposed to responsible government, the panacea Lord Durham recommended for the ills of British North America. Time has proved Durham right and Haliburton wrong ; but Haliburton's judicial analysis in the *Bubbles of Canada* of the situation in Canada, particularly of the Ninety-Two Resolutions, is still worthy of perusal by students of Canadian political history.

While Haliburton has been included among writers of fiction, a novelist in the generally accepted sense of the word he was not. There is only the thinnest thread of plot in his works, but his characters are among the best imaginative creations of modern times, one of them, Sam Slick, taking rank with such immortals as Pickwick, Tartarin of Tarascon and Huckleberry Finn. Indeed he is, in a way, better done than any of these, for while he is drawn with fine humour, his language sparkles with wit and wisdom that are lacking in the creations of Dickens, Daudet and Mark Twain. Sam Slick, while 'dressed in cap and bells' by his creator, is, like Touchstone and the other 'fools' of Shakespeare, a preacher of wisdom and right-eousness by means of extravagant drollery. *The Clock-maker; or, The Sayings and Doings of Sam Slick of Slick-ville, The Attaché; or, Sam Slick in England, Wise Saws and Modern Instances* and *Nature and Human Nature* are the 'Sam Slick' books proper. *The Clockmaker* first made its appearance serially in Joseph Howe's *Nova Scotian* in 1835-36. It is in three series, the first published at Halifax in 1837, the second and third in London in 1838 and 1840 respectively. In 1840-42 *The Clockmaker* was translated into German and published at Brunswick.

The Attaché was published in 1843-44; Sam Slick's *Wise Saws and Modern Instances* in 1853 and *Nature and Human Nature* in 1855. The main interest of these books is 'Sam Slick.' This shrewd Yankee pedlar is the medium through which Haliburton, with penetrating humour, analyses society, impales hypocrisy, studies life and lays bare the weaknesses of humanity. Aphorism and epigram abound, and wisdom is crystallized in phrases that have not perished with the passage of time. Many, very many, of Sam Slick's flashes of wit and bits of wisdom have become incorporated into our everyday speech. Such cannot be said of any other Canadian author. The first book of the 'Sam Slick' group is the best. The hero of the piece is on familiar soil, and his antics, his humorous hyperbole, his odd manner of speech, his quaint turns of thought, are in keeping with his environment. As the 'Attaché' he is not so good, and his manners and language while moving in English aristo-cratic circles strike one as being decidedly grotesque; but even here in his nonsense there is much sense. Haliburton found the name 'Sam Slick' such a popular one that when he published the *Bubbles of Canada* (1839) and *The Letter Bag of the Great Western; or, Life in a Steamer* (1840) he made Sam Slick the nominal author. His other important works are—*The Old Judge; or, Life in a Colony* (1847), a work

that was translated into both French and German ; *The Season Ticket* (1860), which appeared first in *Dublin University Magazine ;* and *Traits of American Humour* and *Americans at Home,* two works made up of extracts from contemporary American literature and merely edited by Haliburton.

Judge Haliburton is the one early writer of Canada who has won a place in English literature. He was not only the creator of a distinct character and the utterer of words that live ; he was also in a sense the creator of a school of writers. American humour received its impulse from 'Sam Slick,' and Haliburton was, moreover, the first writer to use the American dialect in literature. Artemus Ward, Josh Billings and Mark Twain are, in a way, mere imitators of Haliburton, and he is their superior. He has not, it is true, Mark Twain's power of telling a story and literary art, but as a humorist, in the best sense of the word, he was greater than that distinguished American writer. American humorists produce their effects largely by exaggeration. Haliburton produced his by genial humour, by kindly satire (he smiles even when most sarcastic), by penetrating wit, and most of all by the illuminating wisdom of his detached utterances. His satire is not so much against individuals, to whom he is kindly, as against types ; but at times, when punishment is deserved, he directs his caustic satire against individuals, and he has drawn several characters with the power of a Hogarth, a Cruikshank or a Gillray. He had an affection for Nova Scotia and an ardent hope for a united British Empire, and in satirizing the 'inertia' of Nova Scotians and the 'narrowness' of the people of Great Britain, he did it for the purpose of rousing them to action and to breadth of mind. While it is in aphorism that he is at his best, he could draw a character with inimitable strength. Nothing could be finer than his sketch of Captain Barkins, with countenance weather-beaten but open, good-natured and manly ; and of Elder Stephen Gran, with face 'as long as the moral law, and perhaps an inch longer,' who seemed to feel that 'he had conquered the Evil One and was considerable well satisfied with himself.'

How packed with wit and wisdom are some of Haliburton's sentences ! What could be better than the following ?

'You may stop a man's mouth by crammin' a book down his throat, but you won't convince him.'

'We find it easy enough to direct others to the right road, but we can't always find it ourselves when we 're on the ground.'

'Whenever you make an impression on a man, stop ; your reasonin' and details may ruin you.'

'It is in politics as in horses ; when a man has a beast that is near up to the notch, he had better not swap him.'

'Power has a nateral tendency to corpulency.'

'A joke, like an egg, is never no good except it is fresh.'

What a world of tender feeling, admirably expressed, we have here :

'A woman has two smiles that an angel might envy; the smile that accepts a lover before words are uttered, and the smile that lights on the first-born baby and assures him of a mother's love.'

Thomas Chandler Haliburton, despite much careless, hurried work, coarseness of expression and diffuseness of language, stands high above all other Canadian writers. He possesses to an extraordinary degree that informing personality which makes for greatness. Of him we can say as Ben Jonson said of Shakespeare : 'He was not of an age but for all time.'

The Rev. J. C. Abbott (1789-1863) emigrated to Canada in 1818, and for many years laboured as a missionary of the Church of England in what is now the Province of Quebec. Abbott had the interest of his adopted country much at heart, and was the first enthusiastic advertiser of British North America. He published two works with regard to the country : *The Emigrant to North America, from Memoranda of a Settler*, which appeared in the Quebec *Mercury* (1842) and as a pamphlet in Montreal in the same year ; and *Philip Musgrave ; or, The Adventures of a Missionary in Canada*, printed in London in 1843. The latter work is a story based on the facts and incidents of *The Emigrant to North America*. *Philip Musgrave* was popular in its day and attracted the attention of two of Canada's governors-general, who distributed hundreds of copies of the book among people seeking information about British North America. Abbott's desire was to give information that would be valuable to Old World farmers coming to a country where they would have to face new conditions, and he clothed his information in language and in a manner that are at once strong and pleasing.

About the middle of the last century readers of the *Literary Garland* were familiar with the initials R. E. M. These stood for Rosanna Eleanor Mullins (1832-79) of Montreal, who in 1851 married Dr Leprohon of her native province. This talented authoress wrote a number of excellent stories dealing with Canadian life and manners. Her first novel was published in 1848. It is entitled *Ida Beresford*, and is a remarkable production for a girl only sixteen years old. There are in all some eight novels from her pen, four of which, *Ida Beresford, The Manor House of De Villerai, Antoinette de Mirecourt*—in many ways her best book—and *Armand Durand* were translated into French. Mrs Leprohon was a graceful writer and a skilful portrayer of character. She is particularly strong when moved by the pathos of a situation she has created. From a Canadian point of view *The Manor House of De Villerai* and *Antoinette de Mirecourt* are her most important works. The first appeared in 1859 in the *Family Herald* of Montreal, whose staff Mrs Leprohon joined in 1860. The scene was Canada at the period of the Cession, and the characters are largely the habitants of the Province of Quebec. The simple, kindly lives of these people are sympathetically portrayed ; their quaint, homely manners and customs are given with fulness and exact knowledge.

Mrs Catharine Parr Traill (1802-99) was a member of the famous Strickland family, of which five daughters achieved distinction in literature ; and one son, Lieutenant-Colonel Samuel Strickland (1804-67), although without pretensions to literary power, produced one of the most valuable descriptive works dealing with Canadian life in pioneer days—*Twenty-seven Years in Canada West ; or, The Experiences of an Early Settler.*

Mrs Traill was born in the county of Kent, England, and when thirty years old came with her husband to Canada. Her home was first in the primeval forest near Rice Lake. The conditions of life were hard in the wilderness, but they in no way blunted Mrs Traill's perception of the beautiful in nature and life or detracted from her power of presenting to others what she saw with an artist's eye. She produced two readable novels : *Lady Mary and Her Nurse ; or, A Peep into Canadian Forests* and *The Canadian Crusoes : A Tale of the Rice Lake Plains,* published in London, England, in 1850 and 1852 respectively. These books are better known under the modern titles of *Afar in the Forest* and *Lost in the Backwoods.*

Mrs Traill, however, achieved greater distinction as a writer on nature than as a novelist. Her *Studies in Plant Life; or, Gleanings from Forest, Lake and Plain* is the best popular Canadian botanical book written by a resident of Canada. Trees, animals, birds and flowers were her familiar friends ; it was her faith ' that every flower enjoys the air it breathes.' Her scientific labours received recognition. Lady Charlotte Greville, who was greatly impressed by collections of Canadian ferns and mosses made by Mrs Traill, induced Lord Palmerston to secure for her a grant of £100 for her services as a naturalist, and the Canadian government presented her with an island in the Otonabee River. She continued to write with unimpaired vigour until the end of her long life. Her last two works, *Pearls and Pebbles* (1894) and *Cot and Cradle Stories* (1895), gave insight into the workings of nature, the latter being an excellent collection of simple, imaginative tales for children.

Mrs Susanna Moodie (1803-85), a sister of Catharine Parr Traill, began her literary career at the early age of fifteen. In 1831 she married John W. D. Moodie, a half-pay officer of the 21st Fusiliers, and with him came to Canada in 1832. She and her husband by training and education were totally unfitted for the rough conditions of Upper

Canada ; and their struggle for existence, first near the town of Port Hope and later in the unbroken forest ten miles north of Peterborough, makes pathetic reading ; all the more so as it was the lot of hundreds of people of similar birth and training, who came to Canada in search of riches during the first half of the nineteenth century.

Although a novelist and a contributor of stories to Canadian and American magazines, Mrs Moodie's fame rests largely on her two descriptive works, *Roughing it in the Bush ; or, Life in Canada* (1852) and *Life in the Clearings versus the Bush* (1853)—the former being published later under the title, *Life in the Backwoods.* These works were written largely for the purpose of counteracting the pernicious influence of the extravagant immigration literature that was being spread broadcast through Great Britain by immigration agents and land companies. Thousands of men and women had been induced to come to Canada, there to meet conditions with which they were unable to battle ; and in many instances they had succumbed to the struggle and their lives had been hopelessly wrecked. *Roughing it in the Bush*, in particular, painted in a realistic manner Upper Canada as it really was, and had a salutary influence. It has much literary merit, and, even though the motive that inspired it no longer exists, it still remains a valuable book, a veritable Canadian classic. In it the times are faithfully reproduced. The stories scattered through the pages still entertain, and the characters introduced are depicted with droll humour and tender pathos, and show the author to have had a deep insight into life. Mrs Moodie's novels have not stood the test of time as well as her descriptive works on Upper Canada ; but *Mark Hurdlestone, the Gold Worshipper, Flora Lindsay ; or, Passages in an Eventful Life, Matrimonial Speculation, Geoffrey Moncton ; or, The Faithless Guardian* and *Dorothy Chance* can yet be read with enjoyment.

Mrs Moodie was, too, one of the best of the early Canadian poets. Imaginative, keenly alive to the beauties of nature, sympathetic with suffering, patriotic, she wrote a number of poems which—at least during her lifetime—had a wide appreciation. Some of them were set to music and were popular in Canadian homes sixty years ago.

James de Mille (1836-80) was one of the most voluminous of Canadian writers of fiction. De Mille was born in St John, New Brunswick, and died in Halifax, Nova Scotia. He had an excellent grounding in the ancient and modern languages, and taught classics for some years in Acadia College, and, during the closing years of his life, English and rhetoric in Dalhousie College, Halifax. He wrote in all twenty-eight or twenty-nine stories, besides numerous short stories, and at least one poem, *Behind the Veil*. This poem was found among his papers after his death, and was published under the editorship of Archibald MacMechan in 1893. In artistic and imaginative qualities *Behind the Veil* was much in advance of the poetical work done in British North America before the modern school of Canadian poets began their work, about 1880, the year of de Mille's death.

De Mille's first important book, *The Martyrs of the Catacombs*, was published in 1865, and his last, *A Castle in Spain*, thirteen years later. It is hardly correct to say his last, for ten years after his death, when such weirdly imaginative tales as H. Rider Haggard's *King Solomon's Mines* and *She* were attracting attention, de Mille's *A Strange Manuscript found in a Copper Cylinder* made its appearance. This extravagant tale of adventure, quite as good as many others of its class, had the usual fate of such stories—it was momentarily popular, and then forgotten. De Mille's genius had a wide range. In *The Dodge Club; or, Italy in 1859* he showed a humorous vein. His six volumes in the *B.O.W.C. Series* and the three in the *Dodge Club Series* prove him capable of writing healthy, vigorous stories for the young. Novels with a mysterious setting, romances sentimental in character, and fiction interesting by its thrilling incidents, he wrote with equal ease.

William Kirby (1817-1906), through his book *The Golden Dog (Le Chien d'Or)*, has deservedly won a high place among Canadian novelists. *The Golden Dog* in a way marked the beginning of a new era in Canadian literature. In time it turned the attention of writers to the rich material to be found in the past of Canada for fiction, and it has been followed by a number of romances with a historical foundation. In many respects it still holds the first place among Canadian historical novels.

William Kirby was born at Kingston-upon-Hull and came to Canada with his parents in 1832. For five years the Kirbys resided in Montreal ; they then moved to Niagara, where the rest of William Kirby's long life was spent. For over twenty-five years he edited and published the Niagara *Mail*, and for nearly a quarter of a century longer held the office of collector of customs at Niagara. Kirby was a thorough Canadian and an ardent imperialist, and ever showed a deep interest in the history of the country in which his lot was cast. His first production was a historical poem, *The U.E. ; a Tale of Upper Canada* (1859). In 1888 he published a collection of poems entitled *Canadian Idylls*, a second edition of which was issued in 1894. He is also the author of a historical work, *The Annals of Niagara*, and of several other volumes of prose. But he is remembered solely by his historical romance, *The Golden Dog*, first published in 1877.

For his novel he selected the most magnificent theme this continent afforded—the final struggle between the French and the English for empire in America. His stage is the rocky citadel of Quebec, and his actors are governors and intendants, officers and merchants, noble ladies of New France and the humble habitants. He had a genuine admiration for the French, and his characters are all sympathetically drawn. No French writer could have shown more feeling than did Kirby in his presentation of the unhappy country surrounded by foreign foes and plundered by Bigot and his henchmen, Cadet and de Péan. Kirby had thoroughly saturated his mind with the history of Old France and New France in the days of Louis xv, and his vivid imagination enabled him to give a faithful picture of the times. The officials of Quebec, the seigneurs and their dependants are all faithfully portrayed. Count Philibert and his son Pierre are presented in the grand manner, and the father is probably the best-drawn and best-sustained character in Canadian fiction, while Amélie de Repentigny and Angélique des Meloises—as wide as the poles apart in character—are strongly depicted women. *The Golden Dog* is a mixture of the manner of Scott and the manner of Dumas. At times the story drags, largely due to the desire of the author to give local colour and to detail fully the life of the period with which he is dealing ; but the well-conceived plot and the stirring incidents with which the work is packed sustain interest. *The Golden Dog* is a great book—a book that has turned the feet of thousands of pilgrims towards Quebec. As a historical novel, however, it is not without its blemishes. Many of the characters were not as black as they are painted, and some of the noble Frenchmen who move through its pages are—as the documents that have come down from the times prove— far from being as noble as they are pictured. *The Golden Dog* is highly thought of by French Canadians, and was translated into French by two of the most distinguished writers of the Province of Quebec, Louis Frechette and Pamphile Le May.

Among other Canadian novelists of the earlier period worthy of consideration are : Mrs May Agnes Fleming (1840-80), who was the author of twenty-two novels of a highly sensational character ; John Lesperance, who, in *The Bastonnais : a Tale of the American Invasion in Canada, 1775-1776*, produced a useful and accurate story of the times ; the Hon. Lucius Seth Huntington, whose *Professor Conant* gives an excellent study of English and American political and social life ; Mrs Mary Ann Sadlier, a prolific writer of fiction, biography and essays ; and Louisa Murray, one of the most graceful writers of prose and verse who have ever appealed to the Canadian public.

As we shall see later, a new movement took place in Canadian poetical literature about the year 1880 ; some ten years after this date Canadian fiction entered upon a new stage in its development. It would be quite within the mark to take the definite year 1890 as the dividing line between the early writers, more or less provincial in their art, and the modern school, influenced by world standards. In that year Gilbert (afterwards Sir Gilbert) Parker took up his residence in London, England, and began the stories, many of them dealing with Canadian life in the past and present and with Canadian colour and atmosphere, that were to make him easily the first of Canadian novelists. Two years later his volume of short stories, *Pierre and his People*, was published, and a Canadian writer of more than ordinary force took his place in the world of fiction. It was in 1890, too, that Sara Jeannette Duncan (Mrs Everard Cotes) began her career as a writer of books with *A Social Departure*. In 1891 Lily Dougall's first novel, *Beggars All*, was published, and in 1889 Margaret Marshall Saunders's *My Spanish Sailor* had appeared. During the next decade Charles W. Gordon, Charles G. D. Roberts, Norman Duncan, William McLennan, Blanche Lucile Macdonell, Joanna E. Wood, Allan Richard Carman, Edward W. Thomson and other strong writers of fiction appeared in the Canadian field, producing well-constructed stories, artistic in treatment, and showing a power to make characters of the past and present live on the written page.

Sir Gilbert Parker occupies a high place among writers of fiction. He was born in Camden East, Ontario, in 1860, and spent the first twenty-five years of his life in Canada. His literary training was unique. It was his original intention to enter the ministry, but after studying arts and theology for a brief period at Trinity College, Toronto, he followed his literary bent and took up letters as a profession. In 1885, after some experience as a writer of poems and sketches and as a lecturer on literary subjects, he went to Australia, and for a time was on the staff of the Sydney *Morning Herald*. He has been a persistent traveller, visiting the outlying portions of Europe and every corner of the Empire—Northern Canada, the South Sea Islands, Egypt and the Far East—and wherever he has gone he has been a close observer of life. His books show him to have been influenced largely by his Canadian home and training, and his earlier works all have a Canadian colour and atmosphere; but while he is spoken of as a Canadian, it would be more correct to regard him as a literary product of the British Empire.

Canada, the Channel Islands, Egypt, South Africa—he has studied them all and makes them the stages on which his characters move. Incidentally he was in his youth an ardent student of Shakespeare, and knew by heart the greater part of a number of the poet's dramas. This may account for the fact that his first ambitious literary efforts were dramas, of which he wrote three during 1888-89 ; but he seems to have been discouraged by the reception accorded to his adaptation of his historical romance, *The Seats of the Mighty*, and concluded that it would be wise to give all his energies to the novel.

He first appealed, as already stated, to lovers of fiction in a volume of short stories entitled *Pierre and his People*—a very excellent collection showing much promise. ' Pretty Pierre,' the titular hero, the link that binds the various stories together, a half-breed with whom card-playing was 'a science and a passion,' is not as well done as some of the other characters. Pierre lacks reality and is the creation of the writer's imagination rather than a type of the life to be found in the early days in the Far West. Parker's Indians, too, are either idealized or brutalized, and lack realistic truth. But Sergeant Fones, ' the little Bismarck of the Mounted Police,' who had ' the fear o' God in his heart, and the law of the land across his saddle, and the newest breech-loading rifle at that ' ; and Sergeant Tom Gellatly, a blood-brother of Kipling's ' Mulvaney,'—are powerfully created. The half-breeds, the Hudson's Bay Company's factors and employees, and the men of the Mounted Police are sketched in a comprehensive way, and the moving incidents by flood and field sustain interest. However, *Pierre and his People* can only be considered a tentative effort on the part of the author. Much of the work is slipshod. It is, for example, difficult to imagine that the author of *The Judgment House* could have ended a tragic story with such a sentence as this : ' The hands were wrinkled ; the face was cold ; the body was wet ; the man was drowned and dead.'

During the next three years Parker produced six novels— *Mrs Falchion, The Trespasser, The Translation of a Savage, The Trail of the Sword, When Valmond came to Pontiac,* and

An Adventurer of the North—and one volume of poems, *A Lover's Diary*. In *The Trail of the Sword* he wrote with a verve and dash that remind one of Weyman and Doyle ; but the book was too packed with incident, and the sudden and wide changes of scene marred its construction. In *When Valmond came to Pontiac* he attempted to depict life in a French-Canadian village ; but the life is of his own imagination. Only at times is the habitant truly presented, and on the whole the study is a caricature. All these earlier novels may be considered the work of Parker's apprentice hand ; but in 1896 a powerful and sustained novel appeared from his pen—*The Seats of the Mighty*. In this book, which is not without its faults, there is an artistic repose, a mastery, a fulness of treatment that bespeak the mature artist. The story is of the period of the conquest of Quebec and has a strong plot and vigorously drawn characters. Captain Robert Moray, the hero, obstinate, self-confident, somewhat of a boaster ; Doltaire, with ' the one gift of the strong man,' inexorable when he made for his end, a fine study in contradictions, a heartless roué, yet moved by a true and noble passion, a flippant admirer of the excesses and trivialities of the court, yet a thinker with a penetrating intellect, a man whose self-consciousness is at once his strength and his weakness ; Gabord, a rough soldier, one of nature's poets and gentlemen ; the Chevalier de la Darante, the soul of truth and honour,—are all striking creations.

Bigot, Vaudreuil, Montcalm, Wolfe, and the other historical characters in the piece are sketched in with rapid, vigorous touches. The book is packed with thrilling incidents, sometimes impossible and sometimes highly exaggerated, it is true, but on the whole kept within bounds. There was in this work still something lacking. It has the fault of many historical novels. Parker was unable to project his spirit entirely into the time about which he wrote, and the men and women, despite their dress and manners, are all of the present rather than the past.

In 1897 Parker published *The Pomp of the Lavillettes* and in the following year *The Battle of the Strong*. The latter book was a distinct advance on any of his previous works. In it he shifted the scene of his story from Canada to the Channel Islands, and his descriptions and character sketches are truer to life than in any of his Canadian books. He had evidently studied exhaustively the islands and their inhabitants, which had changed but little since the time portrayed in his story—the close of the eighteenth century. Philip d'Avranche and Ranulph Delagarde, Jean Tousel and Dormy Jamais, Guida Landresse and Maîtresse Aimable Tousel are sympathetically drawn, and the book has touches of true humour, totally absent in his other stories save in isolated passages in *Pierre and his People*. In construction, in workmanship, in descriptive fineness, in its interpretation of life and in ethical value *The Battle of the Strong* showed a distinct advance in power and the artistic handling of his historical and romantic material.

In 1901 came *The Right of Way*. Here the author dealt with a pathological subject. Although the book has been highly praised, it has two leading defects. The scene is laid in the Province of Quebec, but the life is lacking in truth, while the hero is an impossibility. A careful analysis of his character and action will show that no one could possibly have been so clever and resourceful in so many odd directions as was Charley Steele.

In the meantime Parker entered on a new career. In 1900 he was elected in the Unionist interest for Gravesend and has since held a seat in the British House of Commons. His work done in literature received recognition from his sovereign, and in 1902 he was honoured with knighthood.

Parker's next truly great work, *The Weavers*, was published in 1907. The scene of this story is mainly in Egypt, and the book was written evidently after a most thorough study of the country, its problems and its people. The climax of Parker's art was reached in 1912, in the important creation, undoubtedly his masterpiece, *The Judgment House*. The scene of this great story is laid in London and in South Africa. The time is the period before and during the South African War. 'The Partners,' a group of men exploiting South Africa, coarse and strong characters;

Krool, the Hottentot-Boer, patriotic, vindictive, yet to his master as docile as a tamed animal ; Byng, a diamond in the rough, who in the end turned out to be a polished gem ; Jigger, the newsboy, and his sister Lou ; Ian Stafford, philanthropist and statesman, familiar with the international game, with the defects of his qualities ; Jasmine and Al'mah, the heroines of the piece,—are all living beings, men and women of flesh and blood. Parker in *The Judgment House* has attained the heights. He has proved himself capable of giving ' in the man of the day the eternal man,' and he takes his place among the truly great writers of fiction. But in this work he is no longer Canadian : *The Judgment House* is the result of his imperial training and of years spent in the social and political atmosphere of Great Britain.

The Rev. Charles W. Gordon, D.D. (Ralph Connor), was born in 1860 at Indian Lands, Glengarry, Ontario, and his early life was spent among the sturdy Highlanders who did so much of the pioneer work of the Dominion. Gordon is, in every way, a Canadian writer. He was educated in Canada ; he has spent his whole life, save for a very short period as a student in Scotland, in the Dominion ; he has devoted his entire attention to the study of Canada and Canadian men and women. He was educated at the University of Toronto and at Knox College. The mission field attracted his earnest, vigorous nature, and between 1890 and 1893 he worked among the miners and lumbermen of the North-West Territories. He began his literary career in 1897 with a brief sketch entitled *Beyond the Marshes*. In 1898 *Black Rock* won him a wide audience. It touched the popular heart with its rapid, terse style and its mingled humour and pathos, its sympathy with men half brutalized by their work and environment, and its admiration for the noble and self-sacrificing in life.

In his introduction to *Black Rock* Professor George Adam Smith wrote : ' He [Ralph Connor] has seen with single eye the life which he describes in this book, and has himself, for some years of hard and lonely toil, assisted in the good influences which he traces among its wild and often lonely conditions.' And he adds that he ' writes with the freshness and accuracy of an eyewitness . . . with the tenderness and hopefulness of a man not only of faith but of experience.'

The heroes of Gordon's books, whether in the mines or the lumber camps, in the pulpits or the universities, in the cities or on the prairies, are all, each in his own way, ' fighting out that eternal fight for manhood, strong, clean, and God-conquered.'

In *Black Rock*, and in *The Sky Pilot* produced in the following year, the details of life in lumber and mining camps are well given, and the motley crews of vigorous, sometimes brutal manhood—Irish, Highland, French-Canadian, English —and the missionaries—Craig, Moore and Father Goulet— pious, manly, self-sacrificing, are portrayed with sympathy and insight.   There is invariably the typical feminine guardian angel in all Gordon's books, but the weakness is that the author never varies her; and Mrs Mavor of *Black Rock* and Mrs Murray, the mistress of the Glengarry manse, are one and the same woman under different names.   In these two early books the author shows that he understands French-Canadian life, at least in the lumber camps : Baptiste and Latour are quite as true to life as are the faithfully drawn characters of William Henry Drummond.   In the ' strange medley of people of all ranks and nations ' Gordon finds men with vices due rather to the circumstances of their lives than to the natural tendencies of their hearts.   To him sin is largely ' energy gone wrong,' and evidently the purpose in his books is by their presentation of life and action to direct this energy properly.

Gordon, in his romances, is a teacher of ethics ; a preacher by profession—in his novels he merely makes mankind at large his congregation.   In *The Man from Glengarry* (1901) the characters are the men he was familiar with in his boyhood days, now playing their parts in the lumbering operations on the Ottawa River and the Gatineau.   In the introduction to his book he has very clearly given his main reason for writing it : ' Not wealth, not enterprise, not energy, can build a nation into true greatness, but men and only men with the fear of God in their hearts and no other, and to make this clear is also a part of the purpose of this book.'

Theoretically Gordon is something of a Calvinist, but even a casual reading of his stories will show that by *fear* of God he really means *love* of God—love is made the impelling force for good in all his books. In *The Man from Glengarry* the characters Big Macdonald, Dannie Ross, Findlay Campbell, Louis Le Noir are men of ' hardness of frame, alertness of sense, readiness of resource, endurance, superb self-reliance, a courage that grew with peril, and withal a certain wildness which at times deepened into ferocity.' This book has preserved in vital form rough conditions and characters that are rapidly passing away under the influence of civilization and education.

In *Glengarry School Days* the crude conditions of life and education in the backwoods of Canada in the middle of the nineteenth century and even later are faithfully reproduced. In *The Prospector* (1904) and *The Doctor* (1906) the lives of a healer of souls and a healer of bodies in a new country where hardships have to be faced in the performance of duty are convincingly presented.

In 1909 Gordon hit on a happy title, *The Foreigner.* Admirable material for tragic and romantic use lies ready at hand for the investigator who will take the trouble to look into the lives of the foreign element in the cities or ' in the melting-pot of nations,' the Canadian North-West. The author of *The Foreigner* set out with high aims : ' Out of breeds diverse in traditions, in ideals, in speech, and in manner of life, Saxon and Slav, Teuton, Celt and Gaul, one people is being made. The blood strains of a great nation will mingle in the blood of a race greater than the greatest of them all.' There is much that is realistic, indeed, much that is after the manner of Zola and his followers of the naturalistic school, in *The Foreigner* ; at times it is even repulsive in its details, but it has purple patches of great power.

In *Corporal Cameron* (1912) the action begins in Scotland, moves to the Province of Quebec and then to the North-West. The characters are largely repetitions, under other names, of the men and women of the early books, as are the incidents, save for the well-described Highland games.

Gordon's power lies not so much in his ability as a constructive artist as in his strong, isolated passages. His gentler action is commonplace ; but his incidents, such as football matches and bar-room brawls, are masterly bits of work.

Norman Duncan is one of the Canadian authors who, at an early age of their literary career, were drawn away by the larger and more profitable markets of the United States. Duncan was born in Brantford, Ontario, in 1871, and was educated in that city and at the University of Toronto. In 1896, when twenty-five years old, he took a position on the New York *Evening Post*, and until 1901 he did all his best work for that journal. He first proved himself a master of the short story, and in his volume *The Soul of the Street* gave a series of sketches which for insight into life and for character drawing are as fine as anything done in the short story in America, and indeed compare favourably with the short-story work of the greatest of British short-story writers. These sketches, dealing with one section of the foreign element in New York city, show the author at the outset of his career to have had a genius for interpreting life. He presents in a masterly manner one phase of New York life, and he was able to do so because he had gone down into the street and into the homes and studied at first-hand the men and women he depicted.

But Duncan was soon to work in a new field. As a special writer he went to Newfoundland, a region he has made peculiarly his own. Hardy fisher-folk, traders and seamen—hospitable, tender, simple, willing for toil—and sturdy lads ' who know hardship and peril when the boys of the city still grasp a hand when they cross the street,' appealed to him, and he has drawn them with fidelity and strength, with tender pathos and grim humour. The rocky, rugged, storm-beaten shores of Newfoundland and the Labrador coast gripped his imagination. The North Atlantic ocean, with its icebergs, field-ice and ' growlers,' with its ' frothy fangs ' and ' soapy seas,' has never been presented so ' deeply and faithfully '—to use the words of Frank Bullen, himself a master in portraying the ocean and the characters of the men who go down into the deep.

Dr Luke of the Labrador gave Duncan a distinct place in modern literature. In it the life of a hardy people playing their part on a hard stage is exhaustively treated. He found, too, the heroic in commonplace life ; a healer of men working among humble, grateful, illiterate folk gave him as fine an opportunity for his genius as others have found amid the clash of arms and in the courts of nations.

Norman Duncan produced in *The Adventures of Billy Topsail, The Cruise of the Shining Light* and *Billy Topsail and Company* a series of healthy, manly books for boys. They abound in adventures on rocky coasts, in blinding fogs and in the ice-pack. Through all there is a sea movement that is unexcelled by the best work of such trained seamen turned novelists as Russell and Bullen. In Duncan's books Newfoundland and the Labrador coast have been given a prominent place in literature. *The Measure of a Man* (1912) is laid in a different field. The hero, John Fairmeadow, is a reformed drunkard, a recruit from Jerry M°Auley's mission in Water Street, New York. Fairmeadow had chosen for his work, in the capacity of a lay missionary, the lumber camps of Minnesota. He is a well-drawn, virile character who, when occasion demanded it, was quite capable of stepping from his pulpit and thrashing a disturber in his congregation into a respectful attitude. But Duncan has lost something of his power in this new field and with these new characters. There is not the definiteness, the reality in his landsmen that is to be found in his sea-folk. There is a vagueness in his character studies in this book, a lack of firmness of touch and an extravagance in incident that detract from its merits. He handles, it is true, the elemental passions with power. From the rough human rock there can be carved either a brute or an angel, and he has brought out both. But, though John Fairmeadow in this book appears ' in the measure of his service, in the stature of his soul, a Man,' he impresses one rather as a product of the author's imagination than a being of flesh and blood.

Charles G. D. Roberts has already been considered as a writer of animal stories, and will later be dealt with as a poet, but it is also necessary to consider him briefly as a writer of fiction. He has worked mainly in a somewhat narrow field, the Maritime Provinces, but, so far as external nature is concerned, he has treated that region exhaustively. In *The Raid from Beauséjour*, *The Forge in the Forest*, *A Sister to Evangeline*, *The Prisoner of Mademoiselle*, and a volume of short stories, *The Marshes of Minas*, he has graphically pictured the ' romantic period in Canadian history when the French were making the very last struggle to retain their hold upon the peninsula of Acadie—now called Nova Scotia.'

Roberts is without an equal in Canadian literature as a writer of mellifluous prose ; sea, sky, landscape—he has caught their rhythm and colour and described them in exquisite passages that read like a succession of lyrical poems ; but his pictures of Acadian life are *couleur de rose*. The characters he draws in *A Sister to Evangeline* are not borne out by history. He lacks dramatic force, and the language of his men and women, in the light of the times in which they lived, is unnatural ; but his style is inimitable and the local colour of his descriptions of such regions as Annapolis Basin, Minas Basin and the Isthmus of Chignecto would be hard to excel. Apart from his character portrayal, he has, in his Nova Scotian stories, as truly pictured the face of that part of the Dominion as has Hardy his Wessex coast or Egdon Heath.

In his short stories, each a prose poem, he has been influenced largely by the modern French school of whom Daudet and de Maupassant are the ablest representatives ; but some of his work is distinctly original. In his studies in *Earth's Enigmas* dealing with lumber camps and lumbering operations he is peculiarly good. His residence on the St John and Miramichi—great lumber rivers—has well fitted him to handle these themes. In ' Within the Sound of the Saws ' he has succeeded in making the mill town a reality to any one born within the sound of the saws, to whom the news that the mills were to close down was very much as if the sun were about to be removed for a season ; and who measured the return of the spring, not by the first robin, but by the buzz of the saws, the dull clang of the deal on the piles, and the heavy clatter of the mill carts. No second-hand observation could ever have produced the following paragraph :

> In the middle of the mill worked the 'gang,' a series of upright saws that rose and fell swiftly, cleaving their way with a pulsating, vicious clamour through an endless and sullen procession of logs. Here and there, each with a massive table to itself, hummed the circulars, large and small ; and whenever a deal, or a pile of slabs, was brought in contact with one of the spinning discs, upon the first arching spirt of sawdust-spray began a shrieking note, which would run the whole vibrant and intolerable gamut as the saw bit through the fibres from end to end. In the occasional brief moments of comparative silence, when several of the saws would chance to be disengaged at the same instant, might be heard, far down in the lower storey of the mill, the grumbling roar of the great turbine wheels, which, sucking in the tortured water from the sluices, gave life to all the wilderness of cranks and shafts above.

It is the same with 'The Butt of the Camp' and 'At the Rough-and-Tumble Landing.' In the one Roberts has given with great truth the boisterous life of a lumber camp ; in the other, with graphic power, the most perilous task— breaking a log jam—that an ax-man can tackle.

William Wilfred Campbell,[1] another of Canada's widely known and appreciated poets, has been drawn aside from a field in which he peculiarly excelled and has written several descriptive works and two excellent novels—*Ian of the Orcades* and *A Beautiful Rebel*. The latter is on a Canadian theme, the War of 1812, but is not as good as the former, which has Scottish ground for its stage and Celtic characters as actors. *Ian of the Orcades* had not the enthusiastic reception it deserved. Had S. R. Crockett, for example, written it, it would have been hailed as an exceptionally powerful historical novel. The style is elevated, the characters are strongly drawn, the incidents are striking, given with intensity but without exaggeration ; and, as in Roberts's work, where the author is interpreting nature the story abounds

---

[1] See pp. 578-9.

in prose poems. There are in it passages of profound thought, and what has been said of Campbell's poetry might with equal appropriateness be said of this novel—through the tragic story ' there runs a deep undertone of haunting, mysterious suggestiveness which naturally links the restless phenomena of nature with the joys and sorrows of the h . nan heart.'

Campbell is a Celt, and in *Ian of the Orcades* there are passages abounding in natural magic, that peculiar gift of Celtic writers. The dramatic passages, too, are well done ; there is in them a naturalness, a vigour and truth that are lacking in many Canadian books that have had a wider audience.

No writer has possessed more enthusiasm for Canada or greater hope in Canada's future in material and spiritual things than William Douw Lighthall of Montreal, and no one has done more to make known to the world Canada's past and what Canadians of the present have been doing. His collection of poems, *Songs of the Great Dominion,* with his excellent introduction and notes, showed that a fine body of poetical work was being produced in Canada. Lighthall has also done much historical and antiquarian work, and has written three books of fiction of a high quality— *The Young Seigneur, The False Chevalier* and *The Master of Life.*

The Young Seigneur is not properly a novel, but rather a race and politico-sociological study. Its chief aim was, as the author says in his preface, the ' perhaps too bold one —*to map out a future for the Canadian nation,* which has been hitherto drifting without any plan.' Lighthall's plan evidently was not widely accepted. *The Young Seigneur* was published in 1888 under the nom de plume ' Wilfred Chateauclair,' and ' the Canadian nation ' continued to drift, and, judging from the parliamentary discussions during 1913, it is still drifting. Another aim of the author was to make the ' atmosphere of French Canada understood by those who speak English.' Few, we imagine, for whom the book was intended, have benefited by the study, but that is the fault of the reading public and not of the author. *The*

False Chevalier was published in 1898 and is a distinctly abler book. It has a well-worked plot, and the historical material both of Old France and of New France is skilfully handled. Several of the characters are drawn with dramatic insight. It would be hard to find in Canadian fiction a better or more truthfully portrayed character than the merchant Lecour of St Elphège, a fine type of prosperous habitant—simple-minded, honest, generous, industrious— or than his wife—romantic and ambitious for her son. Germaine Lecour, the son, is likewise well portrayed, but there is a disappointing unreality about him while he plays his part on the European stage. Lighthall is only at his best when on the firm and familiar ground of Canada. *The Master of Life* is an exceptional book, a unique book. It is a novel of Indian life without a white man in it ; a story ' of woods and water and prehistoric times.' The central figure is Hiawatha, the founder of the League of the Five Nations, and the main interest of the story for Canadians centres round the destruction of Hochelaga, the town vividly described by Jacques Cartier in 1535, which had been wiped out of existence by the beginning of the seventeenth century. It is the destruction of Hochelaga that forms the principal theme of the book. *The Master of Life* is the product of years of study and reflection. It displays extensive archæological research ; and the primitive manners, the customs and mode of life of the Indians are reproduced with a fidelity that convinces. No other work that we know shows so well the stoicism, the melancholy, the fatalism, the poetical imagination, the indifference to life of the Indians, to whom all nature was a living thing through which and over which was the Master of Life.

William McLennan (1856-1904) was the author of three notable books of fiction, of an excellent volume of translations, *Songs of Old Canada*, and of original stories and essays of a high order. His collection of short stories, *In Old France and New*, portrays French character on two continents, subtly distinguishing between the life in France and in Canada. *Spanish John* is his best-known book ; the style is good, the characters possess reality ; it is crowded with stirring incidents and the life of the time dealt with is faithfully reproduced. *The Span o' Life*, a historical novel of the days of Prince Charlie, was written in collaboration with Jean N. McIlwraith. It is a most readable story, with a romantic colour that is heightened by the bursts of song scattered through its pages.

W. A. Fraser first appealed to the public in his book, *The Eye of a God and Other Stories*, published in 1892, and has since produced many short stories and several novels. He is strongest in his short stories, several of which take rank among the best of modern times. The influence of Kipling is to be found in his work, and evidently he has closely studied the method of that master. Fraser has made the race-track his peculiar field. Among his best-known books are *Mooswa and Others of the Boundaries*, *The Outcast*, *Thoroughbreds*, *Brave Hearts* and *Sa'Zada Tales*.

Edward W. Thomson is a Canadian writer of varied experience. In 1865 Thomson, then a mere boy, enlisted in the American army and served with the Federal forces on the Potomac. In the following year, 1866, he was at Ridgeway doing duty against the Fenian invaders. He began his business career as an engineer and later joined the staff of the Toronto *Globe*. He is widely known as a sound writer on political questions, and also as a writer of excellent verse. He is seen at his best in his stories : *Old Man Savarin and Other Stories*, *Walter Gibbs*, *The Young Boss and Other Stories*, *Between Earth and Sky* and *Peter Ottawa*, while being mainly for boys, can be enjoyed by both young and old. The characters are types of vigorous Canadian boyhood and manhood. Canadian forests, fields and streams are the theatre, and the incidents are depicted with a strength that could only be given to them by a man of action.

Robert Barr (1850-1912) was born in Glasgow and received his early education in Ontario, and for a few years taught school in that province. From 1876 until 1888 he was on the staff of the Detroit *Free Press* ; and after that, until the time of his death, he lived in England. He could not be called a great novelist, nor is there in his work much

Canadian atmosphere. Indeed, his only story on a Canadian theme is *In the Midst of Alarms*, a story of the Fenian raid. He depends not so much on plot as on incident and on touches of humour that brighten his pages. His brother, James Barr (Angus Evan Abbott), was born in 1862 in Wallace-town, Ontario, but has since 1883 lived in England, where he has been engaged in journalism. He has written several excellent novels, which, however, are not widely known in his native land.

James Macdonald Oxley (1855-1907) wrote numerous boys' stories based on historical incidents, travels and adventures. These stories cover a wide range of territory. *Fife and Drum at Louisburg* deals with the siege of the fortress conducted by the New England troops under William Pepperrell and the British fleet under Admiral Warren in 1745. *Archie of Athabasca* takes the reader into the Far North of the Dominion, and *Up among the Ice-floes* gives thrilling adventures in the Arctic regions. All of Oxley's books are virile and healthy—excellent stories, fine in their descriptive passages and character drawing.

Arthur J. Stringer was born in London, Ontario, in 1876. After studying at the University of Toronto and at Oxford, he served his apprenticeship to literature in that excellent school, journalism, and was for a year on the staff of the Montreal *Herald*. In 1898 he moved to the United States, and, while still remaining a summer resident of Canada, has made New York city his home, and has written verse and prose largely in a manner suited to the taste of the magazine-reading public of the United States. He has produced much dainty verse, fine in thought and excellent in technique. Several of his novels, such as *The Silver Poppy* and *The Wire Tappers*, have been very popular, but they have little of the permanent value of Parker's *Battle of the Strong* or *The Judgment House* or of Duncan's *Dr Luke of the Labrador*.

One of the latest to enter the field of romance is the Rev. Robert Knowles, pastor of Knox Church, Galt, Ontario. He is a writer of the religio-sentimental school, and though his books are widely read they do not appeal to thoughtful men and women. *St Cuthbert's, The Undertow, The Attic Guest*, etc., lack variety. Incidents, situations, characters are too often mere repetitions.

Mrs Everard Cotes (Sara Jeannette Duncan), who began her literary career under the nom de plume ' Garth Grafton,' was born in Brantford, Ontario. Mrs Cotes is the most voluminous of Canadian women writers, having written in all nearly twenty volumes. She first attained distinction in 1890 by her delightfully humorous travel book, *A Social Departure ; or, How Orthodocia and I went round the World by Ourselves*. This book is vivid in its description, kindly in its humour, delightful in its genial sarcasm. Mrs Cotes has long lived in India, and has done much to make the native and official life of that important part of the Empire known to the world. Her books have not Canadian themes or Canadian characters : *An Imperialist*, published in 1904, is her only story with a Canadian setting. She has a place well towards the front rank of modern humorists. Mrs Cotes is a keen observer of life, with exceptional descriptive powers, and a style that sparkles and scintillates, her pages bubbling over with incisive wit. She holds easily the first place among women writers of fiction born in the Dominion.

In the little fertile island province washed by the waters of the Atlantic and inhabited by a people of simple manners and customs, a novelist appeared in the closing years of the nineteenth century who was to make Prince Edward Island, its inhabitants and external nature, known to the world as they never had been before. Lucy Maud Montgomery, at that time a school-teacher in the province, sprang suddenly into fame by her first book, *Anne of Green Gables*. In 1911 Miss Montgomery married the Rev. Ewen McDonald, and has since resided in Ontario. *Anne of Green Gables*, published in 1908, took the reading public by storm. It won eulogies from such appreciative critics as Mark Twain— who called it the ' sweetest creation of child life yet written ' —and Bliss Carman, who said that Anne, the heroine, must ' always remain one of the immortal children of fiction.' Other books by this author are *Anne of Avonlea, Kilmeny of the Orchard* and *The Story Girl*. Sympathy with child life and humble life, delight in nature, a penetrating, buoyant imagination, unusual power in handling the simple romantic material that lies about every one, and a style direct and pleasing, make these books delightful reading for children and, indeed, for readers of all ages.

Alice Jones, daughter of the late lieutenant-governor of Nova Scotia, A. G. Jones, is one of the noteworthy women writers of fiction in the Dominion. Her naturally fine intellect was sharpened and broadened by study in France and Italy. She first won a place in public estimation by her story, *A Hazard of Hearts*—which appeared in Frank Leslie's *Monthly*. This author has written five other stories : *The Night Hawk*—which she wrote under the nom de plume ' Alix John,' *Bubbles We Buy*—issued in England under the name Isabel Broderick, *Gabriel Praed's Castle, At the Harbour's Mouth* and *The Consul's Niece*. *Gabriel Praed's Castle*, published in 1904, is undoubtedly her strongest book both in plot construction and character portrayal.

Joanna E. Wood was born in Scotland, but came with her parents to Canada when a child. Her home is on the picturesque heights of Queenston, a spot unexcelled for beauty in Canada and replete with historical and romantic material. This author has produced in all seven novels : *Judith Moore, The Untempered Wind, The Lynchpin Sensation, A Daughter of Witches, Where Waters Beckon, Farden Ha'* and *Unto the Third Generation*. In her works she shows an intimate acquaintance with early conditions in Canada, and treats her subjects with artistic fineness and praiseworthy seriousness.

Lily Dougall, formerly of Montreal but now for over twenty years a resident of Great Britain, should, like Robert Barr, be classed among purely British writers. She is one of the most cultured women writers of the day ; all her novels have a purpose and have as their motifs social or moral problems.

Among other Canadian women worthy of special note who have written novels are : Blanche Lucile Macdonell, Agnes Maule Machar (' Fidelis '), Jean N. McIlwraith, Emily P. Weaver and Mrs S. F. Harrison.

VII

POETRY

THE chief glory of Canadian literature is its poetry. Scarcely had the guns ceased thundering against the walls of Louisbourg and Quebec before Canadian themes attracted the attention of writers. But the first poets who dealt with Canadian subjects were Canadian in no true sense of the word, and it was not until the beginning of the nineteenth century that Canadian-born writers began to express themselves in verse. In 1759 a poem entitled *The Reduction of Louisbourg* was published, and in 1766 another appeared under the name of *The Conquest of Canada ; or, the Siege of Quebec: a Tragedy.* These heroic themes stirred the imagination of sojourners in Canada.

There is much in British North America to inspire poets. No country in the world offers material for more varied themes. Broad rivers, leaping rapids, vast forests, fertile plains, eternal hills—every variety of scene is to be found in the Dominion of Canada and all have had their singers. The struggles of the pioneers against the savage wilderness, the dangers experienced by the hardy fisher-folk by the sea, the battling of the first inhabitants against the Indians, the fight for national existence during the Revolutionary War and the War of 1812, offer many themes. Poets, for the most part inadequately equipped, have essayed in humble, faltering verse to deal with every phase of Canadian nature and Canadian life.

It is not easy to say who was the first strictly Canadian poet worthy of mention. The honour would seem to belong to Oliver Goldsmith—a significant name. Goldsmith was a Nova Scotian, a distant connection of the immortal Oliver, and was born in Annapolis County in 1787. He held several important government positions in his native province, and died in Liverpool, England, in 1861. His poem, *The Rising Village*, published in 1825, is in many ways a remarkable one. It deals very fully with pioneer life in Canada. The struggle with rude nature is admirably described. From the breaking of the soil until the peaceful village, prosperous and happy, stands fair to the eye, each step is told in verse, showing perhaps no high degree of art, but vigorous and correct. The poem is an imitation of Goldsmith's *Deserted Village*, and is eighteenth-century in manner and feeling. The following passage will serve to show its character :

> Here the broad march extends its open plain,
> Until its limits touch the distant main ;
> There verdant meads along the uplands spring,
> And grateful odours to the breezes fling ;
> Here crops of grain in rich luxuriance rise,
> And wave their golden riches to the skies.
>
> .   .   .   .
>
> The farmer's cottage, bosomed 'mong the trees,
> Whose spreading branches shelter from the breeze :
> The winding stream that turns the busy mill
> Whose clanking echoes o'er the distant hill ;
> The neat white church beside whose walls are spread
> The grass-clad hillocks of the sacred dead,
> Where rude-cut stones or painted tablets tell,
> In laboured verse, how youth and beauty fell.

In these simple yet finely descriptive lines English-Canadian poetry may be said to have had an appropriate beginning. In humble verse Oliver Goldsmith recorded the hopes and fears, the struggles and victories, of the pioneer settlers in Canada.

John Fleming of Montreal was even earlier in verse-making than Oliver Goldsmith, but he was not Canadian-born, and his verse (it can hardly be called poetry) was in no sense of the word Canadian. The only poem by which he is remembered is ' An Ode on the Birthday of King George III.' This poem is stiff, wooden, stilted. It has little poetical feeling and abounds in hackneyed poetical phrases.

Robert Sweeny, a native of Ireland, published in 1826 *Odds and Ends*, a volume containing many dainty lyrics. Adam Kidd, born in Ireland in 1802, published in 1830, one year before his death in Quebec, a volume *The Huron Chief and Other Poems*. The theme makes this volume distinctively Canadian. Kidd sang the sorrows of the unfortunate Hurons, and his lines prove him to have been an enthusiastic admirer of the sublime and beautiful in Canadian scenery. In his minor poems he shows the influence of Tom Moore and echoes his music.

Charles Dawson Shanly (1811-75) and James McCarroll (1815-96) both did excellent work in verse. Shanly was born and educated in Dublin, Ireland, and remained for only a brief period in Canada. McCarroll was likewise an Irishman, born in the county of Longford. He came as a boy of sixteen to Canada, and during a busy official and journalistic career, ' amid the thunder of the presses and the myriad-voiced confusion of public office life, he has found a quiet place within himself full of flowers and sun-light, the notes of birds and the murmur of streams.'[1] McCarroll's ' The Humming Bird,' ' The Grey Linnet ' and ' The Vesper Hymn ' are worthy of a place in any collection of Canadian verse.

It was not, however, until 1856 that a poet of more than ordinary skill in art, and one who was to hold a prominent place in Canadian literature, appeared. In this year Charles Sangster (1822-93) published by subscription *The St Lawrence and the Saguenay and Other Poems*. Sangster was born in Kingston, Upper Canada. He held a position in the ordnance office in his native town and for a period was engaged in newspaper work in Amherstburg and Kingston—two places which from their historical associations could not but stir the national pride and the imagination of a man of talent.

Sangster's early volumes showed an intense love of Canada and Canadian institutions, a pleasing poetical taste and fine singing qualities, but a lack of imagination and vigour. In 1860, in *Hesperus and Other Poems and Lyrics*, he struck a loftier note. He showed a deeper insight into nature and her moods, and in his patriotic poems, 'Brock,' ' Wolfe ' and ' A Song for Canada,' did much to foster the

---

[1] From Charles L. Hildreth's Introduction to McCarroll's *Madeline and Other Poems*, 1889.

national sentiment that seven years later culminated in Confederation.

Although even his most enthusiastic admirers could hardly call his work great, Sangster will ever be valued by Canadians. His poetry is simple, humble, unpretentious, patriotic; but so thin is the vein he worked that during the last twenty years of his life he wrote but very little poetry. It could hardly have been otherwise. He had a small stock of ideas on which to draw; his early education had been very limited, and he was without the energy that gave such men as Burns and Whittier the power of educating themselves. They had, too, what he had not —the contact with literary minds more widely cultivated than their own. However, one of his poems at least has had a wider acceptance than any other by a Canadian poet. His stirring lyric on ' The Rapid ' is a vivid, rousing bit of work. In language and rhythm it is splendidly imitative of the rush and sweep of the tumbling, leaping stretch of water so characteristic of Canadian streams.

In 1857 a poem that was to attract the attention of scholars in Canada, in England, and in the United States was published in Montreal. *Saul* was as much apart from other Canadian literary efforts as was Saul in Israel from the men of his time. It had a vigour, an intensity, a dramatic excellence that no other Canadian poem before its time, or indeed until the closing years of the nineteenth century, approaches. *Saul* was from the pen of Charles Heavysege, who, at the time of its publication, was a cabinet-maker working at his trade in Montreal. Heavysege was born in Huddersfield, England, in 1816 and did not come to Canada until 1853. While in England he had already tried his hand at literature and had published one book, *The Revolt of Tartarus*. Four years after his arrival in Canada *Saul* appeared. It was a drama—the purest and most difficult form of literary composition—a massive piece of work, divided into three parts of five acts each, and contained in all about ten thousand lines. The poetry throughout was in the grand manner. Heavysege was not educated in the ordinary sense of the word, but had saturated his mind with the Bible and Shakespeare's dramas, and his ideas, borrowed largely from these sources and his own broodings over the problems of life and death, were presented with a dignity, austerity, epic grandeur and dramatic intensity such as are to be found in few poetic compositions first published in Canada, or, for that matter, on the American continent.

The characters in the drama, such as Saul, Malzah (Saul's evil spirit), David and Samuel, are magnificently sustained. Heavysege had thoroughly grasped the Hebrew spirit, and his language, if somewhat prolix, has a prophet-like majesty, a seer-like intonation which helped to give *Saul* a place among the few really powerful dramas in English literature since the age of the great Elizabeth. It was never intended for the stage, but it has at times—though rarely, it is true—a force that recalls some of Shakespeare's most dramatic passages. Saul's vision, during his visit to the Witch of Endor, on the eve of his death is not unworthy of a place beside Richard III's on the eve of Bosworth Field. His sword had slain many; his victims rise before him and he vainly strives to shut out the spectacle with the words :

> Who comes before me yonder, clothed in blood?
> Away, old man, so sad and terrible ;—
> Away, Ahimelech, I slew thee not !—
> Nor these—nor these thy sons, a ghastly train.
> Nay, fix not here your dull, accusing eyes,
> Your stiff tongues move not, your white lips are dumb ;
> You give no word unto the ambient air ;
> You see no figure of surrounding things ;
> You are as stony, carven effigies. . . .
> Out, vipers, scorpions, and ye writhing dragons !
> Hydras, wag not your heads at me, nor roll
> At me your fiery eyes.

Of *Saul* the *North British Review* said : ' Indubitably one of the most remarkable English poems ever written outside of Great Britain.'

Heavysege is commonly classed as a Canadian author, but erroneously so. The circumstance of his residence in Canada and the fact that his work was printed there are in no way essential; he might have resided anywhere and have written the same book. He was thirty-seven years old when he arrived in Canada. *Saul*, as we have seen, was published four years later. The length of the poem and its general characteristics and finish would indicate that years were spent in its preparation. It is probable that it took shape in Heavysege's mind early in life and that the poem was composed before he left England; but, even granting that it may have been written in Canada, Heavysege was an English rather than a Canadian writer.

Besides *Saul* Heavysege published a volume of sonnets in 1855, *Jephthah's Daughter* and in 1860 *Count Filippo; or, The Unequal Marriage*. During the later period of his life he was engaged in journalism. He died in Montreal in 1879, lamented by all who knew him.

Alexander McLachlan (1818-96) was a poet of a very different stamp. He was a native of Scotland and came to Canada in 1840 at the age of twenty-two. He was a tailor, and while working at his trade composed poems that gained him an appreciative audience. His first volume of verse appeared in 1845 and was followed by *Lyrics* in 1858, *The Emigrant and Other Poems* (1861), and *Poems and Songs* (1874). In 1900 a complete edition of his poems, carefully edited and with numerous notes and a glossary, was published. McLachlan's love of man and of nature won him many admirers, but, while his verse appeals to the heart, every poem he penned has serious flaws due to a lack of education and of the power of self-criticism. Had he devoted much of the time he gave to composition to studying the masters of English verse, he might have achieved something really fine in poetry, but his work as it stands is commonplace and defective and adds nothing to Canadian literature, even though, from the great heart of the poet and the mind eager to enjoy nature and to cause others to enjoy it with him, he will continue to find readers among those who care much for feeling and little for art.

Thomas D'Arcy McGee (1825-68) was a poet of considerable power, despite the fact that he was a busy publicist and a hard-working politician. He spent only eleven years of his life in Canada, and, although he was one of the Fathers of Confederation and a minister of the crown, and published a volume of poems entitled *Canadian Ballads and Occasional Verses,* Canadians have no right to claim him as one of their poets. His volume of verse was published one year after he arrived in Canada. D'Arcy M\cGee, therefore, must be classed as an Irish poet. An Irishman he was by birth and at heart. His work is steeped in Irish feeling and his poetry has in it much of the music of Moore.

The year 1880 marks what has not unfittingly been called by J. D. Logan the Canadian Renaissance. A new era began with the publication of *Orion and Other Poems.* This volume was the work of a mere boy, Charles G. D. Roberts, who was born in New Brunswick in 1860, and at the time of its publication was teaching school in Chatham, in that province.

Orion and Other Poems attracted wide attention on its appearance, for it differed from all previous attempts at poetry in Canada. Here was verse of a high order, carefully done, showing scholarship and with something of the atmosphere of Shelley, Keats and Tennyson. There was nothing provincial about it. It was rich in itself and rich in promise. The themes were largely classical ; the young poet had not dared to venture into original fields. It was serious verse throughout, and was free from the crudities that had marred the greater portion of Canadian poetry. Except for a too evident striving after literary conceits, a superabundance of epithets and an ornateness to be expected of a youth under twenty, the poems were, indeed, almost flawless.

Six years later Roberts's second volume, *In Divers Tones,* appeared. In this volume the poet showed a vast step in advance of his earlier work. His style was more subdued. He had largely broken away from classical subjects, and had his eye fixed on nature as he saw it about him. In 1893 his *Songs of the Common Day* was given to the world. This collection of poems showed still further growth : the art was finer and more mature, and inspiration was found largely 'in common forms' and 'the soul of unregarded things.' The volume *Songs of the Common Day* contains Roberts's most ambitious and sustained effort in verse— 'Ave' (published separately in 1892), an elegy written to commemorate the death of Shelley. Not only is this ode great as a Canadian poem, but it is also important as an English elegy and is worthy of study alongside of such a poem as Matthew Arnold's 'Thyrsis.' 'Ave' has a virile force, a sensuous splendour, an artistic excellence that make it compare favourably with the best work done in the United States and with the work of any of the recent singers of Great Britain. Its power can be judged from the following stanza :

> Thyself the lark melodious in mid-heaven ;
>   Thyself the Protean shape of chainless cloud,
> Pregnant with elemental fire, and driven
>   Through deeps of quivering light, and darkness loud
> With tempest, yet beneficent as prayer ;
>   Thyself the wild west wind, relentless strewing
> The withered leaves of custom on the air,
>   And through the wreck pursuing
> O'er lovelier Arnos, more imperial Romes,
> Thy radiant visions to their viewless homes.

While this poem is in memory of Shelley, and while it characterizes with power and fidelity the work and life of that master genius, it is of peculiar interest as a truly Canadian poem with Canadian atmosphere and colour. Shelley had been an inspiration to Roberts, and with Shelley was associated in the poet's mind the spot in nature that first lifted his heart above the material aspect of things and made song vibrate in his brain. Those vast Westmoreland flats, 'miles and miles, level, and grassy, and dim ' ; that red sweep of weedy shore, the blue hills, the sea mists, 'the sting of buffeting salt '—his life is full of them. Shelley strikes ' with wondering awe his inward sight,' and these are the very words he uses to describe the influence of the Tantramar marshes on his being. 'Ave' to be appreciated must be studied as a whole, but there are in it many passages that stand out with peculiar lyrical prominence. A few will serve to show the poetic gems it contains :

> And speechless ecstasy of growing June.

> Again I heard the song
> Of the glad bobolink, whose lyric throat
> Pealed like a tangle of small bells afloat.

> The common waters, the familiar woods,
> And the great hills' inviolate solitudes.

> But all about the tumult of his heart
> Stretched the great calm of his celestial art.

The other poems in *Songs of the Common Day* are all worthy of close study. About his nature verse there will be found an aroma of marsh and salt sea air, a delight in Canadian woods and Canadian fields.

In *The Book of the Native*, published in 1897, Roberts made a still further advance. The influence of the years that bring the philosophic mind was manifest, for the author now grappled with deeper problems. In such a poem as ' Origins ' he showed the action of the modern scientific spirit upon him. In this study he brings man into vital, physical contact with nature, and poetically awakens the mind to the influence of heredity and the kinship of all created things.

In 1898 *New York Nocturnes* was published ; and in 1901 a volume of collected verse appeared containing all his poems written before 1898 that Roberts wished to preserve. *The Book of the Rose* was given to the public several years later, and showed that though he was devoting himself largely to the writing of fiction and animal stories, he had lost none of his delicate art or his refined fancy. It must be said of Roberts, however, that his work has not an ethical centre, nor is he to be considered as an interpreter of life. But his poetry is something that should give pride to his fellow-countrymen. In *Roberts and the Influence of his Time*, already mentioned, James Cappon unhesitatingly says of Roberts that he ' is certainly the most distinguished of our

Canadian poets, those, at any rate, who use the English language.' In commenting on a number of passages selected to show the genius of the poet, Cappon remarks : ' If these passages were found in Wordsworth, say in the series of sonnets on the Duddon, they would be quoted by every one as fine and subtle renderings of the moods of Nature.' This is high praise from a critic of acknowledged authority, and ought to bring Canadians to study the work of Roberts ; but this money-worshipping age, this age of prose and reason, is impatient of poetry.

Archibald Lampman was a spirit of the rarest excellence. Of him William Dean Howells wrote : ' His pure spirit was electrical in every line ; he made no picture of the Nature he loved in which he did not supply the spectator with the human interest of his own genial presence, and light up the scene with the lamp of his keen and beautiful intelligence.' And again : ' The stir of leaf, of wind, of foot ; the drifting odours of the wood and the field ; the colours of the flowers, of skies, of dusty roads and shadowy streams and solitary lakes, all so preciously new, give his reader the thrill of the intense life of the northern solstice.' On account of the beauties that Howells found in Lampman's work many critics have given that poet the first place in Canadian literature.

Archibald Lampman was born in Morpeth, Ontario, in 1861. He was of United Empire Loyalist stock on both his mother's and father's side. His father was a clergyman of the Anglican Church, a scholar, and himself no mean poet. From his earliest days Archibald Lampman was delicate. While a child his parents moved to Gore's Landing, a small village on the shore of Rice Lake. Here in his seventh year young Lampman contracted rheumatic fever, which left him a cripple for four years and physically weak for the rest of his too short life. He received his education at Trinity College School, Port Hope, and at Trinity College, Toronto. In these institutions he laid the sound foundation of the scholarship that marks his poetical achievement. For a brief period after graduation he taught school, and then entered the civil service at Ottawa, where he spent the remainder of his days faithfully doing the drudgery of office work, but ever keeping his sunrise aim, devotion to poetry. In February 1899, while the winter blasts swept his loved Ottawa valley, Lampman's spirit went to its eternal rest. His death at the age of thirty-eight was a most severe loss to Canadian literature. He was the one poet who had been altogether faithful to his art. He was a dreamer of poetical dreams and would allow nothing to turn him aside from clothing his dreams in exquisite verse forms.

During Lampman's lifetime he published two volumes: *Among the Millet and Other Poems* in 1888 and *Lyrics of Earth* in 1896. At the time of his death another volume, *Alcyone*, was in press. In 1900 his complete poems were brought out. The work of editing this volume was entrusted to his friend and fellow-poet, Duncan Campbell Scott. The excellent memoir by the editor is in itself a fine piece of work, both as biography and as appreciative literary criticism.

Archibald Lampman undoubtedly ranks high as a nature poet. Every season, every month in the year, every phase of nature seen along the Ottawa valley has been interpreted by him. He saw beauty in life's commonest things. Even the harsh croaking of the frogs gave him a subject for most melodious verse. A selection from the poem ' Heat ' will serve to show his genius better than could any descriptive notes :

> From plains that reel to southward, dim,
>   The road runs by me white and bare ;
> Up the steep hill it seems to swim
>   Beyond, and melt into the glare.
> Upward, half-way, or it may be
>   Nearer the summit, slowly steals
> A hay cart, moving dustily
>   With idly clacking wheels.
>
> By his cart's side the wagoner
>   Is slouching slowly at his ease
> Half-hidden in the windless blur
>   Of white dust puffing to his knees.

This wagon on the height above,
From sky to sky on either hand,
Is the sole thing that seems to move
In all the heat-held land.

Beyond me, in the fields, the sun
Soaks in the grass and hath his will;
I count the marguerites one by one;
Even the buttercups are still.
On the brook yonder not a breath
Disturbs the spider or the midge.
The water-bugs draw close beneath
The cool gloom of the bridge.

With a rapid pencil the poet has here limned a common Canadian country scene with the vigour and truth of a Millet. Lampman continually lived close to the heart of nature, and nature revealed herself to him and gave him the power to reveal her to others with a natural magic. He was, too, a consummate artist. He knew the value of words, and an examination of the passage quoted will show with what aptness, with what imaginative force he was able to use language. There is a pictorial splendour in such a poem as 'Heat,' a power of painting a broad landscape and giving at the same time its minutest details. Nor is it without its humanistic touch. That wagoner 'slouching slowly at his ease' adds human interest to the scene. In the background of it all there is ever the poet himself with his illuminating mind—'his keen and beautiful intelligence.'

Lampman was a master of the sonnet. Through this little instrument he breathed out some of his most beautiful and serious thoughts. Such sonnets as 'Truth,' 'Prayer,' 'Knowledge' and 'Sight' show the intense earnestness of the poet. His first desire was to be true; his prayer was for power to do worthy work and for the knowledge that gives insight. Lampman's work has not the splendid sensuousness of Carman's verse, nor has he handled as many and varied themes as Roberts; he lacks, too, the moral profundity of William Wilfred Campbell in that poet's inspired moments, but as an interpreter of nature in all her gentler phases he stands by himself. A knowledge of his verse will open the eyes and ears of all who read it to the marvellous beauties of the fields and streams and woods that lie about them.

William Wilfred Campbell is another of the recent Canadian poets who have attracted many readers. He was born in Ontario in 1860, and was educated in Toronto and in Cambridge, Massachusetts. In 1885 he was ordained to the ministry of the Church of England. He gave up the ministry in 1891 and entered the civil service at Ottawa. He first came into literary prominence by his volume *Lake Lyrics and Other Poems*, published in 1889. This was followed by *The Dread Voyage* and *Beyond the Hills of Dream*, volumes showing no great advance in art but a firmer grip on the problems of existence. His tragedies *Mordred* and *Hildebrand* are powerful in thought. Although both dramas are somewhat loosely constructed, they have the distinction of being the ablest dramatic work produced in Canada. In *Mordred* the poet deals with an Arthurian theme, but he was unhappy in his selection of a subject. The unspeakable crime of Arthur does not make pleasant reading. Again, in a field so thoroughly exploited by such a master poet as Tennyson, it was difficult to avoid imitation. The Tennysonian note is prominent throughout the drama, and characters and manner are often little more than echoes. Dramatic force is frequently lacking, and in its place there is the epic note. In 1905 Campbell published his *Collected Poems*, a volume of some three hundred and fifty pages. He is undoubtedly a poet of power. He has a profundity of thought, a seriousness and an ethical purpose which no other Canadian poet possesses to the same degree. To him art is secondary.

One of his poems at least is pre-eminently great in idea and workmanship. 'The Mother' ranks with the very finest poems of modern times. 'A Present Day Creed,' 'The Blind Caravan,' 'Soul,' 'The Glory of the Dying Day' are among his most characteristic lyrics. 'Lazarus' is one of his strongest and most typical poems. The thought in it is the essential thing. Whittier, in 'The Cry of a Lost Soul,' has in his simple manner developed the same idea—

the cry of a lost soul reaching the ears of a spirit in heaven would cause suffering where it is generally supposed no suffering can be. Lazarus, in Campbell's poem, as he listens to an agonized voice rising suppliant, says :

> This is no heaven with all its shining hosts ;
> This is no heaven until that hell doth die.

In ' Lazarus,' as in most of his other poems, the poet is so much preoccupied with the idea beating in his brain that he is not always careful of his art, and there are lines that need polishing and thoughts that need recasting ; but these are the knots in the oak.

Bliss Carman is a Canadian poet who is held in the highest repute in the United States. By many he is considered the most eminent lyrical poet of the North American continent, and not a few agree with Arthur J. Stringer when he calls him ' the sweetest lyrist of America.'

Carman was born in Fredericton, New Brunswick, in 1861 and is of United Empire Loyalist descent. He received his early education under George R. Parkin at the collegiate institute in his native city. After a brilliant career in the provincial university he spent several years in post-graduate work in Edinburgh and Harvard Universities. In 1890 he began his literary career in New York city as literary editor of the *Independent*. He was afterwards connected with the *Atlantic Monthly* and the *Cosmopolitan*, and in 1894 published the *Chap Book* in Chicago. He later engaged in literary work in Europe, and his experience in Old World cities and scenes has done not a little to colour his verse. In everything his equipment is an ideal one for a poet: he is a good scholar ; he has had wide experience with life in the New World and the Old, and excellent opportunities for studying nature in all her moods. His first volume of verse appeared in 1893, and between that date and 1913 he has given the world nearly thirty volumes in verse and prose. His first book was entitled *Low Tide on Grand Pré*. This was followed by three volumes entitled *Songs from Vagabondia*, written in partnership with Richard Hovey. His more important volumes of verse are *Behind the Arras* (1895), *Ballads of*

Lost Haven (1897), and the series of five volumes under the general title *Pipes of Pan*, which contained his best work done between 1897 and 1905. He has also written several prose works which from the point of view of style are admirable.

Carman has a song for every mood, and passes with ease from the grim, ghastly, grotesque force of ' The Red Wolf ' to the rich beauties of the songs of the *Pipes of Pan* series or the exquisitely suggestive, longing plaintiveness of ' Exit Anima.' He has not written, save in his early tentative efforts, on distinctively Canadian themes, but the colour of much of his work is Canadian. Even in *Pipes of Pan*, Greek in tone and colour, when he deals with nature, the voices of the birds and beasts that reach his ear, the colours that flash before his eyes from meadow, forest and hillside, are those with which he was familiar in his New Brunswick home. In ' Beyond the Gamut ' his two lines,

> Dared the unknown with Blake and Galileo,
> Fronted death with Daulac's seventeen,

show how his heart feels towards Canada. Instead of Daulac we might have expected some such name as Leonidas in this combination, but the hero of New France appealed to Bliss Carman with more force than the hero of Thermopylae.

It is not an easy task to characterize Carman's work. He is a sort of twentieth-century blend of Omar Khayyam, Shelley and Robert Browning, with Tennyson's art thrown in to give delicate flavour to the whole. Not that he is as supremely great as any of these, but his thought and manner of expression suggest no lesser creative artists. He has Omar's love of sensuous beauty, Shelley's lyrical power, Browning's force and often his vagueness, and something of Tennyson's skill in concentrating an idea or scene into a uniquely obtrusive word or phrase. At times he combines imaginative power with realistic force. There is also a Norse atmosphere to much of his work. ' The Yule Guest,' ' The Last Watch,' parts of ' Outbound,' and ' The Tidings to Olaf ' have something of the feeling inspired by the Norse sagas. ' Marsyas ' and ' Beyond the Gamut ' are exquisite pieces of lofty music and compare favourably with Browning's masterpiece in music, ' A Toccata of Galuppi's.' They have much of Browning's manner, while they are at the same time the distinctive product of Carman's own individuality. But the poem ' Pipes of Pan ' in *From the Book of the Myths* is in many ways his supreme effort. It is Greek, pagan, and gives an excellent interpretation of nature. The poet has entered thoroughly into the spirit of the early world in which men saw naiads, nymphs, dryads and oreads in every stream, grove, tree and mountain. It has, too, a colour and movement that suggest the Elizabethan renaissance, and is in many ways not unlike Milton's ' L'Allegro ' and ' Il Penseroso.' Although the groundwork of the poem is Greek, Pan in this poem is wandering through and piping in Canadian scenes. ' Pipes of Pan ' is of its kind a perfect piece of work ; no jarring note is heard ; thought, rhythm and language make a harmonious whole.

George Frederick Cameron (1854-85) is one of the most spontaneous of Canadian singers. Cameron was born in New Glasgow, Nova Scotia, but when fifteen years old he became a resident of Boston, and the greater part of his literary life was spent in that United States centre of culture. Even before going to Boston he had produced some excellent verse. The lyrical cry is to a marked degree present in every line he wrote. When pleasure or pain smote upon his spirit he burst into song. Love, liberty, the mysteries of life and death—these were his themes. There is nothing of a dramatic character in his work and but little that is descriptive. Characteristic of his best work are the two stanzas entitled ' Standing on Tiptoe,' which appeared in the volume *Lyrics*, published after his death :

> Standing on tiptoe ever since my youth,
>   Striving to grasp the future just above,
> I hold at length the only future—Truth,
>   And Truth is Love.
>
> I feel as one who, being a while confined,
>   Sees drop to dust about him all his bars :—
> The clay grows less, and leaving it, the mind
>   Dwells with the stars.

Much of his work was written in the cause of liberty. Wherever he saw oppression—in Ireland, Russia, or Cuba—he raged in song against it. There is a lyrical force and fire in his songs written between 1868 and 1872 on Spanish oppression in Cuba that may have done something to keep alive the fire of indignation which burst into flame twenty-five years later, and this humble Canadian singer may have played his part in driving Spain from the American continent. These poems were popular when published and are the best lyrics written on suffering Cuba. Cameron returned to Canada in 1882, and during the last three years of his too brief life did some of his best work—calmer in tone, deeper in thought and finer in workmanship than his early verse, yet with all its lyrical rush and sweep and spontaneity.

Robert Service is one of the most popular of the poets who have written in the Dominion, and though he is not a Canadian, his poems are distinctly a product of Canada and have to be considered in any review of Canadian verse. Service is of Scottish descent and was born in England in 1876. He came to Canada in 1897, and, while in the employment of the Bank of Commerce in the Yukon, was inspired by the grandeur and tragedy of that region to write three volumes of verse: *Songs of a Sourdough, Ballads of a Cheechako* and *Rhymes of a Rolling Stone.* His power lies in depicting rugged mountain scenery, the awful sublimity of the Arctic world, the vast beauty of such natural phenomena as the 'silver dance of the mystic Northern Lights,' and the rough, brutal, vicious life of a primitive mining region. There are in his work isolated passages of great power. The masculine force and dramatic intensity of his lines, the strong music of his stanzas, the admiration for the heroic in man attracted the public, and he found wide appreciation. He has nothing of the artistic fineness of the work of Roberts, Carman or Lampman, but he drives home some eternal truths with sledge-hammer blows. Other Canadian poets play pleasing songs on their rustic pipes, but Service has a whole anvil chorus. He has, however, the defects of his qualities to a marked degree. He too often forgets that vulgarity is not strength, that brutality is not force. Some of his subjects are unspeakable, and many of his best poems are marred by unnecessary coarseness.

William Henry Drummond (1854-1909) was born in Ireland, but at an early age he came to Canada, and the whole of his literary work is Canadian. His distinction lies in his having created, or rather discovered, a striking and, in many respects, an original character in literature. True, the habitant had been presented in prose and verse before his day, but although such writers as William McLennan had made careful studies, charming in their simplicity and truth, of this picturesque figure of Canadian life, Drummond made him his own, and gave an exhaustive interpretation of his homely, kindly character. The broken English of the habitant is used as the vehicle for the poet's expression, and Drummond handles it with skill and makes his characters living beings. He had a genuine affection for the French-Canadian peasants, and, while presenting them in verse inimitable for its humour, he never caricatures them. He studied them on their farms and in their homes, and, through his sympathy, he was able to depict their lives with great fidelity.

During his lifetime Drummond published four volumes of verse : *The Habitant and Other French-Canadian Poems, Johnny Courteau and Other Poems, Phil O'-Rum's Canoe and Madeline Verchères* and *The Voyageur and Other Poems.* In 1909, shortly after his death, another volume was issued. The public never tired of Drummond's work. His wit and humour, the kindly smile that played through every line, and his tender pathos when dealing with the sorrows of the habitants gave him a wide audience of enthusiastic admirers. The habitant of Drummond will live in Canadian literature. Johnny Courteau, the members of the Laramie family, and the crew of the wood-scow *Julie Plante* will go down the ages hand in hand with ' Sam Slick.'

Charles Mair as a poet is as old as the Dominion. He was born in Ontario in 1840 and in 1868 published his first volume of verse, *Dreamland and Other Poems.* He is best known as the author of *Tecumseh,* a drama in five acts, first published in 1886. *Tecumseh* abounds in noble sentiments and shows insight into Indian life and character. The language of the Indians, however, is not natural ; sentiments and form of speech are those of a cultivated Englishman rather than of such Indians as Tecumseh and the Prophet. The movement of the verse has not the freedom, the conversational overflow essential to dramatic utterance. Too much of it is in the epic rather than the dramatic manner, but it has many fine passages and striking lines. Mair's poems ' A Ballad for Brave Women,' in which he sings the courage and patriotism of Laura Secord, and ' The Last Bison ' are in many ways finer than *Tecumseh*. His description of the bison is most impressive :

> His shining horns
> Gleamed black amidst his fell of floating hair;
> His neck and shoulders, of the lion's build,
> Were framed to toss the world.

Frederick George Scott of Quebec has been one of the most persistent of Canadian poets, having published six or seven volumes of verse. His work has no distinctive note. He is a careful artist, and writes almost exclusively in a lyrical vein. Once or twice, as in ' The Frenzy of Prometheus ' and ' Justin,' he strikes an epic note, and Miltonic and Tennysonian echoes are heard in his lines. He is at his best in such a poem as ' A Song of Triumph,' where he sings man's conquest of his environment.

> In his hands are the sands of the ages, and gold of unperishing youth,
> On his brow, even now, is the shining of wisdom and justice and truth ;
> His dower was the power to prevail, on the lion and dragon he trod,
> His birth was of earth, but he mounts to a throne in the bosom of God.

Among other men who have a prominent place in Canadian song are John Reade, author of *The Prophecy of Merlin*, a poem showing imagination, scholarship and culture ; Arthur Weir (1864-1902), author of three volumes of verse rich in music and good in their interpretation of the changing moods of nature ; John Hunter-Duvar (1830-99), of Prince Edward Island, who wrote several dramas with lyrical interludes, quaint and sweet, and having a mediæval tone and colour ; and Duncan Campbell Scott, the author of several collections of lyrics, Canadian in colour and with a music rich in tone and splendidly interpretative of nature.

In 1884, on the receipt of Isabella Valancy Crawford's *Old Spookses' Pass, Malcolm's Katie, and Other Poems*, Lord Dufferin wrote the author a letter in which were the following words : ' It is time now that Canada should have a literature of its own, and I am glad to think that you have so nobly shown us the way.'

Isabella Valancy Crawford (1850-87) was born in Dublin, Ireland, and came with her father, a physician, to Canada in 1858. Dr Crawford settled with his family first in the village of Paisley on the Saugeen River, and later at Lakefield, near the Kawartha Lakes—picturesque spots, where the father, a man of ' wide reading and culture, waged an unsuccessful war against poverty.' His daughter had a keen, well-stored mind and a penetrating imagination. She saw poetry in life's common things and is, in a sense, the best of the interpreters of the typical life of pioneer days who have yet written prose or verse in Canada. As J. W. Garvin, the editor of her collected poems (1905), remarks, 'a great poet dwelt among us and we scarce knew her.' She died at the early age of thirty-six and she did her work among a people caring little for art, but she left behind her a body of work that is seldom commonplace, and which at times has a sincerity and a virility that are the gifts of only the greatest singers. ' The Helot ' is a fine example of her genius. In it music, diction and ideas are in perfect harmony. Not one of its ninety-seven stanzas is weak. Its power is best shown by an example :

> Bruteward lash thy Helots, hold
>   Brain and soul and clay in gyves,
> Coin their blood and sweat in gold,
>   Build thy cities on their lives,—
>
> Comes a day the spark divine
>   Answers to the gods who gave ;
> Fierce the hot flames pant and shine
>   In the bruised breast of the slave.

' Old Spookses' Pass ' is a dialect poem possessed of great

dramatic force, rugged humour and good character interpretation. The sublimity of the elements at war in a mountain region and the wild rush of a herd of frightened cattle
are depicted with a power and truth all the more astonishing
as they are described by a woman unfamiliar with such
scenes and are purely the product of an intense creative
imagination. Through it all, too, thoughts such as are
contained in the following stanza pulsate :

> An' yer bound tew listen an' hear it talk,
>> Es yer mustang crunches the dry, bald sod,
> Fur I reckon the hills an' stars an' crick
>> Are all uv 'em preachers sent by God.
> An' them mountains talk tew a chap this way :
>> 'Climb, if ye can, ye degenerate cuss !'
> An' the stars smile down on a man, an' say,
>> 'Cum higher, poor critter, cum up tew us !'

'Malcolm's Katie,' a pastoral idyll, is the only Canadian
poem of any length that has taken as its subject the struggle
of the pioneer with the primeval forest. It abounds in
nature touches, its imagery is rich and in keeping with the
characters and their environment, and the dramatic passages
are varied and strong. The delicate love-song beginning
'O, Love builds on the azure sea' is as artistic as some of the
lyrics with which Tennyson brightens his idylls ; and nothing
stronger has been done in Canadian verse than the song in
which the pioneer is shown doing 'immortal tasks' :

> Bite deep and wide, O Axe, the tree !
> What doth thy bold voice promise me ?
>
> I promise thee all joyous things
> That furnish forth the lives of kings ;
>
> For every silver ringing blow
> Cities and palaces shall grow.
>
> Bite deep and wide, O Axe, the tree !
> Tell wider prophecies to me.
>
> When rust hath gnawed me deep and red
> A nation strong shall lift his head.

His crown the very heavens shall smite,
Æons shall build him in his might.

Bite deep and wide, O Axe, the tree!
Bright seer, help on thy prophecy!

Isabella Valancy Crawford's poetry has vigour and artistic excellence; it evinces a deep insight into nature in all her moods, faithfully interprets life, and is a worthy, if slight, contribution to the poetical literature of the English-speaking peoples.

E. Pauline Johnson (1862-1913) has a unique place in Canadian letters. In her veins was the blood of the Mohawks, the most renowned among the Indians of the Six Nations. She published in all three volumes of verse : *The White Wampum, Canadian Born* and *Flint and Feathers*, the last including the poems published in the earlier volumes.

Pauline Johnson was born on the Grand River Indian Reserve, and was the daughter of Chief Johnson of the Mohawks. Though her mother was an Englishwoman, the poetess ever prided herself on her Indian origin. She is at her best when portraying the savage instincts of the Indian heart, and such poems as ' A Cattle Thief ' and ' A Cry from an Indian Wife ' have much dramatic force. Her volumes abound in verse distinctively Canadian in subject ; nor is she limited to one district. All the vast Dominion from Halifax to the Pacific Ocean was her ' stamping ground.' The tide-fretted shores of the Atlantic, the rapids and streams of the east and west, the cattle country, the Rockies, the Arctic regions have all had tributes from her. ' The Song my Paddle Sings ' is one of her finest and best-known lyrics, a delightful bit of music with thought and rhythm in perfect harmony.

The beauty of Canadian scenery, the varied seasons, and the aspirations of a pioneer people have produced an astonishingly large number of women writers. Among those who have published volumes of verse are : Sarah Anne Curzon (1833-98), whose drama *Laura Secord,* a somewhat heavy and stilted performance, has given permanent form to one of the most heroic deeds of the War of 1812 ;

Agnes Ethelwyn Wetherald, who has to her credit no fewer than four books of poetry, all of which are rich in art and thought; Agnes Maule Machar ('Fidelis'), whose peculiar poetic domain is the Thousand Islands, and in whose verse there is a fine rendering of the restful beauty of that summer dreamland ; Jean Blewett, strong in her portrayal of domestic life and homely scenes and incidents ; S. Frances Harrison ('Seranus'), a maker of verses refined in colour, music and language ; Kate Seymour MacLean, whose work is serious in thought and who has more than usual skill in expression ; and Marjorie L. C. Pickthall, whose volume, *The Drift of Pinions*, published in 1913, shows subtle and delicate music and pictorial distinctness.   At times—too frequently, indeed —Miss Pickthall's meaning is obscured by the fervour of her imagination, but one lyric at least, 'Dream River,' is a perfect bit of work.   Its closing lines give an excellent idea of its qualities :

> O, every morn the sparrow flings
> His elfin trills athwart the hush,
> And here unseen at eve there sings
> One crystal-throated hermit thrush.

From this rapid review it will be seen that a body of literary work distinctively national and worthy of serious consideration has been produced by Canadians.   When the recent settlement of British North America is considered, when account is taken of the backward condition of education for many years and the exceedingly limited reading public that native authors have had to appeal to, the literary achievement must appear remarkable.   Moreover, Canadian authors have been handicapped in having to compete in their own market with—it must be admitted—better creations than theirs by British and American authors.   Again, as has been shown, many Canadian writers secure an appreciative audience in the United States and ultimately take up their residence in the republic ; others are attracted to the mother country.   In either case these self-expatriated Canadians shape their style and feelings into harmony with their new conditions.   They in time lose their Canadian

colour and atmosphere and become a literary part of the
country in which they have made their home. Parker,
Carman and Duncan have lost to a large extent their Canadian
identity.

The Canadian literary domain, too, has been invaded
by foreign writers, and much of it has been worked by mere
visitors to the Dominion. Parkman has written the early
history of Canada with a fulness and in a manner that make
it difficult, though not impossible, for any writer to do original historical work in the same field. Much of the storehouse
of romance has been exploited by American and British
writers of fiction. Mary Hartwell Catherwood, Conan
Doyle, Jack London, Silas Weir Mitchell, Kirk Monroe,
Mary N. Murfree (' Charles Egbert Craddock '), Charles
Dudley Warner, Stewart Edward White, Mrs Humphry
Ward and Henry Van Dyke have dealt with Canadian
material better than have most Canadian-born novelists.
But there are still rich literary fields to be cultivated ; and
with the increase of wealth and the consequent increase
of leisure, with better educational establishments, Canadian
authors will have a home market for their productions, and
will doubtless be able to do as good work as is done in other
parts of the English-speaking world.

J. G. Marquis

'French-Canadian Literature'

CAMILLE ROY

FRENCH-CANADIAN LITERATURE

FRENCH-CANADIAN LITERATURE

I

LITERARY ORIGINS, 1760-1840

THE literary history of the French Canadians may be said to date from the year 1760, or, if one prefers, from the cession of Canada to England. Before that time, indeed, there had been certain manifestations of literary life in New France : there had been accounts of travel, like those of Champlain ; interesting narratives, like the *Relations* of the Jesuits ; histories like that of Charlevoix ; studies of manners like those of the Père Lafitau ; and instructive letters, full of shrewd observations, like those of the Mère Marie de l'Incarnation. But these works were, for the most part, written in France, and all were published there. Their authors, moreover, belong to France much more than to Canada, and France, rather than Canada, is entitled to claim their works as her patrimony.

During the hundred and fifty years of French domination in Canada the colonists were unable to devote much attention to intellectual pursuits. All the living forces of the nascent people were engrossed by the ruder labours of colonization, commerce and war.

Nor was it even on the morrow of 1760—the morrow of the treaty that delivered New France to England—that the first books were printed and the first notable works written. There was other work to be done, and the French under their new rulers betook themselves to action. While repairing the disasters to their material fortunes, they numbered themselves, consolidated themselves, and set themselves to preserve as intact as possible their ancient institutions and the traditions of their national life.

From this effort to preserve their nationality the first manifestations of their literary life were soon to spring; and it was through the newspaper—the most convenient vehicle of popular thought—that the French-Canadian mind first found expression. Only colonial literature could begin in the newspaper article. The older literatures were born on the lips of the ædes, the bards or the troubadours: it was the human voice, the living song of a soul, that carried to attentive ears these first untutored accents. But in Canada, in America, where machinery is at the beginning of all progress, the Press is naturally the all-important instrument for the spread of literary ideas. In the years immediately following the Cession there were established in Quebec and Montreal several periodicals, in which the unpretentious works of the earliest writers may be found.

The following are some of the journals that appeared at the end of the eighteenth century and the beginning of the nineteenth, and that mark the true origin of French-Canadian literature :

La Gazette de Québec (1764); *La Gazette du Commerce et littéraire*, of Montreal, named almost immediately *La Gazette littéraire* (1778); *La Gazette de Montréal* (1785); *Le Magasin de Québec* (1792); *Le Cours du temps* (1794); *Le Canadien*, of Quebec (1806); *Le Courrier de Québec* (1807); *Le Vrai Canadien*, of Quebec (1810); *Le Spectateur*, of Montreal (1813); *L'Aurore*, of Montreal (1815); *L'Abeille canadienne*, of Montreal (1818).

These journals were not equally fortunate. Most of them—*La Gazette littéraire, L'Abeille canadienne, Le Magasin de Québec, Le Courrier de Québec, Le Vrai Canadien*—struggled for life for a few months or a few years, and disappeared one after the other. With the exception of *La Gazette de Québec, La Gazette de Montréal, Le Canadien*, and *Le Spectateur*, the first newspapers succumbed after a valiant struggle for existence. To reach the greatest possible number of readers, several of these journals—*La Gazette de Québec, La*

Gazette de Montréal, *Le Magasin de Québec* and *Le Cours du temps*—were written in both English and French.

The French newspapers may be divided into two distinct categories. There were those that were mainly political, or contained political news, like *La Gazette de Québec* and *La Gazette de Montréal* ; and the periodicals that were distinctly literary, such as *La Gazette littéraire* of Montreal and *Le Magasin de Québec*. This last-named journal contained little but reproductions from foreign literature.

La Gazette littéraire of Montreal, published by Fleury Mesplet, on whose staff Valentin Jautard, a native of France, was an active collaborator under the pseudonym of 'Le Spectateur tranquille,' is noteworthy as having given the French Canadians their first opportunity of writing on literary and philosophical subjects. Much literary criticism, sometimes of a decidedly puerile nature, also appeared in it. In this paper, too, are encountered the first manifestations of the Voltairian spirit that had permeated many minds in Canada during the latter part of the eighteenth century.

The first political journals were literary in but a small degree, and it was seldom that they published French articles of any value. Apart from a few occasional poems —of little merit, however—the French contents of *La Gazette de Québec* were, for the most part, merely translations of its English articles. The political literature of this journal is dull and unimportant. William Brown, who, with Thomas Gilmour, was its founder, characterized his journal only too well when he wrote (August 8, 1776) that it 'justly merited the title of the most innocent gazette in the British dominions.'

Nevertheless it was Quebec that became, in 1764, the cradle of Canadian journalism. Before the end of the French régime Quebec was already the centre of a civilization that was polished, elegant—refined even—and often very fashionable. Peter Kalm, the Swedish botanist—who visited New France in 1749, and left such a curious, instructive and faithful record of his journey—observed that Quebec then contained the elements of a distinguished society, in which good taste was preserved, and in which the people delighted to make it govern their manners, their language and their dress. Quebec, moreover, prided herself not only on gathering within her walls the most important personages of the political and the ecclesiastical world, but also on being the chief seat of intellectual life in the new country. From Bougainville [1] we learn that in 1757, towards the end of the French régime, there was a literary club in Quebec. Besides this, the Jesuits' College and the Seminary had for more than a century drawn to Quebec the studious youth of the entire colony. Michel Bibaud, who visited the city in 1841, noted there 'the agreeable, affable manners of her leading citizens, and their French urbanity and courtesy.' [2] For this reason he called her 'the Paris of America.'

It was at Quebec, too, after 1791, when parliamentary government was accorded Lower Canada, that political oratory—timid at first, and modest in expression—was born. There the first groupings of intellectual forces were afterwards organized : the *Club constitutionnel* (1792) ; the *Société littéraire* (1809) ; the *Société historique et littéraire* (1824), founded at the Château Saint-Louis, under the presidency of Lord Dalhousie ; and the *Société pour l'encouragement des Sciences et des Arts* (1827), which soon amalgamated, in 1829, with the *Société historique et littéraire*.

Montreal, in the nineteenth century, was not backward in seconding, propagating and developing those movements of intellectual life which were gathering force in Quebec. At Montreal people read both poetry and prose. Joseph Mermet, a French military poet, who came to Canada in 1813 and took part in the war then in progress, had a large number of admirers in the city. There Jacques Viger pursued his historical studies on Canada ; and Denis Benjamin Viger, who at certain moments thought himself a poet, published his ponderous verses in *Le Spectateur*.

---

[1] Bougainville, Louis Antoine, Comte de (1729-1811), came to Canada in 1756 as Montcalm's aide-de-camp. He kept a careful journal of the campaign ending with the surrender of Quebec. He returned to France and joined the navy. He made a voyage round the world (1766-69), and later fought with distinction against the British during the Revolutionary War.

[2] *Encyclopédie canadienne*, i. 309 : ' Mon dernier voyage à Québec.'

In 1817 H. Bossange established in Montreal a fairly considerable bookselling business. The City Library is said to have contained eight thousand volumes in 1822.[1] The inhabitants might also nourish their intellectual curiosity in the newspapers and the literary miscellanies published about the middle of the nineteenth century, such as—*La Minerve* (1827), *L'Ami du Peuple* (1832), *Le Populaire* and *La Quotidienne* (1837), *L'Aurore des Canadas* (1839), and *Le Jean-Baptiste* (1840). To these may be added the miscellanies of Michel Bibaud—*La Bibliothèque canadienne* (1825 to 1830), *L'Observateur* (1830), *Le Magasin du Bas-Canada* (1832), and *L'Encyclopédie canadienne* (1842).

At this period Quebec and Montreal, with their associations, their journals and their literary miscellanies, were not as yet, of course, powerful centres of intellectual life, nor was the energy they radiated either very active or brilliant. In tracing the real origins of a literature, however, it is not unprofitable to indicate briefly the historical environment in which that literature was to have its birth. By this means the relative value of its earlier efforts is more justly appreciated.

With the French Canadians, song appears to have been the first form of poetry. Some verses written in 1757 and 1758[2] are still to be found ; many may be read in the journals which made their appearance later. The popular song flew quickly from mouth to mouth when, in 1775, or again in 1812, the people were fired with a fine patriotic ardour to defend the soil of their invaded country. New Year's Day also supplied the rhymesters with matter for a few verses, mainly intended for newsboys' addresses. Needless to say, these poems—interesting as they are from the point of view of literary origins—have in themselves scarcely any literary value. The same may be said of many lyrical, pastoral and satirical pieces that appeared anonymously in the early journals.[3]

---

[1] *Histoire du Canada*, by Michel Bibaud, ii. 403.

[2] *Le Foyer canadien*, 1865 : article on ' Nos chansons historiques,' by Dr Hubert Larue, pp. 17-18.

[3] On this subject see the author's work, *Nos Origines littéraires*, pp. 70-83 and 111-23, in which several extracts from these early poems are given.

At this period, however, two poets stand out from all others—Joseph Quesnel and Joseph Mermet. Although they were of French origin, they so deeply impressed Canadians of their time, and exercised such an influence upon later writers of verse and men of letters, that we cannot but take account of them in a history of the beginnings of French-Canadian poetry.

Quesnel was born at St Malo in 1749, and died at Montreal in 1809. He came to Canada from France in 1779. He was a village merchant at Boucherville, and afterwards lived in Montreal. He employed much of his leisure in writing verses and music. His principal work consists of a large number of poems, epistles, hymns, epigrams and songs. He also left a dialogue in verse, *Le Rimeur dépité* ; a comedy in verse, *L'Anglomanie* ; and two prose comedies— *Colas et Colinette*, the text of which is embellished with ariettas, and *Les Républicains français*.

Quesnel's poetry was for the most part light and playful. His muse never tires of pleasantry, in which he often indulges with delicacy and grace. To fine badinage he readily adds a piquant irony. In his epistle to M. Généreux Labadie he pokes fun playfully both at the public, for not sufficiently encouraging literature, and at Labadie himself. *Le Rimeur dépité* is another example of this raillery, at once light and biting. In these two pieces, however, there is a lack of care in regard to form and of scholarly dignity.

Quesnel concerns himself more with the quality of his verse and the trueness of its tone when he writes idyllic poetry and sings of nature. He had a keen appreciation of that beauty of nature which the descriptive poets of the eighteenth century made popular. He was probably the first French-Canadian poet to sing in praise of running brooks and blossoming flowers.

Quesnel's two most important works, however, are *Colas et Colinette*, the text of which is preserved in *Le Répertoire national*, and *l'Anglomanie*, a little comedy in verse which has not been published, but has been included by Jacques Viger in his *Saberdache*.

Colas et Colinette is a comedy, and is French rather than

Canadian. Traces of the customs of Canada are rare. Apart from certain psychological observations on love, which may be applicable to any country, the piece has little interest except as a picture of popular manners in provincial France. The old and gallant *bailli*, who wishes to rob the rude, rustic Colas of his delicate and graceful Colinette, resembles a Canadian magistrate but distantly ; while Colas himself, with his strange and faulty speech, in no way represents a young peasant of Lower Canada.

Quesnel's *L'Anglomanie*, or *Le Dîner à l'anglaise*, is frankly Canadian in inspiration. The subject was suggested by a caprice that affected the upper ranks of French-Canadian society about the beginning of the nineteenth century. At that time certain families allowed themselves to be too easily fascinated by English fashions and customs. They abandoned the old French domestic traditions, in order to adopt the habits of their British compatriots. *L'Anglomanie* is not, of course, a powerful work, but it is nevertheless interesting. It is to be hoped that it may yet be printed and submitted to the curiosity of the public. Quesnel's light comedies and his copious poetic output led his contemporaries to regard him as the model of elegant and witty versifiers.

A few years after Quesnel's death another French poet arrived in Canada, and in turn succeeded in getting his work read and admired—sometimes with a too generous admiration. This was Joseph Mermet, lieutenant and adjutant of de Watteville's regiment. Mermet came to Canada in 1813 with his regiment, composed mainly of Swiss soldiers and officers. Watteville's regiment took a prominent part in the War of 1812-14. It was sent to Kingston, and in that town the poet-lieutenant employed his leisure in writing verse. There he made the acquaintance of Jacques Viger, and the two became friends. It was Viger who made the poet's work known to his friends in Montreal, and got his poems published in *Le Spectateur*.

In these poems Mermet sang of war—the war that American cupidity had just brought close to Canadian homes, and that had summoned the brave militia beneath the colours. Several of his pieces owed their success chiefly to the actuality of the subject treated rather than to their artistic merit—for example, the lyrical verses in which he essayed to sing the victory of Châteauguay.

The hymn of the ' Victory of Châteauguay ' secured its author the friendship of the hero of that day. De Salaberry, wishing to meet the poet who had extolled his military deeds, invited him to his table. The soldier-poet went to Chambly ; he passed a few hours in the colonel's retreat there, and on returning from the visit wrote his poem on ' Chambly.'

During his travels on Canadian soil Mermet could not but admire the magnificent spectacles presented by nature. He is, we believe, the first Canadian poet to sing of Niagara ; he set himself to describe it, and his lines possess the special merit of precision.

It is not, however, in Mermet's poems of patriotism and war, nor even in his descriptive poetry, that the author's best and most characteristic spirit is to be found. The adjutant of de Watteville's regiment loved raillery above everything. This French soldier is merry. He loses no opportunity of throwing off a humorous couplet or of distributing impromptu rhymes among his friends. To him everything is matter for amusing or satirical verse. In the *Saberdache* of Jacques Viger many of these light and often carelessly written poems may still be found ; although of little value, they were received enthusiastically by the readers of 1813.

Mermet returned to France in 1816. In Canada, therefore, he was merely a visitor. Nevertheless it is plain, from certain literary discussion in which he took part in *Le Spectateur*,[1] that his influence upon the poets of his time was considerable.

Mermet has given us several examples of that sprightly, bantering literature so long practised by Quesnel. He is not, of course, a great poet ; he did not even take pains to be a second-rate poet. Yet he stimulated the ambition of those who at the beginning of the nineteenth century were endeavouring to make the new-born literature of Canada lisp in numbers.

[1] *Le Spectateur*, September 16 and 23, and October 21, 1813.

In Quesnel and Mermet we see the expression of the French muse, which has become Canadian for a brief period. In their poems, too, we see a reflection—dim though it be— of those light, graceful and terse forms of poetry, frequently idyllic, that flourished in France during the eighteenth century.

While these poets were still making their influence felt at Quebec and Montreal, a Canadian poet—Canadian by birth—essayed to capture public attention. This was Michel Bibaud, who was born near Montreal, at the Côte des Neiges, in 1782, and died at Montreal in 1857. To Bibaud must be accorded the honour—if honour it be—of publishing the first miscellany of poems in the history of French-Canadian literature. This collection, which appeared in 1830, is entitled *Épîtres, Satires, Chansons, Épigrammes, et autres pièces en vers*. It is composed of pieces that had appeared several years previously, the first satire dating from 1817. It contains no poems that are really good. It was seldom given to Bibaud himself to be a poet ; and the pieces he published are more interesting from the point of view of the history of manners and ideas than from that of art, which in him is usually commonplace.

Michel Bibaud and Denis Benjamin Viger, who con-tributed to *Le Spectateur*, were the representatives of French-Canadian poetry at the moment when it was venturing on its first flights. It is true these men were not great poets, but we must be thankful to those who, at the beginning of a country's history, venture to do something, and who, at the cost of their own failure, point the way to others who may yet follow and excel them.

The most important chapter of French-Canadian literary origins—dull though it often is—is composed of the prose matter in the early newspapers. Among the first to write for the journals and to influence the public mind in their diverse degrees were—Pierre Bédard and François Blanchet in *Le Canadien* ; Jacques Labrie and Louis Plamondon in *Le Courrier de Québec* ; Denis Benjamin Viger in *Le Canadien* and *Le Spectateur* ; Michel Bibaud in *L'Aurore des Canadas* and later in his collected works ; and Jacques Viger in *Le*

Canadien and in the literary journals and miscellanies of Michel Bibaud. After these came Étienne Parent, who, by virtue of his forceful thought and the vigour of his articles, merits a place apart.

This newspaper prose was almost the only literary matter printed at the close of the eighteenth and the beginning of the nineteenth century; it was also the only literature, or nearly so, that expressed Canadian thought. It was this literature that engaged the attention of the citizens, directed their political sympathies, and often moulded their judgment on public affairs. This prose is by turn passionate and calm, fiery and restrained, aggressive and patient. It is full of those agitations that at certain periods troubled the national life—when, for example, Craig was the dupe of the evil counsellors who surrounded him, and the French Canadians were at once irascible and bold in their demands. Throughout this political literature are to be found the deep traces of those increasing recriminations excited during nearly forty years by topics that so often irritated, such as supplies and the reform of the legislative council.

The political oratory of the first parliaments had naturally much of the qualities and defects of the journalism. Usually we find the same men speaking from the political platform and writing in the journals. Their style varies greatly : it is generally temperate, terse and precise ; but frequently it is confused, ponderous and solemn. The oratory, like the written prose of the time, was substantial rather than artistic, vigorous rather than pliant, firm rather than passionate. The name of Louis Joseph Papineau stands out among all those who earned applause as political orators during the first half of the nineteenth century. Papineau's name is still popular among French Canadians, for he long embodied the highest aspirations of his countrymen. This is not the place to discuss the excesses into which he was sometimes led by his ardent patriotism. It is well worth remembering that, more than any other in his day, he was an orator and a political tribune. He knew and could use those expressions that strike the imagination of a people. From the platform, where he himself fought like a soldier, he impetuously sounded the charge, at once restraining and inflaming popular passions.

While Papineau was making speeches, a journalist was writing articles in which the very soul of the French-Canadian people was expressed with an eloquence by turns commanding, ironical, rugged and light. It may be said that Étienne Parent portrayed the most intimate thoughts of the people for a longer time than Papineau, and more faithfully. In Parent, indeed, we encounter the man who, during the period of the literary origins of French Canada, was the most sagacious of the politicians and the greatest of the writers.

Parent was born at Beauport, near Quebec, on May 2, 1802. On the completion of his classical studies at the College of Nicolet and the Seminary of Quebec, he entered the profession of journalism. In 1822 he became editor of *Le Canadien* in Quebec. After the temporary cessation of this journal in 1825, the young editor pursued his law studies, and was admitted to the bar in 1829. He was unable to devote himself long to the practice of law. His literary temperament, his well-stored mind, his desire to discuss ideas, and his taste for controversy drew him once more to journalism. In 1831 a group of young deputies demanded the establishment of a fighting journal, and suggested the revival of *Le Canadien*, whose very name was a watchword. Parent undertook the task of resurrecting it, and on May 7, 1831, the initial number appeared. On the first page a new device was inscribed : ' Our Institutions, our Language and our Laws ! '

In Montreal, at that time, *La Minerve*—a very violent patriotic organ—was read. At Quebec, it was *Le Canadien* that undertook to scatter the seed of those political truths with which it was desired to imbue all minds.

The office of *Le Canadien*, in which Parent reigned, became a sort of centre where politicians gathered, and where the plans of attack and defence of the parliamentarians were arranged. Parent retained the conduct of his journal until 1842. In the preceding year he had been elected member for the county of Saguenay. In consequence of serious deafness, contracted in the state prisons in which he was confined with so many other patriots during the winter of 1837-38, he considered it necessary in 1842 to resign his seat. He accepted the post of clerk of the executive council. He ceased to direct *Le Canadien*, therefore, in the same year. He reappeared frequently, however, and still conducted lively controversies, in its columns.

From 1842 it was chiefly by means of lecturing that Parent sought to continue among his countrymen the educative ministry to which his journalistic activity had accustomed him. To the members of the Canadian Institute of Montreal and Quebec, at the reading-room of Saint-Roch, Quebec, and before the Society for the Early Closing of Shops, Quebec, he delivered courses of public lectures that testify to the extent of his knowledge, and especially to the philosophic penetration of his mind. He became under-secretary for the Province of Lower Canada in 1847, and retained substantially the same functions under Confederation, with the title of under-secretary of state. He retired from office in 1872, and died at Ottawa on December 22, 1874. On the day of his death *Le Courrier de l'Outaouais* declared that Parent ' created the journalistic style of this country.' This eulogy suggests the high and authoritative place that the editor of *Le Canadien* had won. By his brother journalists he was called ' the Nestor of the Press,' as a tribute to the prudence he generally exercised in his writings.

Moreover, Parent the journalist was more than any other of his contemporaries a courageous and clear-sighted patriot. A master-thought directed all his ideas. ' A pole-star led me,' he used to say in his later years.[1] This star—the guide of his spirit—was the motto which he inscribed at the head of *Le Canadien* : ' Our Institutions, our Language and our Laws ! ' Whatever had no concern with this patriotic programme was banished from the journal's columns. Parent had well-defined political principles, and it was upon these principles that he founded his journalistic activity, and sought to achieve the liberty of his compatriots. What were the principles he professed ? Upon what rights did he wish to base the stability and progress of the nation ?

[1] Words quoted by Benjamin Sulte, in *La Minerve*, December 23, 1874.

He considered, in the first place, that in a country endowed with a parliamentary system the House of Assembly ought to have a certain and decisive influence upon the policy of the government. He could not conceive this influence being sufficient without the absolute control of supplies. This famous question of supplies, it will be remembered, was, in both Upper and Lower Canada, for more than thirty years the cause of the most violent public controversies. Parent combined this principle of the control of supplies by the assembly with the higher principle of the responsibility of the executive. The latter, he held, ought to be responsible to the people or to their deputies. It is especially interesting to note with what precision the editor of *Le Canadien*, in 1833, demands this responsible government :

> We now ask that the Executive Council be assimilated to the cabinet in England. . . . Thus, instead of influential members of one Chamber or the other being summoned and made mere political councillors, we now desire that they be made heads of departments, severally and jointly responsible to the Chambers.[1]

It was to secure a more complete application of this governmental responsibility that Parent, and all the patriots of his day, conducted their agitation against the legislative council, then composed of members nominated by the crown. In place of irresponsible councillors he demanded elective councillors. He regarded the constitution of the legislative council, as defined by the constitution, as a great error on the part of Pitt. ' The minister,' he declared, ' ought to have seen that he was bringing into the lists against the people a class of men who could never have anything in common with them, since the former ran necessarily towards liberty, and the latter towards absolute power and privilege.' [2]

In the exposition and defence of his political principles Parent always displayed a calm and appropriate moderation. He was never a lover of excess, either in words or deeds.

[1] *Le Canadien*, June 19, 1833.   [2] *Ibid.*, May 1, 1833.

Although he long fought by Papineau's side, and was long one of 'the sullen guard of the agitators '—in the phrase of that day—he was unable to follow the leader of the patriots to the end. He broke away when it seemed to him that Papineau was about to abandon the paths of prudence and legality.

In his study of social questions, no less than in politics, Parent displayed the lucidity and penetration of his intellect. Both by taste and by virtue of his remarkable mental qualities he was a philosopher. His contemporaries did not hesitate to call him ' the Victor Cousin of Canada,' at a time when Cousin was exercising in France a very great influence on philosophic thought.

In his lectures Parent set himself to popularize those philosophical and social ideas, inspired by Christianity, towards which his sympathies and intellect naturally drew him. In order to present some idea of the wide range of his studies, it will suffice to cite the subjects of the speeches or lectures delivered by him in Montreal and Quebec. At the Institut Canadien, Montreal, he gave the following lectures : ' Industry as a Means of Preserving our Nationality' (January 22, 1846) ; ' The Importance of the Study of Political Economy' (November 19, 1846) ; ' Human Labour' (September 23, 1847) ; ' The Priest and Spirituality in their Relation to Society' (December 17, 1848) ; and ' Considerations on our System of Popular Education, on Education in general, and the Legislative Means of providing for it' (February 19, 1848). At the Institut Canadien of Quebec he delivered two lectures on ' Intelligence in its Relations to Society ' (January 22 and February 7, 1852) ; before the Society for the Early Closing of Shops, Quebec, he spoke on ' The Importance of Commerce and its Duties ' (January 15, 1852) ; and at the reading-room of Saint-Roch, Quebec, he lectured to an audience of workingmen on ' The Condition of the Working Classes ' (April 15, 1852). This last lecture puts very happily, from a Christian standpoint, the necessary social conditions of labour, and formulates the principles that ought to regulate the relations of masters and men.

At this conference Parent thus exhorted his hearers to make Catholic doctrine the rule of all economic progress :

> Ouvriers, mes amis, pour qui je parle, vous qui êtes les abeilles travailleuses de la ruche sociale, voulez-vous éviter les maux dont souffrent vos semblables ailleurs, tenez fort et ferme à votre système catholique, et à tout ce qui en fait l'essence. Repoussez les adeptes du jugement privé, qui cherchent à vous en éloigner. Le catholicisme, voyez-vous, c'est l'association dans sa plus haute et sa plus vaste expression, et cela au profit du pauvre et du faible, qui ne peuvent être forts que par l'association. Celle-ci en les réunissant en un faisceau saura les rendre plus forts que les forts. Je ne nierai pas que, humainement parlant, le principe du jugement privé, qui est, en pratique, l'individualisme appliqué aux choses morales, ne tende à augmenter la force des individualités ; mais cela ne peut profiter qu'au petit nombre d'individus fortement trempés. L'individualisme est comme le vent qui anime un brasier, mais qui éteint une chandelle. Aux masses il faut l'association d'idées, l'unité, et par conséquent l'autorité. Je prie ceux de mes jeunes auditeurs qui seraient, comme on l'est trop souvent à leur age, enclins à se révolter contre toute espèce d'autorité, de bien réfléchir là-dessus, avant de jeter le doute et le trouble dans l'esprit du peuple, à l'endroit de ses anciennes institutions. Les anciennes institutions d'un pays, ses croyances religieuses surtout, il ne faut jamais l'oublier, sont à un peuple ce que sont à un individu sa constitution physique, ses habitudes, sa manière de vivre : en un mot, c'est sa vie propre. Et dire qu'il se trouve des hommes, de soi-disant patriotes, prêts à faire main-basse sur tout cela, sous le prétexte de réforme et de progrès ! Les malheureux ! ils ne voient pas que c'est la destruction et la mort. Réformons, mais ne détruisons pas : avançons, mais sans lâcher le fil conducteur de la tradition.

In these lectures, as in his articles in *Le Canadien*, may be seen the impressive, forceful and clear language of which he was master. True, it has not always the freedom and grace that might be wished ; but it is often coloured by vivid and striking images that fix the idea in bold relief. It readily becomes ironical, incisive and caustic. In *Le Canadien* there are articles, directed against the Montreal *Herald*, the *Mercury*, and even *L'Ami du Peuple*, that are little master-pieces of invective and sound sense.

Parent's contemporaries did not fail to recognize his high intellectual value and his practised taste as a man of letters. He was often consulted, and his judgments were highly esteemed. He was not only a political leader, but also the literary leader of his time. He loved to welcome, encourage and stimulate talent; and, as Hector Fabre said in those days, ' no one dared to think himself a writer unless he had his patent from Parent's hands.'

It would be impossible, then, to accord this father of French-Canadian literature too large a place in the history of its origins. His is incontestably the finest, most worthy and most expressive figure of that time. While Parent belongs to the origins of the literature, he is also a prophet of the following period—that of more fruitful growth; he even merits a place beside the most illustrious in any period of the literary history of French Canada, for he is still recognized in the Dominion as one of the highest representatives of French thought and culture.

While Parent held the public mind by his journalism and lectures, another writer—at first by journalism and later by literature—was seeking to attract attention. This was Michel Bibaud, whose heavy and dull poems have been mentioned; but he succeeded better in prose than in verse. Public sympathy, however, was meted out to him but sparingly. We have already recalled the literary miscellanies that he successively edited between 1825 and 1842. Here must be mentioned the *Histoire du Canada*, which at first appeared fragmentarily in these miscellanies, and was afterwards published in three volumes, the first of which was given to the public in 1837, the second in 1844 and the third—long after the author's death—in 1878.

This *Histoire du Canada* comprises the whole course of the political life of the country from its first settlement until 1837. It had not the good fortune to please French-Canadian readers, and this explains the silence with which the work was received. Bibaud was not one of the patriotic school. He did not agree with such men as Papineau, Morin, Viger and Parent; in politics he held aloof from his French-Canadian fellow-citizens. He rather sided with those who at that time approved the conduct of the English functionaries, governors or councillors—collectively termed ' bureaucrats.' Bibaud, a bureaucrat, wrote the history of Canada from the point of view of a friend of the administration : on nearly every page of his narrative he censured the attitude and conduct of the patriots. He reproached them especially with their irreconcilability, complacently set forth certain errors in their tactics, and devoted himself, for the most part, to defending the policy of the oligarchy by which Lower Canada was governed. It will be readily understood that such a history could not be acceptable to the public. Although it occasionally contains judicious observations, it is evident that the work is written with prejudice. It was, therefore, condemned to failure at the outset.

The matter, especially in the second and third parts, is not well assimilated, or presented with sufficient skill. Bibaud is too often content merely to pile documents and official papers on the top of each other. Frequently confusion and obscurity are the result. The narrative might well have been freer, more spirited, and more precise.

II

LITERARY DEVELOPMENT, 1840-1912

HISTORY

SHORTLY after the publication of Michel Bibaud's *Histoire du Canada*, another work appeared which was at once to eclipse it and cause it to be forgotten—the *Histoire du Canada* (1845-48) by François Xavier Garneau. With this work the second period of French-Canadian literature opens—the period of its development. This book was soon to be followed by others, not less important, which were to make the years following

1840 a remarkable epoch from the point of view of progress in Canadian letters.

The conditions of the political life of the country were such as to bring about this literary growth. The struggles which the French Canadians had to maintain for the defence of their legitimate liberties, the bloody issue of that long agitation, the designs of diplomatic repression which the Act of Union of 1840 sufficiently disclosed—gave them to understand that they must more than ever concern themselves with strengthening their separate and distinctive public life. As nothing expresses better, or stimulates more effectually, the forces of national consciousness than literature —history, poetry, oratory, books and publications of every kind—several minds determined to devote themselves to the development of French-Canadian letters. Men felt a need to write the history of their past, the better to illumine the future ; to sing the ancient glories in order to inspire new courage ; to relate the old and venerable traditions, that their memory might be imprinted ineffaceably on the hearts of the young. François Xavier Garneau appears first on the list of those who then made the literature of French Canada shine with a fresh brilliance. National history has for him a distinct claim on the Canadian conscience.

Born at Quebec in 1809, Garneau belonged to a respectable artisan family, industrious but not well-to-do. His people were unable to give him the education he would have liked. He attended the day-schools of Quebec, but he was unable to enter the Petit Séminaire for his classical course. Entering the office of Archibald Campbell, notary, at the age of sixteen, young Garneau began his apprenticeship, studying Latin and French classical authors by himself in his spare time. It was while thus engaged that his vocation as historian was revealed to him. It was then, at least, that, moved by a natural feeling of irritation, he one day conceived the project of writing his history of Canada. There were some young English clerks in Campbell's office ; and, as the rivalries of race were at that time warm, arguments frequently arose on questions of Canadian history. The young patriot's opponents did not scruple

to offend his pride. After all, was he not but a son of the
vanquished, and did not every one know that the French
Canadians had no history ? One day, driven beyond all
bounds by some such insult, young Garneau retorted :
' Our history ! Very well—I will tell it ! And you will
see how our ancestors were vanquished, and whether such
a defeat was not as glorious as victory ! ' The work that
Garneau wished to write demanded much labour and preparation. Unexpected circumstances occurred, however,
to enable him to qualify himself gradually for the task.

Garneau became a notary in 1830. He employed his
leisure in collecting historical notes on Canada ; and soon,
on June 20, 1831, by dint of stringent saving, he was enabled
to go to England. There he applied himself to the study
of English institutions, and attended the sittings of parliament. After a short visit to France he returned to London,
and had the good fortune to become secretary to Denis
Benjamin Viger, who was then diplomatic agent for the
French Canadians to the English government. The young
secretary spent two years in London. He had an opportunity of meeting some of the great men in the English and
French world of letters ; he learned at what cost the literary
glories of Europe had been built up, and he was astonished
at the influence and prestige accorded to intellectual authority in the enlightened Old World centres of culture. Returning to Quebec on June 30, 1833, Garneau endeavoured
—but only for a short time—to pursue his profession as a
notary. He then became an accountant in a bank, and
was at length appointed translator to the legislative assembly
of Lower Canada. It was in an official position that he was
to find the time necessary for carrying into effect his project
for a history of Canada.

The first volume appeared in 1845, the second in 1846
and the third in 1848. These volumes brought events down
only to 1792. In 1852 the author published a second edition,
in which the narrative reached the year 1840. In 1855
Garneau published his *Voyage en Angleterre et en France.*
But already a serious malady, epilepsy, was gradually under-
mining his health. Since 1844 he had been secretary of the

city of Quebec ; he was obliged to resign in 1864, when his malady attacked him in a more violent form. He died at Quebec in 1866. The ashes of the 'national historian' of French Canada rest in the Belmont cemetery, at the gates of the city, near the battlefield of Ste Foy, the glory of which he has so eloquently told.

Garneau's *Histoire du Canada* gives the story of all the French colonies of North America from their origin to the treaty of 1763. From that date the author confines his narrative to Canada proper. The sustained effort necessary to the construction of a work so extensive and so fine cannot be overestimated. Garneau wrote at a time when it was very difficult to get access to the sources of the history of Canada. Obviously, his documentation could not be so abundant as that of later historians. But he set himself to turn to account all the materials and historical information he was able to collect. Out of these materials, hitherto rare, he made a work that, although incomplete and capable of improvement in many respects, excited the admiration of his contemporaries by its general excellence. Written during the political turmoil that came to a head in 1837, and published on the morrow of the insurrection and the establishment of the inacceptable union of the two Canadas, Garneau's work is plainly a work of defence and of attack. Yet the spirit of moderation by which it is animated deserves praise. Some of his contemporaries even reproached him for not having written panegyrics on the French Canadians. Garneau preferred, while honourably acquitting his compatriots in respect of certain historic accusations made against them, to indicate also the political errors into which they fell.

One of the most important sections of the *Histoire du Canada*, and one awaited with the greatest curiosity and impatience, was that devoted to the account of the conquest of Canada by England. Garneau had himself suffered from the accusations sometimes lightly cast at the conquered Canadians. Happily, and very justly, he brought out the value of such a conquest, and opportunely rectified the military history of those painful years.

Garneau's chief aim was to write the political history of his country. Educated in the school of Augustin Thierry and Guizot, he took delight in philosophical speculations ; he loved to trace the principles governing historical development, and his work clearly bears the mark of his intellectual sympathies. His history is not merely dramatic by reason of the stirring recitals it contains ; it is also a work of philosophy.

Unfortunately, the philosophy of Garneau is not always very safe. Not having followed the lessons of the masters, and having acquired his ideas on government in the course of studies that were often ill-chosen, he sometimes allowed theories derived from French liberalism to find their way into his work—for example, the principle of the absolute freedom of conscience, for which he has been so keenly reproached. Garneau, moreover, did not sufficiently appreciate the part played in Canadian history by the Catholic Church or the clergy. He did not see with sufficient clearness the very special conditions under which the church's intervention in the political life of the colony took place. Nor did he sufficiently know or understand the efforts made by the clergy for the instruction of the people. These errors of the historian prevent his work from being as perfect as it might otherwise have been. If, however, we forget these defects and remember only the work as a whole, we are obliged to acknowledge that such a monument could have been conceived and executed only by a great mind.

The literary style, moreover, heightens the interest. Garneau's phraseology is free, ample and eloquent. On occasion it is warm and vibrating. If it is hampered at times by heaviness, it is incontestably capable of grace and vivacity. The study of the *Histoire du Canada* produced the greatest enthusiasm in the middle of the nineteenth century. The young especially were stirred as they turned the pages in which they felt the soul of their country throb. Garneau founded a school. Under his inspiration the historians and poets of the ensuing years worked.

Garneau was still alive when another historian essayed to rival him in public favour—the Abbé Jean Baptiste

Antoine Ferland, who was born at Montreal in 1805. A diligent student at the Collège de Nicolet, and gifted with the most varied talents, he became in turn professor at Nicolet, vicar, curé, and finally, in 1850, a member of the archiepiscopal staff in Quebec. He devoted his later years to the study of Canadian history, and from 1856 to 1862 delivered at Laval University lectures which were well attended. These university lectures he began to publish in 1861. He was able to issue only one volume ; the second was published by his friends. Illness and death prevented the continuation of his work. He died at Quebec in 1865.

Ferland's *Cours d'Histoire du Canada* comprises only the years of the French domination, and it is to be regretted that the author was unable to carry his work further. He possessed, indeed, the best qualities of the historian. He is specially distinguished by the most scrupulous scientific method ; he was a tireless seeker for truth. He visited the archives of London and Paris to consult documents at first hand. The sole object of his stay in Europe, during the years 1856 and 1857, was to obtain materials for his history from original sources. In his work he did not sufficiently indicate his references to authentic documents, but he rarely wrote without basing his information on such documents. Thus he was able to rectify a great many dates which, before his history appeared, were uncertain, and to throw a fresh light upon incidents that had not always been properly judged. He understood better than Garneau the religious nature of the historical origins of Canada, and rendered greater justice in this regard to those who were their principal creators.

Ferland carefully examined the details of the life and manners of New France. He also made a very full study of the character and the curious customs of the Indians. He took special pains in his narration of the circumstances attending the establishment of the colony, and the first developments of its national life. After a preface dealing with the early inhabitants of America, and the explorers who were the first to touch the American coast, he addresses himself to the subject of his laborious study, and lays bare, with the most ample and interesting details, the foundations of Canadian history.

Ferland has not the brilliant literary enthusiasm of Garneau. He aims less at the development of general considerations, he has a better grasp of vital details, and he gets into his book more historical matter. The language he writes is thoroughly French, and is precise, clear and spirited, its one ornament being a fine and frank simplicity.

Certain of Ferland's smaller works and articles are of the greatest interest and deserve mention : *Journal d'un Voyage sur les Côtes de la Gaspésie, Louis-Olivier Gamache, Le Labrador,* and *Notice biographique sur Mgr Joseph-Octave Plessis.* These studies appeared in *Le Foyer canadien* between 1861 and 1863.

Contemporary with Ferland was Antoine Gérin-Lajoie, one of his admirers, who also wrote a considerable chapter of Canadian history. He was born at Yamachiche in 1824, and died at Ottawa in 1882. He was long known chiefly by his novel of colonization, *Jean Rivard.* But in 1888 a valuable work which he had left in manuscript, *Dix ans d'Histoire du Canada, 1840-50,* was published. This work is the best study we have of the period that witnessed the establishment of responsible government. The information is abundant and accurate. Possibly official documents are inserted too copiously in the text, and too frequently impede the course of the narrative. The style is temperate and easy. Although not an artist capable of making his figures stand out boldly, Gérin-Lajoie produced a work that may be read with great interest and profit.

The Abbé Henri Raymond Casgrain, who was born at Rivière-Ouelle in 1831 and died at Quebec in 1904, devoted his entire life to the study of his country's past. He was a most prolific and enthusiastic historian. With Gérin-Lajoie, Joseph Charles Taché and Dr Hubert Larue, he played a large part in the renaissance of French-Canadian letters that followed the year 1860. With them he founded *Les Soirées canadiennes* in 1861, and *Le Foyer canadien* in 1863. The works of Garneau and Ferland had excited his ardent interest, and it was his ambition to continue and complete their task.

In 1860 he began by publishing his *Légendes*, in which he set himself to revive Canadian customs. He then entered upon serious history, and wrote successively—*Histoire de la Mère Marie de l'Incarnation* (1864) ; *Biographies canadiennes*, which were collected in one volume ; *Histoire de l'Hôtel-Dieu de Québec* (1878) ; *Pèlerinage au Pays d'Evangéline* (1885) ; *Montcalm et Lévis* (1891) ; *Une Seconde Acadie* (1894) ; *Asile du Bon Pasteur de Québec* (1896) ; and *Les Sulpiciens et les Prêtres des Missions Étrangères en Acadie* (1897). The work of Casgrain is therefore considerable. It gives evidence of great activity. Yet his eyes had been strained by overstudy, and he had to have recourse to a secretary to aid him in his search for and study of documents. His learning was great, and his books are full of information of the most varied nature. It is generally agreed, however, that he possessed an imagination and sensitiveness which at times injured the accuracy of his narrative and the justness of his judgment. He liked to find in history what he sought. Yet his books are imbued with warmth and life. The language is free and vivid, although sometimes rather overloaded with imagery—especially in his earlier works. It was, indeed, by his literary art that he captivated his readers. Casgrain's works have helped greatly in making Canada known abroad, especially in France.

In the first of his *Légendes*, le *Tableau de la Rivière-Ouelle*, Abbé Casgrain thus faithfully described in a most picturesque manner the home of the French-Canadian habitant :

> Voyez-vous là-bas, sur le versant de ce coteau, cette jolie maison qui se dessine, blanche et proprette, avec sa grange couverte de chaume, sur la verdure tendre et chatoyante de cette belle érablière. C'est une maison canadienne.
>
> Du haut de son piédestal de gazon, elle sourit au grand fleuve, dont la vague, où frémit sa tremblante image, vient expirer à ses pieds. Car, l'heureux propriétaire de cette demeure aime son beau grand fleuve et il a eu soin de s'établir sur ses bords. . . .
>
> Voulez-vous jeter un coup d'œil sous ce toit dont

l'aspect extérieur est si riant ? Je vais essayer de vous en peindre le tableau, tel que je l'ai vu maintes fois.

D'abord, en entrant, dans le *tambour*, deux sceaux pleins d'eau fraîche sur un banc de bois et une tasse de ferblanc accrochée à la cloison, vous invitent à vous désaltérer. A l'intérieur, pendant que la soupe bout sur le poêle, la mère de famille, assise près de la fenêtre, dans une chaise berceuse, file tranquillement son rouet. Un mantelet d'indienne, un jupon bleu d'étoffe du pays et une *câline* blanche sur la tête, c'est là toute sa toilette. Le petit dernier dort à ses côtés dans son *ber*. De temps en temps, elle jette un regard réjoui sur sa figure fraîche qui, comme une rose épanouie, sort du couvre-pied d'indienne de diverses couleurs, dont les morceaux taillés en petits triangles sont ingénieusement distribués.

Dans un coin de la chambre, l'aînée des filles, assise sur un coffre, *travaille au métier* en fredonnant une chanson. Forte et agile, la navette vole entre ses mains ; aussi fait-elle bravement dans sa journée sept ou huit aunes de *toile du pays* à grande largeur, qu'elle emploiera plus tard à faire des vêtements pour l'année qui vient.

Dans l'autre coin, à la tête du grand lit à courte-pointe blanche et à carreaux bleus, est suspendue une croix entourée de quelques images. Cette petite branche de sapin flétrie qui couronne la croix, c'est le rameau bénit.

Deux ou trois marmots nu-pieds sur le plancher s'amusent à atteler un petit chien. Le père, accroupi près du poêle, allume gravement sa pipe avec un tison ardent qu'il assujettit avec son ongle. Bonnet de laine rouge, gilet et culottes d'étoffe grise, bottes sauvages, tel est son accoutrement. Après chaque repas, il faut bien fumer une *touche* avant d'aller faire *le train* ou battre la grange.

L'air de propreté et de confort qui règne dans la maison, le gazouillement des enfants, les chants de la jeune fille qui se mêlent au bruit du rouet, l'apparence de santé et de bonheur qui reluit sur les visages, tout, en un mot, fait naître dans l'âme le calme et la sérénité.

After these distinguished authors, who created and developed the writing of history in French Canada, we need recall only three writers—of much less power, however—who left useful works : Louis Philippe Turcotte (1842-78), author of *Canada sous l'Union* ; Théophile Pierre Bedard

(1844-1900), author of *L'Histoire de Cinquante Ans*, and Joseph Royal (1837-1902), author of a *Histoire du Canada* (1841-67), which deals with the régime of the Union.

The field of history is still that which is most cultivated by French-Canadian writers of to-day. Among these may be mentioned — Benjamin Sulte, who, in addition to his *Histoire des Canadiens Français*, wrote many articles and studies which have been collected in volume form ; Joseph Edmond Roy, author of the *Histoire de la Seigneurie de Lauzon* ; the Abbé Auguste Gosselin, the historian of the church in Canada (L'Église du Canada) ; Alfred De Celles, the elegant monographist who wrote on Papineau, La Fontaine and Cartier ; Thomas Chapais, the author of *Jean Talon* and the *Marquis de Montcalm* ; N. E. Dionne, who gave an account of our colonial origins ; Louis Olivier David, author of *L'Union des Deux Canadas* (1841-67) and the *Histoire du Canada sous la Confédération* (1867-87) ; the Abbé Amédée Gosselin, the erudite archivist of Laval University, who rewrote the history of *L'Instruction au Canada sous le Régime Français* ; and Pascal Poirier, the historian of Acadia. Among the very numerous French-Canadian workers engaged in rewriting, correcting and continuing the history of their country these are distinguished from their fellows by a riper learning and a more perfect art.

POETRY

In French Canada poetry was the daughter of history. It is true that, during the period of literary origins, poetry sang freely of all subjects, but it sang, for the most part, without either inspiration or craftsmanship. About 1840, however, it essayed to do better and to take a loftier flight. It was the breath of history that inspired its voice and sustained its wing. The work of François Xavier Garneau long supplied the verses of the poet-patriots with themes. It evoked before their eyes the image of a country which had never before appeared so great, heroic and beautiful— a country whose many wounds still bled. They set themselves to extol ' that glorious world in which our fathers dwelt.' Garneau himself was naturally the first to be fascinated by the spectacle of the heroic deeds of his ancestors, and he wrote some of the first pieces in the repertory of 1840.

Another influence, however, was about to modify profoundly French-Canadian poetry—the influence of the romantic school. The intellectual relations of Canada with France had long been maintained with difficulty ; they suffered from the mere distance of the motherland, and from the political and social severance of New France from Old France. Thus the literary revolutions that agitated the mind of France were long in making themselves felt in Canada. About the middle of the nineteenth century, however, Octave Crémazie, the poet-bookseller, exerted himself to make the newer works of French poetry known in Quebec. He himself had felt the influence of his eager reading, and he was the first to tune his song to the note of romantic lyricism. Crémazie may justly be called the father of French-Canadian poetry.

Crémazie was born at Quebec on April 16, 1827. After completing his education at the Seminary of Quebec, he became associated with his two brothers, Jacques and Joseph, in their bookselling business. Anxious to instruct himself, and gifted with a fine imagination and keen sensitiveness, Crémazie loved to devote his leisure to reading his favourite authors, particularly the French poets whose works were in his bookshop. He was fond of inviting friends to talk literature in the back shop ; among these were the Abbé Raymond Casgrain, Antoine Gérin-Lajoie, Hubert Larue and Joseph Charles Taché.

About 1854 Crémazie published his first poems in *Le Journal de Québec*. These thrilling utterances of his soul stirred to their depths the hearts of his countrymen. Men felt them to be inspired by the profound emotion of a poet who loved Canada and France above everything. Unhappily, reverses of fortune, in which Crémazie found himself gravely compromised, obliged him to fly from the justice of his country into exile. In 1862 he took refuge in France. He lived there, poor and alone, under the name of Jules

Fontaine, and died at Havre in 1879. During his exile he published no more poetry. He often confided to his friends that he had hundreds of poems in his mind, but he would not give them to the world. The only literary work remaining from these hard years, spent far from his native land, consists of a few letters to friends on questions of Canadian literature, some letters to his mother and brothers, and the detailed narrative, written from day to day, of the siege of Paris. This record is a journal which Crémazie used to write up every evening for his family, and in which he noted down such minor incidents, interesting gossip and fugitive impressions as do not usually figure in serious history.

In Crémazie's letters, and in his *Journal du Siège de Paris*, the whole heart and soul of the writer was disclosed. His letters give evidence of an alert and versatile mind, by turns serious and humorous, playful and sarcastic ; capable of prompt and just judgments, but also of ideas that can with difficulty be accepted. His theories as to the impossibility of creating a Canadian literature, most disputable in principle, have been falsified by facts. In this long correspondence Crémazie displays all the delicate, wounded sensibility of his nature.

It was by the poems collected by his friends in book form that Crémazie was chiefly known, and it is these that still secure him so much lasting sympathy. Not that this poetry is really of a high quality, or that it constitutes a considerable achievement. Crémazie left scarcely more than twenty-five pieces, and one unfinished poem, *La Promenade des Trois Morts*. Into these two hundred pages of verse, however, he infused a generous, patriotic and Christian inspiration that moved Canadian readers. He was able to express so many of the things with which the heart of the people then overflowed, and which were the favourite subjects of popular thought ; and for this he was awarded the warmest and most sincere admiration.

In *Castelfidardo* Crémazie sings of the papacy menaced by the Piedmontese and defended by the heroic zouaves ; in the *Chant du Vieux Soldat canadien* and *Le Carillon* he celebrates the glorious memories of the history of New

France ; in the *Chant des Voyageurs* he recalls certain familiar features of Canadian life ; in *La Fiancée du Marin* he relates, in the manner of Hugo's ballades, a legend of the country. Because, for the first time in the history of Canadian poetry, readers found in these verses of Crémazie something of themselves so fully expressed, they applauded the poet, and his name and his verse were soon on every lip.

Crémazie's work has one rare merit. This is the sincerity of inspiration, and the profound feeling that imbues his patriotic songs. But Crémazie suffers in that he came too soon—at a time, that is to say, when he had himself to discipline his talent and learn to fashion his verses without any master. It was very difficult for the poets of 1850 to perfect their art : they were sadly lacking in the implements necessary to enable them to excel. Crémazie was obliged to pick up the lessons he needed casually in the course of his reading. To this cause are attributable his sometimes rather naïve imitations of the masters of French poetry—for example, of Victor Hugo in his *Orientales*.

Crémazie, moreover, did not sufficiently concern himself with correcting his work and lightening its heaviness. He cared nothing about being an artist. He first composed his poems in his memory; thence he let them drop on paper without altering their often commonplace matter, and without recasting their somewhat ponderous construction. *La Promenade des Trois Morts*, which he left unfinished, is a varied medley of delicate, moving lyricism and of realistic tales which are at times gruesome.

It is noteworthy that Crémazie did not pause to sing of love and the ardour of passion. His lyricism excluded this favourite theme of Lamartine and Musset, and devoted itself to the expression of religious and patriotic sentiments. This lyricism, with its twofold object, religion and patriotism, fascinated Crémazie's young contemporaries, and was continued in some of their works. Most of the poets of this period and the following years were disciples of the author of the *Chant du Vieux Soldat canadien*. They form what may be termed the patriotic school of Quebec.

The first of Crémazie's disciples was Louis Fréchette,

born at Lévis on November 16, 1839. He was a student at Quebec when Crémazie was issuing his first poems and gathering the studious of 1860 into his côterie of the Rue de la Fabrique. Fréchette did not attend these meetings in the back shop ; but he read the poet's verses, he felt the enthusiasm which they excited in the readers of Quebec, and when he was twenty he began to write poetry himself. In 1863 he published his first collection of poems, *Mes Loisirs*. He soon became immersed in politics, a sphere in which he never succeeded. Often disillusioned and embittered by the struggle for life, Fréchette, then a voluntary exile in Chicago, published from 1866 to 1869 the *Voix d'un Exilé*. He returned to Canada, and having at length abandoned political life, after being a member of parliament at Ottawa for a few years, he devoted himself almost entirely to literary work, and published successively—*Pêle-Mêle* (1877); *Fleurs boréales* and *Oiseaux de Neige* (1879) ; *La Légende d'un Peuple* (1887) ; and *Feuilles volantes* (1891). Before his death he prepared a final edition of his poems. Under the title of *Épaves poétiques* he introduced, in addition to the finest poems that had already appeared in *Mes Loisirs*, *Pêle-Mêle* and *Fleurs boréales*, a few unpublished pieces and his great pathetic drama, *Veronica*.

In prose Fréchette published *Originaux et Détraqués* (1892), in which he delineated certain popular types, though sometimes with a little exaggeration ; and his *Noël au Canada* (1900), in which he depicts in simple fashion the believing, faithful soul of the French-Canadian people. After a fuller poetical career than that of any other Canadian poet, he died at Montreal on May 31, 1908.

Fréchette devoted himself chiefly to lyrical poetry. Feeling rather than thought animates his verse. His inspiration, more versatile than that of Crémazie, touched upon nearly all the usual lyrical themes. Fréchette, however, like Crémazie, scarcely ever concerned himself with the passion of love. Crémazie shunned it altogether ; Fréchette skimmed with a light wing over such ardent subjects. The bearing of his muse never ceased to be irreproachable. The author of *Mes Loisirs*, *Pêle-Mêle* and *Fleurs boréales* contents himself with singing of the most delicate ties of friendship and the family, and of all the precious memories which we accumulate in our lives. He sings, too, in praise of nature and her varying expressions. Having studied in the school of the romantic poets dear to his youth, he loved, like them, the spring, flowers, trees, rivers and landscapes, and he sought to portray their colours, lines, depths and harmonies. At times he succeeded well in expressing many of the feelings awakened in us by contact with persons and things, and his verses entitled 'Sursum Corda' in *Pêle-Mêle* and 'Renouveau' in *Fleurs boréales* are full of the most deep and delicate feeling. In these lyric poems of sentiment Fréchette diverges and differs from Crémazie ; in his patriotic songs in *La Légende d'un Peuple* he approaches and resembles him. Like Crémazie, he was a patriotic poet. He shared with his master the readily accorded title of 'national poet.' In *La Légende d'un Peuple* he set himself to relate the epic of French Canada—to write in eloquent strophes the history of his race. From among the events of this history he chose those that seemed to him most representative of a moment or a period ; he celebrates them one after another, without linking them sufficiently, and without sufficiently disclosing, by means of general and essential ideas, their powerful cohesion.

At the beginning of *La Légende d'un Peuple* Fréchette hails in eloquent strophes the America which its discoverers had revealed to the world :

Amérique !—salut à toi, beau sol natal !
Toi, la reine et l'orgueil du ciel occidental !
Toi qui, comme Vénus, montas du sein de l'onde,
Et du poids de ta conque équilibras le monde !

Quand, le front couronné de tes arbres géants,
Vierge, tu secouais au bord des océans
Ton voile aux plis baignés de lueurs éclatantes ;
Quand, drapés dans leurs flots de lianes flottantes,
Tes grands bois, tout pleins d'oiseaux chanteurs,
Imprégnèrent les vents de leurs âcres senteurs ;
Quand ton mouvant réseau d'aurores boréales
Révéla les splendeurs de tes nuits idéales ;

I

Quand tes fleuves sans fin, quand tes sommets neigeux,
Tes tropiques brûlants, tes pôles orageux,
Eurent montré de loin leurs grandeurs infinies,
Niagaras grondants ! blondes Californies !
Amérique ! au contact de ta jeune beauté,
On sentit reverdir la vieille humanité !

All the poet's eloquence found vent in this collection ; along with strongly inspired couplets there are pages throughout which rhetoric lavishes its pompous and easy periods. Rhetorical language and structure too often weaken poetry : under their sway verse constantly becomes commonplace and bombastic, particularly when the poet's native land and its traditional glories are the theme. Great originality alone can triumph over these temptations to swell one's voice, in order to dazzle the reader with grandiloquent words and make him forget the emptiness of sonorous constructions. Fréchette was not always proof against these dangerous temptations, and his lyricism, although often sustained by powerful inspiration, also degenerates, here and there, into mere declamatory harangues. Moreover, he was ambitious to imitate Victor Hugo in his *Légende des Siècles*, and he exposed himself to the charge of copying Hugo's least pardonable faults. Nevertheless, to Fréchette must be ascribed the honour of perfecting the form of French-Canadian verse. More concerned about variety of rhythm and harmonious cadences than Crémazie, he produced a more carefully wrought and more artistic poetry. It was with justice that, about 1880, French Canadians acknowledged Fréchette to be their greatest poet.

By Fréchette's side, sometimes separated from him, but always related to him by common tastes and an equal if not a rarer talent, another poet, Pamphile Le May, lived and wrote. Born at Lotbinière in 1837, he was older than Fréchette by two years. He too received, from that epoch of literary effervescence in which he passed his youth, an influence and an impetus that were soon to make him follow in the footsteps of Crémazie. In 1865 he published his *Essais poétiques* ; in 1870 he translated, in verse, Longfellow's *Evangeline* ; in 1875 he produced *Les Vengeances*, republished in 1888 under the title of *Tonkourou*, the Indian name of one of the chief personages of this romance in verse ; in 1881 he published his *Fables canadiennes*, in 1883 *Petits Poèmes*, and in 1904 *Gouttelettes*. Le May still devotes his laborious old age to writing little comedies, poems that he will doubtless collect some day in volume form.

Le May was not so given to using the file as Fréchette, or, like him, careful to perfect as much as possible his poetical style. Yet he had, perhaps in a fuller measure, the ready inspiration, the vivid imagination, the profound sensibility, the *mens divinior*, that go to the making of true poets. He was also, like Fréchette, a national poet, yet in a different sense : he betook himself naturally, and with irrepressible spirit, to singing of the things that make Canadian life. Into the intimacy of that life he penetrated more deeply than Fréchette—into the details of the customs of the people, into all the picturesque manifestations of their rustic life. It was, indeed, to its charming pictures of country life that *Les Vengeances* owed its success; for, despite its rather hasty and careless workmanship, this poem derives value from its portrayal of Canadian customs.

It was Le May's wish to be the poet of the soil. He could not well be more ' regionalistic,' to adopt the French expression of to-day. Even while his art is being perfected he remains the friend of his country ; he has not forsaken the source of his early inspiration. The best of his collected poems are the sonnets which he published under the title of *Gouttelettes*. These mark the truest progress in his career.

One of the finest poems in this collection is the sonnet in which Le May sings the return, the awakening of spring :

> Laissons l'âtre mourir ; courons à l'aventure.
> Le brouillard qui s'élève est largement troué ;
> La fontaine reprend son murmure enjoué ;
> La clématite grimpe à chaque devanture.

> Le ciel fait ondoyer les plis de sa tenture ;
> Une tiède vapeur monte du sol houé ;
> L'air doux est plein de bruits ; les bois ont renoué,
> Dans les effluves chauds, leur discrète ceinture.

L'aile gaiment s'envole à l'arbre où pend le nid ;
L'enfant rit ; le vieillard n'a plus de tons acerbes ;
Les insectes émus s'appellent sous les herbes.

O le joyeux réveil ! tout chante, aime, bénit !
Un élan pousse à Dieu la nature féconde,
Et le rire du ciel s'égrène sur le monde.

In these carefully wrought little pieces Le May has not confined himself to the artistic treatment of Canadian themes. There are biblical and evangelical sonnets ; there are poems that breathe of religion and of love ; but above all there are rustic sonnets, songs of the hearth and songs of history. The whole mind of the poet is found in this collection. Along with the poet of private life and domestic confidences we have the poet-patriot moved by the noblest inspirations of his race, and the Christian poet extolling that which is most dear to his faith and piety. Because Le May has thus expressed, often with charm and exquisite sweetness, so many things that fill the national consciousness with pride, he stands out as the most sympathetic poet of the school of 1860.

To this school belongs another poet who yields to no one in respect of the oratorical cast of his verse—William Chapman. He has published Les Québecquoises (1876), Feuilles d'Érable (1890), Aspirations (1904) and Les Rayons du Nord (1910). These works do not resemble those of Crémazie, Fréchette and Le May, except in their patriotic and religious inspiration—that correct and austere sentiment which above all characterizes the whole Quebec school. Chapman's verse is also less sincere and more grandiloquent than that of his rivals. He is the poet-rhetorician par excellence, who does not shrink from oratorical displays, however threadbare. Yet, as with all who flutter their wings, Chapman at times takes flight, and soars and hovers, bearing with him the reader's admiration. He has written some very fine verse, stately in movement and proportion. What he lacks is a more constant inspiration, a more fully fledged thought, a less flagging and less wordy versification. He too often delights in enveloping his ideas in needless amplification. *Aspirations* seems, so far, the culminating point of his work.

Adolphe Poisson and the Abbé Apollinaire Gingras, the former in *Heures perdues* (1894) and *Sous les Pins* (1902), the latter in the poems and songs entitled *Au foyer de mon Presbytère* (1881), gracefully carried on the traditions of the Crémazie school. Alfred Garneau and Nérée Beauchemin, although both were the precursors of a new art, may also be included among the poets of this group.

Alfred Garneau, son of the historian, was born at La Canardière, near Quebec, in 1836, and died at Montreal in 1904. He was hardly known as a poet during his lifetime ; he published but little, keeping in his desk the poems that, after his death, were collected in a volume under the title of *Poésies.* He was at once sensitive, timid and artistic, and does not seem to have given out the full measure of his talent. Yet he was especially remarkable for an art more subtle than that of most of his contemporaries, for a more painstaking regard for form, and for a more refined delicacy of feeling.

Nérée Beauchemin, born at Yamachiche in 1851, possessed all the patriotism and piety of the Crémazie group. With these qualities he united a great regard for rhythm and harmony. His *Floraisons matutinales* (1879) contains some very beautiful pieces.

A new school, called ' L'École littéraire de Montréal,' was founded in that city in 1895. It gathered together a few active, enthusiastic spirits—for the most part poets—who sought to lead French-Canadian literature into new paths. The poets of this school, of which Alfred Garneau and Nérée Beauchemin may be regarded as the forerunners, are less circumscribed by patriotic and religious subjects than their predecessors. They may be said to have altogether abandoned these somewhat hackneyed themes, and to concern themselves mainly with the analysis of personal feeling, or the expression of the most diverse emotions of the human soul.

Emile Nelligan and Albert Lozeau are the two best known and most notable members of this group. Nelligan's poetry

comes feverishly from an imagination and sensibility that
are often morbid.   It is inspired too readily by the works
of the French school of Verlaine, Beaudelaire, or Rollinat.
It does not retain the measure and equilibrium indispensable
to enduring work.   Yet it contains accents of profound
sincerity and of poignant sadness, which provoke the most
ardent sympathy.

In the *Vaisseau d'or* Nelligan describes at the outset
the tragic shipwreck of his spirit :

> Ce fut un grand Vaisseau taillé dans l'or massif ;
> Ses mâts touchaient l'azur, sur des mers inconnues ;
> La Cyprine d'amour, cheveux épars, chairs nues,
> S'étalait à sa proue au soleil excessif.
>
> Mais il vint une nuit frapper le grand écueil
> Dans l'Océan trompeur où chantait la Sirène,
> Et le naufrage horrible inclina sa carène
> Aux profondeurs du Gouffre, immuable cercueil.
>
> Ce fut un Vaisseau d'or, dont les flancs diaphanes
> Révélaient des trésors les marins profanes,
> Dégoût, Haine et Névrose, entre eux ont disputé.
>
> Que reste-t-il de lui dans la tempête brève ?
> Qu'est devenu mon cœur, navire déserté ?
> Hélas !   Il a sombré dans l'abîme du Rêve !

Albert Lozeau is more personal than Nelligan ; he is less
bookish, having formed himself by long and solitary medita-
tions.   He prefers to sing of what is external to him, although
his songs are always the expression of the dream through
which all things had to pass to reach his sick-room.   His
verses are also dictated by passion.   Like external nature
and the beauties of art, passion can assume in his lines a
subtle accent, and sometimes a rather quaint form.   In
L'Ame Solitaire (1907) and also in his *Billets du soir* (1911),
which resemble sonnets in prose, and in *Le Miroir des Jours*
(1912), there are, however, the most delicate manifestations
of a fine intellect.

In the following sonnet the poet thus describes the loneli-
ness of his inward life :

Mon cœur est comme un grand paradis de délices
Qu'un ange au glaive d'or contre le mal défend ;
Et j'habite mon cœur, pareil à quelque enfant
Chasseur de papillons, parmi les calices.

Gardé des chagrins fous et des mortels supplices ;
En l'asile fleuri du jardin triomphant,
Pour me désaltérer, dans le jour étouffant,
J'ai ton eau, frais ruisseau du rêve bleu, qui glisse !

Je ne sortirai plus jamais du cher enclos
Où, dans l'ombre paisible, avec les lys éclos,
Par ses parfums secrets je respire la vie.

Car la nature a mis en moi l'essentiel
Des plaisirs que je puis goûter et que j'envie :
C'est en moi que je sens mon bonheur et mon ciel.[1]

Each year sees an increase in the disciples of the École littéraire de Montréal. They seem to be held together by no common doctrine : each develops in the direction of his personal aptitudes. Charles Gill, Albert Ferland and Paul Morin are among those most appreciated by readers. Paul Morin, who published *Le Paon d'Émail* (1912), gives more care to the form of his verse than other Canadian poets. He aims chiefly at producing sonorous lines in which the varied rhythm and rich rhymes charm the ear. From Greek and pagan antiquity he gathers much of his inspiration. He draws landscapes with a glowing pen. There is in his poems more colour than ideas. But his first collection of verse promises a still finer art. Let us hope that ideas may add to his muse the force necessary for true greatness.

FICTION

The novel appeared rather late in the history of French-Canadian literature. This branch of letters, which demands a well-disciplined imagination, a profound knowledge of life, and a most skilful art, suffered from the hard conditions that long affected the development of literature in French Canada. It was not until the middle of the nineteenth century that

[1] *Le Miroir des Jours :* Le ciel intérieur, p. 196.

any one ventured to enter a field in which such rare qualities of mind are necessary for success.

The novel of Canadian life and the historical novel were the first to be cultivated. Works of great merit are not very numerous. In 1853 Pierre Joseph Olivier Chauveau published *Charles Guérin*, which was merely a timid attempt at a novel of manners. Ten years later, in 1863, a work appeared that was to take a permanent place in the history of the Canadian novel—*Les Anciens Canadiens*, by Philippe Aubert de Gaspé.

Born in 1786 at Quebec, de Gaspé, a son of the seigneur of Saint-Jean-Port-Joli, did not enter Canadian literature until late in life. After a career at first mingled with trials, afterwards tranquil and happy at the seigneurial manor, he was suddenly seized with a great longing to communicate to his fellow-countrymen his earliest recollections. It was then 1860, and de Gaspé was in his seventy-fourth year. The literary movement instituted by the intellectual activity of Crémazie, Garneau, Casgrain and Gérin-Lajoie had led to the establishment of *Les Soirées canadiennes*, on the first page of which was inscribed the saying of Charles Nodier : ' Let us hasten to relate the delightful tales of the people before they have forgotten them.' The septuagenarian took Nodier's counsel to himself, and began to write his romance.

Les Anciens Canadiens is at once a novel of manners and an historical novel. As a basis for his narrative the author has used some of the most interesting features of Canadian life. Two young men, one of whom, Jules d'Haberville, is a Canadian, and the other, Archibald Cameron of Lochiel, a Scotsman, become friends during college life. Separated by the necessity of earning their livelihood, they again come together, but under different flags, during the war in which France and England fought for the last time for the soil of Canada on the Plains of Abraham and the fields of Ste Foy. Their old friendship is broken, then resumed with reserve. The author turns to account all the incidents that he gathers about this main theme in relating the life led by his countrymen at the already distant period of the Conquest.

De Gaspé's work is less a novel than a series of historical pictures ; it is, as it were, the first draught—the rough sketch—of a national epic. May not the novel be a veritable epic, and may not the epic, in its turn, be history ?

Les Anciens Canadiens, moreover, was a species of *chanson de geste* in prose. De Gaspé blended history with legend ; he related the heroic actions of the last battles of the Conquest, and their no less poignant dramas of conscience. He introduced the marvellous, without which there is no epic ; he evoked a love-interest, too prudent, perhaps, to satisfy the canons of romance, but capable of recalling the mingled smiles and tears that pervade the *Iliad*, or the passion, ardent yet restrained, that breaks forth only to die at the end of the *Song of Roland*. Thus de Gaspé is at once the most eloquent, the most simple, the most charming narrator of Canada's past—the true epic singer of a marvellous phase of its history.

The life of the seigneurs, interwoven with that of the colonists, is described at length in de Gaspé's pages. The artless simplicity of popular manners is painted with truth. If Père José, as a type of the good old domestic, is a little exaggerated, M. d'Haberville and his son Jules are worthy representations of the seigneur of the old French régime. The scenes of the disaster of Saint Thomas, and the may-pole dancing at Saint-Jean-Port-Joli ; the tales of José, the evocation of the sorcerers of the Isle d'Orléans, and the nocturnal promenades of La Corriveau ; the description of the costumes of the peasants, and the conversations, animated and true to the characters and their time—all reconstruct before the reader's eyes the life of a period whose traditions are rapidly becoming a thing of the past. De Gaspé even shows himself a philosopher : he depicts life and he depicts himself, for in describing the trials endured by the worthy seigneur of the story, d'Egmont, he evidently draws on his personal experience. The style of this novel, unique in French-Canadian literature, breathes simplicity and good-humour. At times there are eloquent passages into which all the author's patriotism is infused. Sometimes these hastily written pages are adorned with classical reminiscences which testify to the writer's culture.

Very different from *Les Anciens Canadiens* is the *Jean*

Rivard of Antoine Gérin-Lajoie. This novel, while containing studies of Canadian manners, is also a social romance—a novel with a purpose. The author published the first part of the book in *Les Soirées canadiennes* in 1862, while de Gaspé was preparing *Les Anciens Canadiens*. He entitled it *Jean Rivard : le défricheur* ; the second part, *Jean Rivard, économiste*, appeared in *Le Foyer canadien* in 1864. Gérin-Lajoie endeavoured in these successive works to persuade his compatriots to remain on their native soil of Canada instead of emigrating to the United States, as they were then largely doing ; to cultivate the rich soil of the Province of Quebec ; to clear the virgin forest without ceasing ; to open up new parishes—in a word, to colonize.

Upon this very real theme of colonization Gérin-Lajoie built up the simplest of romances. As little intrigue and as much agricultural life as possible—such was the rule that this somewhat unromantic novelist imposed upon himself. This did not prevent him from writing a book that was widely read, and creating a type that has remained as an example for all colonists.

Jean Rivard is a young student, prevented by ill-fortune from finishing his classical studies. He passes, willingly enough, from his rhetoric into the forest, where he intends to cut himself out a domain. He becomes a pioneer tiller of the soil. Alone in the woods of Bristol, the forerunner of all his future companions and fellow-citizens, he fells the great trees, clearing them away by dint of the most patient efforts ; he sows his roughly cleared field and builds himself a modest house in the virgin forest—a nest, soon to be brightened by the coming of Louise. The hard-working colonist becomes a rich and contented cultivator. Round about him other young men gather—men who have attacked the great trees with equal ardour. Rivardville is founded. Jean Rivard, who manages his farm with wisdom, is now an able economist after having been an indefatigable farmer. He offers the benefit of his practical experience to whoever will use it. He becomes the leading citizen of the newly colonized region, then the mayor of his village, and finally member of parliament for his county.

In this novel one must not look for profound psychology
or an art practised in narrative. What the author wished
chiefly to portray were pictures of colonization, scenes in
which there passed before the vision, successively and
realistically, the laborious stages, sometimes hard but on
the whole happy, of the Canadian colonist's life. The tale
is told in a simple style—a little dull, perhaps, but always
interesting ; it is enlivened, too, with most picturesque
pages in which are clearly reproduced some of the most
characteristic customs of the French-Canadian habitant's life.

Here, for example, is how Gérin-Lajoie draws the picturesque scene of the *corvée* :

> Quand les matériaux furent prêts et qu'il ne fut plus
> question que de *lever*, Jean Rivard résolut, suivant la
> coutume canadienne, d'appeler une *corvée*. . . .
> Dans les paroisses canadiennes, lorsqu'un *habitant*
> veut lever une maison, une grange, un bâtiment quel-
> conque exigeant l'emploi d'un grand nombre de bras, il
> invite ses voisins à lui donner un coup de main. C'est
> un travail gratuit, mais qui s'accomplit toujours avec
> plaisir. . . . Ces réunions de voisins sont toujours
> amusantes ; les paroles, les cris, les chants, tout respire
> la gaieté. Dans ces occasions, les tables sont chargées
> de mets solides, et avant l'institution de la tempérance
> le rhum de la Jamaïque n'y faisait pas défaut.
> Une fois l'œuvre accomplie, on plante sur le faîte de
> l'édifice, ce qu'on appelle le ' bouquet,' c'est-à-dire quel-
> ques branches d'arbres, dans la direction desquelles les
> jeunes gens s'amusent à faire des décharges de mous-
> queterie.
> Quoique Jean Rivard n'eut invité, pour l'aider à lever
> sa maison, que les hommes de la famille Landry et quel-
> ques autres de plus proches voisins, il vit, le lundi matin,
> arriver avec eux plus de trente colons établis de distance
> en distance à quelques milles de son habitation. . . .
> Chacun avait apporté avec soi sa hache et ses outils,
> et l'on se mit de suite à l'œuvre. Le bruit de l'égouïne
> et de la scie, les coups de la hache et du marteau, les cris
> et les chants des travailleurs, tout se faisait entendre en
> même temps ; l'écho de la forêt n'avait pas un instant
> de répit. . . .[1]

[1] *Jean Rivard*, i. 180-2.

While de Gaspé and Gérin-Lajoie were issuing their works, Georges Boucher of Boucherville (1814-98) published in *La Revue canadienne* another novel, which quickly attracted the attention of readers, *Une de perdue et Deux de trouvées* (1864-65). This was a novel of manners and adventure, and was very successful. The author transports his personages by turns to South America, Louisiana, the Antilles, and finally to Canada. His pictures and descriptions, especially in the first part of the book, are bright and animated. The extravagant and exciting situations that occur in the course of the tale contributed greatly to its popularity.

Joseph Marmette (1844-95), who was a most prolific novelist, devoted himself specially to the historical novel. His principal works were—*Charles et Eva* (1867), *François de Bienville* (1870), *L'Intendant Bigot* (1872), *Le Chevalier de Mornac* (1873), and *Le Tomahawk et l'Épée* (1877).

Marmette's historical studies are generally fascinating; they recreate dramatic periods of the past. In *François de Bienville* he depicts the siege of Quebec by Phips; in *L'Intendant Bigot*, the last years of the French régime. The author had a lively descriptive imagination, not, however, always under control; and his characters are lacking in originality.

The historical novel has had other representatives. In 1866 Napoléon Bourassa published *Jacques et Marie*, which recalls the dramatic story of the dispersion of the Acadians; 'Laure Conan' (Mlle Félicité Angers) wrote *A l'Œuvre et à l'épreuve* (1891) and *L'Oublié* (1902); and in 1909 Sir Adolphe Basile Routhier produced *Le Centurion*, an interesting attempt to reconstruct Jewish and Roman history in the time of our Lord.

Following the example of Gérin-Lajoie, Jules Paul Tardivel (1851-1905) attempted another novel with a purpose. His *Pour la Patrie*, published in 1895, is a work treating of religious thought; in it the author specially attacks the influence of freemasonry, which he denounces as the most dangerous and most subtle evil that can invade the national life of French Canada. Ernest Choquette, who published *Les Ribaud* (1898) and *Claude Paysan* (1899), and Hector Bernier, who wrote *Au large de l'Écueil* (1912), have given us pleasing romances of manners. French Canadians still await writers in the field of fiction who will endow their literature with powerful and original works.

Political, Philosophical and Social Literature

Jules Paul Tardivel belongs to political rather than to imaginative literature. His novel, *Pour la Patrie*, was written chiefly for the purpose of gathering together and systematizing his political and religious ideas. Tardivel was before everything a journalist, and it was in *La Vérité*, the paper which he founded at Quebec in 1881, that he waged his ceaseless combats. He stood apart from political parties, and his one aim was to make the legal principles of the Catholic Church triumph in the conduct of public affairs. He was the irreconcilable enemy of liberalism and free-masonry, and in the three volumes of *Mélanges*, which contain his best articles, one may see his firm and uncompromising cast of thought.

Journalism has from time to time given us writers whose pens were both ready and fertile. The names of Joseph Charles Taché, Joseph Edouard Cauchon and Hector Fabre are well known in the history of French-Canadian journalism. Thomas Chapais, who abandoned journalism for history, collected in a volume of *Mélanges* a number of vigorously written articles, which possess interest in connection with the political history of the last years of the nineteenth century. Those who are incontestably the masters of French-Canadian journalism to-day, who instil most ideas into their writing, and give those ideas the most artistic form, are Henri Bourassa, managing director of *Le Devoir*, Omer Héroux, editor of the same journal, and the Abbé J. A. Damours, editor-in-chief of *L'Action Sociale*. These three journalists are true literary men, whose work undoubtedly bears the mark of high literary culture.

By the side of these journalists may be placed the orators.

Journalists and orators frequently meet in discussing the same ideas; frequently, too, they make use of the same style. The political eloquence of French Canada, however, has nothing of a very high literary value to show. Among those who have disappeared, Honoré Mercier and Adolphe Chapleau were orators who were favourites of the populace, but whose eloquence was by no means uniform. To-day the eloquence that has often thrilled the hearers of Sir Wilfrid Laurier and Thomas Chapais is found with similar intensity and vigour, and with a consummate art which compels admiration, in the speeches of Henri Bourassa.

Sir Wilfrid Laurier, at Paris, in 1907, defined in the following manner the loyalty of the French Canadian:

> Séparés de la France, nous avons toujours suivi sa carrière avec un intérêt passionné, prenant notre part de ses gloires, de ses triomphes, de ses joies, et de ses deuils, de ses deuils surtout. Hélas ! Jamais nous ne sûmes peut-être à quel point elle nous était chère que le jour où elle fut malheureuse. Oui, ce jour-là, si vous avez souffert, j'ose le dire, nous avons souffert autant que vous. . . .
>
> J'aime la France qui nous a donné la vie, j'aime l'Angleterre qui nous a donné la liberté ; mais la première place dans mon cœur est pour le Canada, ma patrie, ma terre natale. . . . Vous en conviendrez avec moi, le sentiment national d'un pays n'a de valeur que par l'orgueil qu'il sait inspirer à ses enfants. Eh bien ! nous l'avons, nous, Canadiens, cet orgueil de notre pays. . . .

The Hon. Thomas Chapais, in 1902, on the day of the national festival of the French Canadians, reminded his compatriots of the reasons that bound them more than all the other races to Canadian soil :

> Mais où sont donc les citoyens du Canada qui sont plus canadiens que nous ? Nous sommes attachés au sol de la patrie par toutes les fibres de notre cœur. Dieu merci, notre nationalité n'est pas ici un arbre sans racine. Pour plusieurs de nos détracteurs, le Canada n'est qu'un pays de passage et d'attente ; pour nous, il est la terre des aïeux, la terre de toutes nos tendresses, de toutes nos espérances. La plupart de nos concitoyens d'origine

étrangère à la nôtre ne voient dans le Canada qu'une
patrie vieille de cinquante ans, de soixante ans, de cent
ans à peine.   Pour nous, c'est une patrie vieille de trois
siècles.   Dans nos vieux cimetières, à l'ombre de la croix
plantée sur les rives canadiennes par Jacques Cartier,
il y a plus de quatre cents ans, dorment six générations
d'ancêtres. . . . Parcourez toutes les provinces de la
Confédération : partout vous retrouverez la trace de
nos héros et de nos apôtres qui ont jeté en terre, avec
leur poussière et leur sang, une semence de civilisation
chrétienne. Ah ! oui, nous sommes les plus Canadiens
des Canadiens.

Henri Bourassa has peculiarly devoted himself to defending the rights of the French-Canadian minority in the Confederation.   At the Monument National in Montreal on
May 9, 1912, he thus expresses himself with regard to secular
legislation in the North-West :

Jusqu'aujourd'hui la Province de Québec a été le pivot
de la Confédération.   Jusqu'aujourd'hui les Canadiens
français ont été le rempart infranchissable contre toute
idée d'annexion aux États-Unis, contre tout projet de
séparation de la Grande-Bretagne.   Ne pensez-vous
pas que cent cinquante ans de loyauté leur méritent un
droit d'égalité politique dans toute l'étendue de cette
confédération ?   Ne pensez-vous pas que les colons que
nous pourrions envoyer sur les bords de la Saskatchewan
ou de la Rivière-Rouge, pour continuer l'œuvre des
ancêtres, mériteraient d'y être aussi bien traités, que
vos co-religionnaires [l'orateur s'adresse aux Anglais
protestants] et vos concitoyens sont traités dans la
Province de Québec ?   Ne pensez-vous pas que des
colonies françaises fortes et prospères, essaimant dans
l'Ouest, préserveraient l'ouest canadien de la pénétration
des idées américaines, comme la Province de Québec a
sauvé le Canada, à trois ou quatre reprises, de l'annexion
aux États-Unis ?
Britanniques, nous le sommes autant que n'importe
quelle autre race du Canada ! Nous ne le sommes pas
par le sang et par la langue, mais nous le sommes par la
raison et par la tradition.
Les institutions britanniques, ce n'est pas la conquête
qui les a faites nôtres, ou du moins ce n'est pas une seule

conquête. Il a y huit cents ans, des hommes qui par-
laient notre langue et dont les veines renfermaient le
même sang que celui qui coule dans les nôtres, sont allés
en Angleterre allier leur génie à celui des Anglo-Saxons.
De cette alliance anglo-normande sont sorties ces institutions magnifiques qui nous sont revenues ici sept
cents ans plus tard.
A ces institutions personne n'est plus attaché que nous.
Mais nous ne sommes pas des chiens rampants ; nous
ne sommes pas des valets, et après cent-cinquante ans
de bons et loyaux services à des institutions que nous
aimons, à une Couronne que nous avons appris à res-
pecter, nous avons mérité mieux que d'être considérés
comme les sauvages des anciennes réserves, et de nous
faire dire : ' Restez dans Québec . . . vous y êtes chez
vous ; mais ailleurs il faut que vous deveniez Anglais.'

Religious eloquence has been careless in preserving its
records. Its utterances have often been powerful and full
of feeling. The Abbé Holmes was one of the most admired
pulpit orators on account of his *Conférences de Notre-Dame
de Québec.* In our own day the sermons of Monseigneur
Paul Eugène Roy, auxiliary Bishop of Quebec, display
literary qualities of precision and grace of the highest order
combined with the utmost dialectical power.

On September 29, 1908, addressing himself to French-
Canadian farmers, sons of families who had occupied for at
least two centuries the ancestral land, and to whom was
restored the ' médaille des anciennes familles,' Mgr Roy
expresses himself as follows :

Elle serait intéressante à raconter et à lire, messieurs,
l'histoire de ces quelque deux cents familles, dont vous
êtes ici les authentiques et heureux descendants ! S'ils
avaient eu le temps et la facilité d'écrire leurs mémoires,
ces braves aïeux ! Si leurs mains avaient su manier la
plume comme elles savaient manier la hache et la charrue,
quelles précieuses archives ils auraient laissées aux
historiens de notre temps !
D'ailleurs, messieurs, la terre qu'ils vous ont transmise,
après l'avoir fécondée de leurs sueurs, n'est-elle pas le
plus beau livre d'histoire que vos mains puissent feuil-
leter et vos yeux parcourir ? Et ce livre, n'est-il pas

vrai que vous le lisez avec amour ? que vous le savez par cœur ?

La préface en fut écrite par ce vaillant chef de dynastie qui apporta ici, il y a plus de deux siècles, votre nom, votre fortune et votre sang. C'était un Breton, un Normand, un Saintongeois, que sais-je ? un Français, en tout cas, et un brave, a coup sûr. Avec cet homme et la femme forte qui vint avec lui ou qu'il trouva sur ces bords, une famille nouvelle venait fortifier la colonie naissante, civiliser le royaume de Québec, et enrichir, d'un sang généreux et de belles vertus, la noble race canadienne-française.

Et l'histoire commence, palpitante d'intérêt, débordante de vie. Que de fois vous les avez vus repasser dans votre imagination, ces premiers chapitres, écrits au fil de la hache, illuminés par les belles flambées d'abatis ? et gardant encore aujourd'hui les âcres et fortifiantes senteurs des terres-neuves, que déchirent la pioche et la herse, et où germent les premières moissons ! Ce sont les années rudes, mais combien fructueuses des premiers défricheurs ; c'est la glorieuse épopée de la terre qui naît, de la civilisation qui trace pied à pied son lumineux sillon à travers l'inculte sauvagerie des hommes et des bois. Chaque coup de hache, alors, est une belle et patriotique action ; chaque arbre qui tombe est un ennemi vaincu ; chaque sueur qui arrose le sol est une semence.

Monseigneur Louis Adolphe Paquet and Father Louis Lalande have also delivered sermons and lectures that, in their ample and harmonious phraseology, bear the impress of true eloquence.

While some writers and orators propagated their ideas by means of journalism or speeches, and examined the religious and social questions of the day, others published books treating of the same subjects and reviewing the same problems. Philosophical and social literature has not yet many representatives ; but there are a few writers who occupy a leading place in these fields.

Edmond de Nevers, who was born at Le Baie-du-Fèbvre in 1862, and died at Central Falls, in the United States, in 1906, published *L'Avenir du Peuple canadien-français* in

1896 and *L'Ame américaine* (2 vols.) in 1900. These two works, which show a wide acquaintance with original documents and are filled with critical observations, have placed Edmond de Nevers in the first rank of Canadian writers. In *L'Ame américaine* the author seeks to analyse the multifarious and dissimilar elements composing the American mind. He examines in turn the origins, the historical life, the immigration movements, and the development of the United States. While there is occasionally a little confusion in the plan, it must be acknowledged that the abundance of information, the ingenuity of the views, and the lofty inspiration of the whole make it a work worthy of preservation.

Among present-day writers Monseigneur Paquet, of Laval University, Quebec, is certainly the most authoritative representative of social and philosophical literature. Prepared for his literary career by long theological study and by his *Commentaria* on Saint Thomas—highly esteemed in theological faculties—he wrote his studies on *Le Droit public de L'Église* with all the competence of a professional. In the first volume he dealt with the 'General Principles' (1908), in the second with 'The Church and Education' (1909), and in the third with 'The Religious Organization and Civil Government' (1912). These two works are methodically planned and ably executed ; they are written in free but carefully chosen language, sometimes eloquent and always well-balanced.

Read, for example, this page where Mgr Paquet demonstrates the necessity of putting religious and moral training at the foundation of instruction :

> Veut-on que l'homme mûr, battu par le flot du doute, blasé, succombant peut-être sous le poids moral qui l'accable, puisse un jour en se retournant vers le passé, puiser dans ses souvenirs d'enfance, dans ses impressions de jeunesse, dans le spectacle d'années heureuses et pieuses, un renouveau de foi, un regain d'ardeur virile et de courage pour le bien ? Qu'on fasse luire, au seuil même de sa vie, le flambeau des doctrines religieuses ; qu'on verse dans son âme encore neuve, comme une coulée de riche métal, les notions élevées, les suggestions salutaires, les persuasions moralisatrices par lesquelles

se forment les habitudes saines, se trempent les carac-
tères généreux, se préparent les fières et triomphantes
résistances aux assauts répétés de l'erreur et du mal.
' Le jeune homme, a dit l'Esprit Saint, suit sa voie ;
même lorsqu'il aura vieilli, il ne la quittera pas.' Cette
voie peut être bonne ou mauvaise ; il dépend beaucoup,
il dépend principalement de l'éducateur et de ses leçons
qu'elle soit une voie d'honneur, de probité et de justice.
La jeunesse est le printemps de la vie. Quand ce
printemps donne toutes ses fleurs, il s'en exhale un
parfum pénétrant de religion et de piété qui embaume
toute l'existence humaine, qui fortifie dans le bien,
console dans la douleur, prémunit l'âme inconstante et
finale contre les enivrements du vice. Pour cela que
faut-il ? plonger l'enfant, l'adolescent, le jeune homme
dans une atmosphère pleine de Dieu et des choses divines ;
purifier la sève qui court abondante dans ses veines ;
faire que toutes ses facultés s'ouvrent avidement à tout
ce qui est bon, à tout ce qui est juste, à tout ce qui est
noble. Saint Thomas cite comme un axiome cette
sentence d'Aristote : ' Un vase garde toujours l'odeur
de la première liqueur qu'il a contenue.' Le jeune
chrétien qui, pendant des années, s'est nourri de la
substance même de la foi ; qui en a, par ses prières, par
ses études, par tous ses actes, aspiré et absorbé les purs
et spirituels éléments, garde, en effet, dans les plus intimes
replis de son âme, même si son esprit se fausse, même si
son cœur s'égare, un reste de bonté surnaturelle et de
grandeur morale qui fera son salut.[1]

Miscellaneous

French literature, to whatever climate it be transplanted,
must produce its *conteurs*, its *nouvellistes* and its *chroniqueurs*,
who express in a light form, generally humorous but sometimes dramatic, caprices of the imagination or picturesque
aspects of popular life. In this varied class of literature
the French genius has always found a field for the display
of its sparkling wit.

The tellers of short stories have not, perhaps, sufficiently
worked the fruitful vein that lies ready for their purpose.

[1] *L'Église et l'Éducation*, pp. 162-3.

French Canada abounds in legends and tales worthy of literary preservation. In 1860 the Abbé Casgrain began the relation of his Canadian *Légendes*. His *Jongleuse* is still celebrated. Joseph Charles Taché (1821-94) continued this task, publishing *Trois Légendes de mon Pays* (1876) and *Forestiers et Voyageurs* (1884). In the latter the life of the woodmen with their merry evenings in camp is told in a style quaint and piquant—a true presentation of life in the shanties. P. J. O. Chauveau (1820-90) published in 1877 *Souvenirs et Légendes*. Pamphile Le May, who is an adept at discovering whatever poetry there is in the popular tale, published his *Contes vrais* in 1899, reissuing them in 1907.

Faucher de Saint Maurice (1844-97), a Gascon born near Quebec, took pleasure in relating the adventures of a life that he thought heroic. He was enamoured of military glory and longed to fight and travel. On leaving college at the age of twenty, he left Canada and placed his enthusiastic youth at the service of the Emperor Maximilian in Mexico. He published successively—*De Québec à Mexico* (1866), *A la brunante : contes et récits* (1873), *Choses et Autres* (1873), *De tribord à babord : trois croisières dans le golfe du Saint-Laurent* (1877), *A la veillée* (1878), *Deux ans au Mexique* (1878), *En route : sept jours dans les provinces maritimes* (1888), *Joies et Tristesses de la Mer* (1888) and *Loin du Pays* (1889).

Doctor Hubert Larue (1833-81), who wrote much in the reviews and journals of his time, left us in the department of the tale and chronicle : *Voyage sentimental sur la rue Saint-Jean* (1879), *Voyage autour de l'Isle d'Orléans*, and two volumes of *Mélanges historiques, littéraires et d'économie politique* (1870 and 1881).

A portion of the work of Sir Adolphe Basile Routhier may be included in this class. *A travers l'Europe*, 2 vols. (1881 and 1883), *En Canot* (1881), *A travers l'Espagne* (1889), and *De Québec à Victoria* (1893) contain impressions of travel recorded in a rapid but instructive fashion. Routhier also set himself to describe and paint *Québec et Lévis* (1900).

Ernest Gagnon, who in 1865 produced a valuable treatise on the *Chansons populaires du Canada*, also published, in

1905, his *Choses d'Autrefois*, in which many interesting recollections are brought together.   Out of history Ernest Myrand, in *Fête de Noël sous Jacques Cartier* (1888), fashioned an attractive order of literature, possessing something of the novel and something of the true narrative.   His *Noëls anciens de la Nouvelle-France* (1899) is also an entertaining monograph.

In the newspapers many *chroniqueurs* have written fugitive sketches—short miscellaneous articles—in which the impressions of daily life were currently recorded.   In Canada the undisputed master of the *chronique* was Arthur Buies, who was born at the Côte des Neiges, near Montreal, in 1840. While he was still very young his parents went to settle in British Guiana, and he was left to the care of two aunts. He led a strange and most eventful life.   During his youth he lived by turns in Quebec and British Guiana ; he then went, against his father's wish, to study in Paris ; and in 1859, to the great scandal of his aunts, he became one of Garibaldi's soldiers.   He returned to Canada the same year to study law, and was admitted to the bar in 1866. The advocate immediately rushed into journalism, and committed the gravest extravagances in thought and language.   Inspired by the influence of French journalists hostile to the church, he delighted in attacking the Canadian clergy in his writings.   This portion of Buies' work is now forgotten, and may be ignored.   Later the *chroniqueur* continued, in various journals that welcomed his collaboration, to write short and sprightly miscellaneous articles, which remain models of their kind in French-Canadian literature. These articles have been collected in book-form—*Chroniques, Humeurs et Caprices* (1873) ; *Chroniques, Voyages* (1875) ; and *Petites Chroniques* for 1877 (1878).

On May 8, 1871, Buies began, in this half-jocular, half-serious tone, his chronicle, dated at Quebec :

> Avez-vous jamais fait cette réflexion que, dans les pays montagneux, les hommes sont bien plus conservateurs, plus soumis aux traditions, plus difficiles à transformer que partout ailleurs ? Les idées pénètrent difficilement dans les montagnes, et, quand elles y

arrivent, elles s'y arrêtent, s'enracinent, logent dans le creux des rochers, et se perpétuent jusqu'aux dernières générations sans subir le moindre mélange ni la moindre atteinte extérieure. Le vent des révolutions souffle au-dessus d'elles sans presque les effleurer, et lorsque le voyageur moderne s'arrête dans ces endroits qui échappent aux transformations sociales, il cherche, dans son étonnement, des causes politiques et morales, quand la simple explication s'offre à lui dans la situation géographique. Si une bonne partie du Canada conserve encore les traditions et les mœurs du dernier siècle, c'est grâce aux Laurentides. La neige y est bien, il est vrai, pour quelque chose, la neige qui enveloppe dans son manteau tout ce qui respire, et endort dans un silence de six mois hommes, idées, mouvements et aspirations. A la vue de cette longue chaîne de montagnes qui borde le Saint Laurent tout d'un côté, qui arrête la colonisation à ses premiers pas et fait de la rive nord une bande de terre étroite, barbare, presque inaccessible, on ne s'étonne pas de ce que les quelques campagnes glacées qui s'y trouvent et dont on voit au loin les collines soulever péniblement leur froid linceul, n'aient aucun culte pour le progrès, ni aucune notion de ce qui le constitue. . . .

Je porte mes regards à l'est, a l'ouest, su sud, au nord ; partout un ciel bas, chargé de nuages, de vents, de brouillards, pèse sur les campagnes encore à moitié ensevelies sous la neige. Le souffle furieux du nord-est fait trembler les vitres, onduler les passants, frémir les arbres qui se courbent en sanglotant sous son terrible passage, frissonner la nature entière. Depuis trois semaines, cet horrible enfant du golfe, éclos des mugissements et les tempêtes de l'Atlantique, se précipite en rafales formidables, sans pouvoir l'ébranler, sur le roc où perche la citadelle, et soulève sur le fleuve une plaine d'écume bondissante. . . . 'Ce vent souffle pour faire monter la flotte,' disent les Québecquois. Et, en effet, la flotte monte, monte, mais ne s'arrête pas, et nous passe devant le nez, cinglant à toutes voiles, vers Montréal.

Ainsi donc, Québec a le nord-est sans la flotte, Montréal a la flotte sans le nord-est ; lequel vaut mieux ? Mais si Québec n'a pas la flotte, en revanche il a les cancans, et cela dans toutes les saisons de l'année. Voilà

le vent qui souffle toujours ici. Oh ! les petites histoires,
les petits scandales, les grosses bêtises, comme ça pleut !
Il n'est pas étonnant que Québec devienne de plus en
plus un désert, les gens s'y mangent entre eux. Pauvre
vieille capitale ! [1]

He also employed his talent for observation in descriptive geographical studies. In this department he has left—
L'Outaouais supérieur (1889), *Le Saguenay et le Bassin du
Lac Saint-Jean* (1896), *Récits de Voyages* (1890), *Les comtés
de Rimouski, Matane et Témiscouata* (1890), *Au Portique
des Laurentides* (1891), and *La Vallée de la Matapédiac*
(1895).

Buies died at Quebec in 1891. His name remains as that
of a writer who well represented the Parisian spirit, ready-
witted and facetious, censorious at times, but also capable
of tenderness and subtle feeling. Buies particularly loved
the French tongue. In Canada he wished to see it freed
from the dangerous contributions of Anglicism. He wrote
a pamphlet entitled *Anglicismes et Canadianismes* (1888), in
which he indicated many new words deserving proscription.
He is one of those who have most skilfully used the French
language in Canada. His *chroniques* are composed of the
impressions of each day, the reflections suggested by events,
the judgments dictated by his wit and his sympathetic
nature ; in them are mirrored all the spectacles of daily
life, and they contain some of the finest pages in the literature
of French Canada.

With less vivacity, but also with wit, Napoléon Legendre
(1841-1907) and Hector Fabre (1834-1910) wrote newspaper
chroniques on all the subjects of the day. The former collected some of his best articles in two volumes entitled
Échos de Québec (1877), and the latter published under the
title of *Chroniques* (1877) pages in which are to be found
the light and entertaining qualities of his ready talent.

Alphonse Lusignan (1843-92), who, at the outset of his
career, was responsible for some very fiery journalism, left
a volume of *chroniques* entitled *Coups d'œil et coups de plume,*
which was much relished by readers. Oscar Dunn (1845-85)

---

[1] *Chroniques canadiennes : Humeurs et Caprices,* i. pp. 11-12.

collected his reminiscences and his principal journalistic writings in *Dix ans de Journalisme* (1876) and *Lectures pour tous* (1878). The Abbé Camille Roy collected under the title *Propos canadiens* (1912) stories and studies dealing with Canadian life. These are in turn rustic, moral, patriotic, scholarly and literary in their tone and colour.

The *chronique* is also represented among us by two women, although their work is rather superficial : 'Françoise' (Mlle Robertine Barry), author of *Chroniques du lundi* (1891) and *Fleurs champêtres* (1895), and ' Madeleine ' (Mrs Gleason-Huguenin), who in 1902 published her *Premier péché*.

Criticism was the last branch of literature to make its appearance, although in the *chronique* and newspaper article it had long been in evidence. P. J. O. Chauveau, whose mind was distinguished by delicacy and good taste, encouraged letters in his *Journal de l'Instruction publique*, and he himself published a literary monograph on *François Xavier Garneau, sa vie et ses œuvres* (1883). Edmond Lareau, in 1874, wrote a first *Histoire de la Littérature canadienne*, and Routhier wrote a study of *Les Grands Drames* (1889). But these were only isolated efforts. Of recent years French-Canadian literature is developing most abundantly, and literary criticism watches over the productions of the writers more assiduously, and especially with more method. The Abbé Camille Roy was one of the first to make a speciality of this branch of study ; he published in 1907 a first series of *Essais sur la Littérature canadienne*, and in 1909 the history of *Nos Origines littéraires*. Henri d'Arles (Father Henri Beaudé), who had already entered upon art criticism in *Propos d'art* (1903) and *Pastels* (1905), applied himself in turn to literary criticism in his *Essais et Conférences* (1910). The Abbé Emile Chartier also devoted a portion of his *Pages de Combat* (1911) to literary criticism. Finally, in the *Bulletin de la Société du Parler français au Canada*, Adjutor Rivard, the learned general secretary of the society, assigned the writers of French Canada their meed of praise or blame, mingled with the wise counsels of his own trained mind.

Such is French-Canadian literature, viewed as a whole and in the persons of some of its best representatives. Intellectual masterpieces, it is true, are rare. We cannot demand of literatures in their infancy such works as can be the glory of old literatures alone. Nevertheless, French-Canadian writers have produced, in almost every branch except the drama, works that do honour to the spirit that conceived them, and that may still be read with profit.

The literature that we have been describing is chiefly notable for its method and clearness, and for the enthusiasm for ideas and the delicacy of feeling that are qualities of the French mind. Sometimes a little heavy, it goes on unburdening itself, freeing itself from cumbersome forms, and perfecting itself in proportion as the writers and their readers are able to devote themselves more and more to intellectual culture.

French-Canadian literature is eminently moral. It bears the stamp of the Christian spirit in which its works are conceived. In it catholic thought is expressed without timidity—with that apostolic boldness which is its characteristic. Further, it generally draws its inspiration from the abundant springs of the national life. At times it has sought unduly to imitate the artistic forms of French thought ; it has often been too ready to reproduce that which is most characteristic, and least capable of assimilation, in the literature of the ancient motherland. Yet it must be acknowledged that, taken as a whole, the literature is indeed Canadian, and that in it the life of the people is reflected and perpetuated. Many of its works, the best in prose and in verse, breathe the perfume of the soil, and are the expression —original, sincere and profound—of the Canadian spirit.

Camille Roy, ptre